To Orville - Enjoy the book.

Wesley Arlin Brown
970 - 353 - 3412

COKER

A Mountain Man's Story

COKER

A Mountain Man's Story

By

Wesley Arlin Brown

Senior Press
Hilton Head Island, South Carolina

Only one person is possible for this dedication and that is the one person who has stood by my side for forty-seven years. When a horse sent me to intensive care for a month, she saved my life more than once. She read and corrected my story and was my best critic. I could say she is the wind beneath my wings, but that would not be accurate. She is the real star of the story. Therefore, this first book is dedicated to my beautiful wife, Jackie.

ACKNOWLEDGMENTS

I can never fully express my gratitude to James Hobbs for giving me permission to use the song he wrote called "Just One More Ride." When I heard the piece, I knew it captured the feeling I had in my heart. Most of the actions and touching scenes were written with the song in mind.

A special thanks goes to Miriam Bush, editor of Senior Press, for her patience and good advice. She put in many long hours to get the book ready to publish.

Mary Hunsaker, my sister-in-law, read my story and gave me a great deal of encouragement. She knew I listened to music while I wrote and sent me a number of recordings that helped me concentrate.

Also, Bob Gibson, the draftsman who constructed the map of Coker's travels, deserves my appreciation for his work.

Colorado

1906

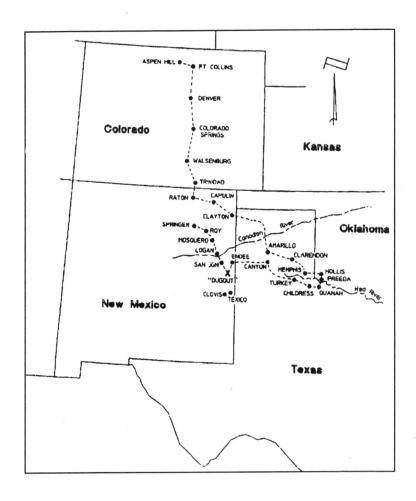

Coker's Journey

Broken line shows route taken by Coker Owen Ford on his special mission 1906-07. He started in the Rockies at Aspen Hill (top), site of the cabin he shared with Rufe Cantrell. Dugout house where he spent some time is located above Clovis and Texico in New Mexico.
Map by Bob Gibson.

1

Aspen Hill

There was that feelin' again, like somethin' was wrong or somethin' about to happen and maybe he hadn't got a handle on it. Wasn't no elk for he would take care of that right off. Nope, they would eat that winter for sure. Jest somethin' not right. But what?

Coker Owen Ford kept shaking his shaggy head as he stooped to come through the door into the cabin.

"Must be gettin' old, mind not workin' the same. Too many years of livin' gone by, damn it, you can tell that from this here beard, been gray and now turning white."

It was natural for him to talk to himself that way. Broke the silence when Rufe wasn't around.

"Think I'll get the stove ready so's I can have it going fast tonight. We got some little sticks here... somewheres." He was reaching down into the kindling box when he saw a folded piece of paper. Good to start a fire.

Crumbling the sheet, he started to drop it in the stove, then stopped and stared. "Hold on now. Where'd we get a piece of paper? I ain't brought no paper up here. Rufe must've brung it up and throwed it in the box."

1

He went out on the porch, sat down and studied the thin wrinkled sheet. "Huh! There's writin' on it. Must be a letter. Wish I could read."

For some time he pondered the words, rubbing them with his fingers as if to absorb their meaning. "Cain't figger this out so I better go see if I can get a elk. Gotta have two more to be sure we can make it through the winter."

He went to pick up his rifle and laid the paper on the table. On the way out, he stopped and stared at it. "How come that ended up here? Rufe must've brought it the last time he got supplies. Wonder why he didn't say nothin'. Looks like a letter I seed once. Well, I cain't waste no more time."

The mountain mists were clearing so he moved fast into the depths of the forest. No long wait, either. Within minutes, Coker, stealthy and silent, crept slowly through the trees, stalking a spike elk that moved warily along, nose to the ground. The early morning sun at his back made Coker's moving shadow nearly invisible. Every few yards the animal looked cautiously around before it grazed. Each time the head went down, the shadow floated a little closer. Somewhere in the forest a buck snorted and the elk jerked its head up to look for the cause of the noise. For a fatal instant the animal froze, then collapsed. The bullet from Coker's Winchester had zoomed through an opening in the trees and shattered the bone in the elk's neck.

From habit formed over many years, Coker stepped behind a large spruce. Like a hunted animal he scanned the forest before he went to the elk. He did not go straight to the dead animal, but circled through the timber looking for movement to see if his shot had attracted the attention of another man.

As he moved from one tree to another, he said, "Ain't seed no Injuns in a long time. And ain't supposed to be no thievin' renegades, but a man don't get to be past seventy bein' dumb."

Coker had gutted hundreds of elk and more deer. He could disembowel an elk in fifteen minutes except, while he was gutting the animal, he usually stopped every minute or two to look around him. When he finished the job, he kept talking to himself. "So 'bout one more'll be 'nough for the winter. This fellow will weigh nigh on to four hundred pounds. Might get us through the winter, but one more'll do it for sure."

He left the elk to fetch his mule tied back in the woods a few yards away. As he approached, Thunder Red watched every step.

"Well, ole feller, I can see those long ears and those big eyes keepin' track of me. You're harder to sneak up on than a big buck. Hope you don't mind carryin' a whole elk for a little ways. He ain't too big."

Drifting through the forest with the same vigilance as always, he led the mule back to the elk. He tied the reins over the saddlehorn, took a rope off the saddle and threw it over a limb. Then he tied the other end around the hind legs of the animal. He cut a three-inch slot between the third and fourth ribs and led Thunder Red beside the carcass. When Coker stopped, the mule wrinkled his nose at the smell of blood, but stood like a statue and waited for Coker to load the dead animal on his back.

The front legs of the elk were placed around the rump of the mule and across the saddle. He slipped the opening made between the ribs over the saddlehorn, took the rope off the legs of the elk and led the mule on a winding path through the forest. Thunder Red followed along, often looking back to keep the legs of the elk from catching on limbs, bushes or rocks.

As he worked his way through the trees, Coker touched many of them with his hands. Because of his

3

long years in the wilderness, he revered the trees and plants as friends, friends who provided him with camouflage, shelter and firewood.

No trail led through the dense forest, but like a bee returning to its hive, he climbed unerringly up a long sloping hill until he reached a clearing. There he paused and looked over at a small grove of aspen where the little cabin perched on the crest of a knob overlooking a vast canyon with a river in its bottom thousands of feet below. A pine squirrel skittered from tree to tree scolding him for encroaching on his territory.

His eyes soft, he gazed at his home. "Aspen Hill. Never get tired of lookin' at those quakies and smellin' the pines. 'Specially this time of year when them aspen leaves are all yeller and gold." He rubbed one big ear with his left hand and studied the color around him with devout eyes. "Wonder how many more times I'll look at 'em."

As he walked to the cabin, his eyes flicked to a corral and the pasture inside. "Wish Rufe would ride one of my mules so he could get them supplies faster. Don't know why he rides that damned old horse he's so set on. It's a wonder he ever makes it down and back on that plug. He'll have to camp down in the Poudre tonight."

Leading Thunder Red under a cross pole between two trees, he threw a rope over the pole and hoisted the elk off the mule's back. Then he unsaddled Red and turned him into the corral he and Rufe had built by tying saplings between aspen trees. It covered only an acre, but it was a place where they could keep their animals close by in case they wanted them quickly.

He started working on the carcass, chopping it in half with a hatchet. He carried the front quarters to a long table nearby, sliced strips with his Bowie knife and hung them on a rack he and Rufe had fashioned to dry meat for jerky.

4

A flock of ubiquitous Rocky Mountain jaybirds, known as camp robbers, gathered in the trees waiting to snatch a piece of meat and fly away. Coker threw them bits to keep them from the meat on the rack.

"Here, eat these, you pesky critters," he said and tossed a handful of scraps on the ground. "That'll keep you busy until I get the net over the meat."

Now and then he paused in his work listening for any danger, but mostly he couldn't keep from listening for Rufe. "No, he cain't get back 'til tomorra." As he cut the last strip of meat, he glanced at the sun. "It's already dinner time."

A jar holding a mixture of salt and pepper stood on the table. Coker sprinkled the meat liberally with the preservative then stretched a fine net over it to keep off the flies and camp robbers. Satisfied, he ambled to the corner of the log hut, squatted by a spring running from under the porch and washed his hands in the cold water. He picked up another armload of sticks and went inside. As he put wood into the old stove, he paused. "I don't want to go to the trouble of cookin' somethin' just for me."

He replaced the lid and went back outside to the rack. Lifting the net he selected three strips of meat that had come from the loin of the elk, returned and sat on the porch with his back against one of the corner posts. He chewed off a piece of the raw flesh and said, "Good eatin'. Might oughta saved some of it for steaks."

He took his rifle into the cabin and put it on wooden pegs set in the wall. As he passed the table his eyes rested on the letter. Picking it up he ambled outside and again sat down.

From his spot on the corner he could watch the trail heading along the ridge across a small saddle where it forked. The left fork went down the side of the massive mountain. Years before, Coker and Rufe Cantrell had worked their way through the timber on the side of the great hill, switching back and forth up the steep slope of the mountain. They made twenty-five switchbacks to reach the ridge. Twenty-four traversed the side of the mountain, but the twenty-fifth one cleared the forest at the last turn and climbed to the saddle. No one could be seen approaching on the trail until he reached this last switchback.

Coker and Rufe took turns going to Fort Collins to get flour, meal and other necessities. Countless times one of them had watched for the other to come out of the timber so he could wave and get ready to hurl all the insults he could muster about the other's animals.

How many times had he sat here waiting for Rufe? Damn, they were both getting old. The planks were worn smooth from years of use. He would glance at the last switchback and then stare at the letter. He looked over the top of the paper intending to focus only on the trail coming up the mountain, but in spite of himself his pale, gray eyes followed the other trail straight up the ridge away from the saddle. He caught himself and jerked his eyes and thoughts away, but his gaze would soon wander to the same spot again. Finally, his eyes riveted on that path and he whispered, "Misty, Misty Valley."

Then his spirit left his body and followed the trail over the mountain to a valley on the other side. Not feeling the hard porch or knowing where he was, Coker sat almost rock still for hours.

The sun hung low over the ridge of pines west of the cabin when a piercing howl brought him out of his trance and caused him to jump off the porch.

"Featherfoot, you ornery old coyote. You damn near scared me to death." Looking at the sun filtering through the trees to gauge the time, he walked toward a coyote sitting on a big rock just a few yards from the porch. "Hey, old man, what are you doin' out so early?

You cain't catch nothin' this time of day, and it ain't time to howl for Rufe 'cause he ain't gonna make it back today. What you howling at anyway?"

Stretching the stiffness out of his muscles, he walked close to the little wolf, but it showed no fear. He stopped a few feet away and looked fondly into the coyote's eyes. "How long you been watchin' me, old pardner? You feel what I been thinkin', Featherfoot?"

Sitting like a sculpture on the mound of dirt, the animal returned Coker's gaze. The old man waited as if he expected him to answer. He had never touched the coyote, but the bond between them could have been no stronger if the animal had slept under his bed every night. Coker had fed him for years and Featherfoot always howled and let them know when any moving thing came up the trail.

A sound from the timber caused Coker to look down the mountain. For a moment he saw nothing, then a black horse came out of the trees.

"You're right again, Featherfoot. It's Rufe! And he's pushin' old Blackie hard. How'd he get back so fast on that nag? Wonder why he's in such a big hurry."

He strode to the hitching post by the corral and studied his old friend. When the black gelding turned from the switchback onto the ridge, Rufe kicked him out of his walk. Blackie trotted to the hitching post and stopped.

Rufe Cantrell, a wiry man two inches short of six feet, lifted a stiff leg over the cantle and slid to the ground. Tiny ears set close against his head made his wrinkled, skinny face resemble the blade of a knife. Normally, his eyes sparkled through eyelids in a perpetual squint, but now they were serious. Struggling off his horse, he limped toward his friend as he tried to work out the stiffness from the long ride.

"You've got that horse in a hell of a lather," Coker said. "If you'd trade that nag for a mule, you wouldn't have to kill him to get here."

"I ain't about to trade Blackie for no stupid, stubborn jackass . . . don't rile me about mules."

"You ain't got no supplies. Why did you turn around and come back?"

"Well, I was over half way to Fort Collins when some dry leaves rattled, and I remembered the last time I went down there the postman hollered me down and give me a letter for you. You wasn't here when I got here so I laid it on the corner of the stove and forgot about it. When I remembered it, I was afraid you'd use it to build a fire. Who would be writin' to you?"

"I don't know. I don't know nobody who'd write to me."

Coker realized he had the letter in his hand and shoved it toward Rufe. "Lucky I found it. I almost used it to build a fire. Did you get somebody to read it to you?"

"Yep, I got the postmaster which hollered me down to read it to me. It sounded important. So when I thought about it I nearly killed my horse gettin' back."

"Well, then, what does it say and who's it from?"

Rufe dropped his eyes to the ground, fidgeted and scratched his head. "I cain't recollect much of it now. Thought I would, but it's been two weeks ago. I can just think of a little of it."

"Well, hellfire, tell me what you do remember, you broke down old codger."

"All I can remember it said was, 'They're goin' to take my babies.' Does that mean anything to you?"

"Naw, not unless I knowed who wrote it, it don't. Did it have a name on it?"

"The guy which read it to me said somethin' I thought was a kinda odd. Oh, yeah. It was Misty Valley. Ever hear of it?"

Coker's head jerked as though he had been hit with a rifle butt. Stunned, he stared without seeing anything. Shaking his head like a wounded bear, he sank to the porch and pressed the letter to his head.

"What's the matter, man?" Rufe asked. "You look like you've seed a ghost."

His friend's grizzled and bearded face seemed frozen in shock. The large watery gray eyes stared. His wide usually smiling mouth behind the thick gray whiskers and mustache hung slack.

Suddenly, Coker stood up determinedly as if he were lifting a tremendous load. He straightened his wide shoulders and towering over Rufe, said loudly, "I've got to go, Rufe. I've got to get packed and go in the mornin'."

2

Watch For Me, Rufe

Eyes blinking, Rufe stared up at Coker's face. His chin dropped and his lower jaw worked as he tried to speak and then sputtered, exploding with questions. "What in tarnation are yuh talkin' about? Are yuh addled? Where yuh goin'?"

"No, I ain't any more addled than I've ever been," Coker said as he rubbed his chin. "I don't know for sure where, and I don't know why 'cause you cain't remember what's in this here letter. But what I know is I got to go."

"You don't make no sense atall. If you don't know where or why, then why do you have to go?"

"Set down, Rufe, and I'll tell you all I can stand."

They sat on the edge of the porch while Coker collected his thoughts. Time and again he started to speak, but shook his head and chewed his lips. At last, husky words came from his tight throat. "Rufe, you see that dim trail goin' from the saddle on over yonder side of the hill?"

"Yeah, I see it ever' day."

"That trail winds around for about five miles and comes to a ridge that circles 'round a little valley. Down in that valley is a big meadow with a crick runnin' through it, and it makes a pond on each end. The little one at the lower end of the meadow is filled with black, sour mud. The big one at the other end is clear as a mirror. You can drink out of it."

"I been there. It's a purty spot. There's a little cabin all fell down in the edge of the timber."

"That's where we lived."

"Who? You . . . That's where who lived? You been here thirty years. I thought you come up from the plains. Never told me much about your folks though. Who's Misty Valley?"

"Misty Valley ain't nobody's name. That's what we called the valley I just talked about."

"Maybe if I listen long enough, you'll make some sense, but you ain't yet. You keep sayin' 'we' but you ain't never said who the other part of that 'we' is."

Coker's eyes focused on Rufe, then shifted to the trail leading over the hill. Tears appeared, but he wouldn't let them flow. "The 'we' is me and Trissy Renn," he whispered.

"Who in the hell is Trissy Renn?"

Coker choked, ducked his head and tried, but words wouldn't come. Rufe put a hand on his shoulder and squeezed. "If you cain't talk about it, that's all right. Just wait a while."

Coker tried to clear his throat several times and said, "Trissy Renn was my wife."

"Wife! Good godamighty! I didn't know you was ever married! Why didn't you ever tell me? What kind of a pardner is it that you cain't talk to?"

"You've been the best pardner a man could have, Rufe. But the reason I didn't tell you is I just couldn't talk with nobody. After thirty-one years it still hurts awful bad to talk about it."

He paused to blow his big nose which had turned red. "I come to these mountains when I was thirty. I rousted around for a couple of years until I found the valley. I built that cabin you seen. I lived there by myself and didn't figger I'd ever do nothin' else. Oh, I did take nearly a year goin' back east with a guy named Johnny Quondell to look for his folks and try to find mine. Didn't have no luck.

"One time after I got back, I decided to go to the big city and see the sights and get some flour and stuff. Well, I got tired of the sights purty quick and decided I'd get my supplies and go back to my valley which was a hell of a lot purtier than them lights in Denver.

"When I went for them supplies, I seen this girl by the door when I went in the store, but I didn't pay her no mind. I carried out a bag of flour, and, lo and behold, she follered me out to my mule. I turned around to get on my horse I was ridin' at the time, and she was just a standin' in front of me real close. All I could see was two big, blue eyes lookin' right through me. I turned as soft as a new deerskin, and I couldn't think of nothin' to do but get on my horse, but that little slip of a thing stepped in my way and asked me what my name was. I couldn't figger out why she wanted to know, but I stammered around and finally told her 'Coker.'"

"'Coker what,' she says then. My tongue was as limber as a old rope, but I finally squeaks out, 'Coker Owen Ford.'

"'Coker Owen Ford,' she says. 'Coker Owen Ford, I'm goin' to marry you.'"

The big man sighed and shook his head.

"Well, then my brains scattered all over and they wasn't no use to me atall, and I went all to pieces. I tried to get on my horse and light out of there, but she held the stirrup and wouldn't let me get on until she told me where she lived and made me promise to look her up next time I got to Denver."

Rufe frowned in disbelief. "Just like that, she said she's gonna marry you?"

"I couldn't figger it out then, and I still cain't figger it out neither. Even then I was ugly enough to scare the bark right offen a tree. I told her Denver was too big, and I probably couldn't find her house so she made me stand there while she drew me a map and put it in my pocket.

Well, now, if you'd seed those eyes, you'd understand it better.

"I couldn't forget 'em, and it seemed I needed to go back to Denver right soon. When I got there and found the house on the map, I walked back and forth in front of the place where she lived with her aunt until she seen me and come runnin' out. Well, we starts talkin', and she was real easy to talk to. It didn't seem we'd ever stop. I found out she was twenty years old and her folks was dead. She lived with her aunt which she didn't like much, but she didn't have nowhere else to go."

"What happened?" Rufe asked softly. "Did you get married then?"

"Naw, that aunt of hers come out there and told Trissy to get back in the house. Then she called me a foul smellin' mountain man and told me to leave. I couldn't think of nothin' to say to her, but I stood there thinkin' I could cut her head clean off with one swipe of my long knife. But she was kin to Trissy so I knowed I couldn't.

"Anyway, I stayed in Denver. Ever'day I watched her house from the end of the street. About the third day she spotted me and sneaked out and we went where her aunt couldn't see us and talked. Trissy told me she loved me, and by that time I sure as hell loved her. I told her about the mountains where I lived and she was real innersted, but someone told her aunt Trissy was talkin' to me and she found us."

Coker paused while he thought about the rest of the story.

"She had the marshal with her, and he threatened to lock me up. I didn't want to cause Trissy no trouble, so I told 'em I'd leave. Just as I turned to go, Trissy run up to me afore they could stop her and whispered real quick that the next time I was in Denver she'd go back to the mountains with me.

"I went right to my valley and saddled a mule and caught another horse. I rode the mule and led my horse and went straight back to get her. I told myself I didn't have no business goin' back to get that little gal, but I couldn't no more stop than I could jump over Long's Peak. I was lucky. Leastwise I thought I was lucky, but sometimes I think maybe not. Her aunt didn't figger me to come back so soon, so she had gone off visitin' for the day.

"Well, when Trissy saw me with the extra horse, she grabbed some things and come runnin' and told me she was ready to go. I set her on the horse and we lit out for the hills. Just afore we cleared Denver, Trissy said that we oughta get married. I told her we could sneak down to Fort Collins and get married someday, but she looked at me real soft and said, 'No, we're married.' And that was that. We was married.

"I cut across a back way to make sure that nobody could foller us so we wasn't on no trail. The first night we stayed in the mountains and slept under a buffalo skin on pine needles. I thought that might be enough to make her want to go back, but it didn't faze her none. We spent another night and seed the valley early the next mornin'. When we come to the ridge, the sun had just rose and fog was driftin' up off the pond there by the cabin. Trissy seed it and said, 'What a lovely, misty valley' and she named it Misty Valley.

"We lived as happy as we could be for two years. Then Trissy had a baby girl. She had a terrible time havin' her, and there wasn't no way to get a doctor there in time. But we managed to get her born, and we named her Bonnie Thankful because we was so happy she was alive.

"Trissy didn't have no more kids, but we was happy enough with Bonnie Thankful. She was as purty as her mama. Trissy taught her to read by the time she was four. I'd get books when I'd go to Fort Collins, but we stayed away from Denver. Trissy tried to teach me to read, but I was too dumb or too stubborn. She wasn't sure which.

"'Cept for marryin' me, Trissy was awful smart, and she teached Bonnie about g'ogerphy and hist'ry and 'rithmetic. She knowed about music too and showed Bonnie how to play a guitar. "Rufe . . . Rufe . . ." Coker struggled to continue his story. Mountain shadows settled around them while they sat silently on the porch. He looked away from Rufe to the west where Featherfoot sat as if he were listening too. Getting control of his sobs, he wiped his eyes on the back of his sleeve and went on. "Then . . . when Bonnie was eight, Trissy . . ." Coker blew his nose again. "Trissy died."

Rufe put a trembling arm over the shoulders of his friend. "I never knowed, Coker, I never knowed. What happened to Bonnie?"

"Well, she was as happy as she could be there with me, just the two of us. But like a damned fool I thought she needed to go to school because when I was a kid I always wanted to go to school. I figgered Trissy's aunt would help her so I went to Denver intendin' to live there durin' the winter so Bonnie could get some learnin'. I had enough gold dust to pay for it."

Coker jumped from his seat. Clenching his fists tight, he paced back and forth. His jaw muscles knotted and he said, "That old hag went to court and took Bonnie away from me. I couldn't come up with no marriage license so the judge give my girl to that old hawk-faced woman.

"Rufe, there ain't nothin ever gonna hurt you as bad as losin' your own little girl. If I'da knowed what they was goin' to do and how bad it'd hurt, I'da killed 'em all and run for Canada.

15

"I nearly went crazy, and I looked ever'where I knew to look for two solid years. Never could find a trace of her."

"Who wrote this here letter?"

"Bonnie Thankful did, I'm sure of it. Trissy's aunt took her away from Denver. That's the reason I couldn't find out where she went. She must've got married and had some kids, and it sounds like somebody's about to take 'em away from her. I got to find her and keep it from happenin'. I cain't let her go through the kind of hell I've been through. I've got to go Rufe."

"Yeah, I reckon you do. Where you goin'?"

"I don't know. I'll stop in Fort Collins and get somebody to read me the letter. Then I'll know. No matter, I'll find her. Help me get some things together, and I'll leave first thing in the mornin'."

No other words were spoken by the old men as they got the packs together for the journey. Coker picked out two sawed-off, double-barreled shotguns, one to go on a thong behind his saddle and the other to tie on a pack just under the elkskin cover. He folded several large elkskins waterproofed with bear grease, and Rufe bundled a bedroll and jerky inside. Fast and thorough, the mountaineers had two packs ready to go in a couple of hours.

"I'll need some of the money we got stashed away I reckon," Coker said. "I'm glad we sold our gold. It'll save me havin' to stop in Denver."

Rufe went to a box under the one window and pulled out two leather bags. "Reckon this will be enough?"

Coker hoisted the bags in his huge hands. "I think I put around five thousand dollars in 'em so one oughta be more than enough."

"Naw, we got five of 'em. You better take three," Rufe said and got another bag.

16

At the urging of his partner, Coker finally accepted two, but refused the third. He wrapped the bags in a piece of skin and put them in the bottom of one of the packs, keeping out a roll of bills for immediate use.

Good old Rufe, Coker thought as the two of them lay on their bunks and talked through the long hours of darkness.

When the first light filtered through the window, Coker went out to the corral and caught his three mules. Rufe was waiting as he led them to the hitching post.

"Which one you goin' to ride?"

"I reckon I'll start off on Thunder Red, then change to Switchback, then to Stranger in a day or two when he gets a little tired."

Coker struggled getting a pack on Stranger. He pushed him against the porch railings so the mule couldn't move away from him and hoisted the baggage in place.

Watching thoughtfully as Coker tied the last strap, Rufe shifted his weight to his good leg and said, "Reckon I'll go along."

Coker put a hand on his shoulders. "No, Rufe, you're the onliest friend I got and these mountains are the only place I can live. Somebody'd probably move into our cabin if we both left so you got to watch it and be here when I get back. I got 'nough meat in for this winter easy, and I'll be back before the next one no matter what."

Rufe nodded. "I reckon as stove up as I am I'd just be in the way so I'll wait."

Coker stepped onto Thunder Red and looked down at his partner of thirty years. Gray eyes locked on brown and a third of a century of experiences passed between them. Slowly, Coker turned Thunder Red's head and pulled away , saying, "Watch for me, Rufe."

To keep from breaking into tears which would have been unmanly for a sixty-five-year old, Rufe was flippant. "I'll watch the switchback until you and those worthless mules get back."

Coker grinned at him. "Got to get in the last word, don't you. Whittle your chains and take care of your mangy nag, you hidebound old cuss."

Touching Thunder Red with his heels, he went down the trail. He waved as they reached the saddle and turned down the canyon. He was nearing the timber at the end of the switchback when the piercing, coyote howl echoed through the hills from the saddle. Coker twisted around and looked at the figure in the saddle at the fork.

"Bye, Featherfoot," he yelled. "You watch out for me too."

Rufe stood on the porch for a long time. "Yeah," he said. "Me'n old Featherfoot'll watch for you, but I got a powerful feelin' it ain't à gonna do no good. I think we're lookin' at our pardner for the last time."

Grabbing the corner post, he pulled himself up on tiptoe and watched until the three mules faded into the early morning blue hanging in the trees.

3

Bonnie's Letter

Thirty years with Rufe tugged at the mountain man as he made his way down the switchbacks. Thirty years of memories lifted the hair straight on the nape of his neck, made goosebumps on his back and threatened to carry him back to the cabin in the little grove of aspen. Thirty years of riding, fighting together and living with Rufe Cantrell made his arms ache to turn his mule back up the mountain.

He felt Rufe's eyes until he entered the timber at the end of the last switchback. Rufe feared for him to leave he knew, and Coker also felt the fright. He had to go. The memory of his long lost daughter whom he still imagined as an eight-year-old with her mother's blue eyes pushed him on with a force too powerful to resist. Still, as he rode down the switchbacks, Aspen Hill filled his mind.

The letter rattled in his pocket. Bonnie! Where was she? Thinking about his daughter made his chest tighten and he fought a great sadness welling up within him. He cried for a mile before he gained control.

"Glad they ain't nobody along. I'd hate for 'em to see me blubberin' like this."

For all those years Coker had lived, fighting his grief, trying to pretend that he had never been married, never had a daughter. The feelings he had suppressed overwhelmed him and a torrent of blinding hate exploded, driving him toward his goal.

"Goddam that old bitch," he swore as he thought of Trissy's aunt. "I shoulda killed her the first time I seen

19

her. If someone's tryin' to take Bonnie's kids, I'll cut the bastards up a little bit at a time."

The thought drove him frantic. Usually disciplined, he lost any semblance of control. He pushed his mules down the switchbacks past the golden-leafed aspens covering the vast mountains this last week in September. Every year Coker and Rufe spent days riding the ranges in the fall to see the leaves and delight in the crisp air, but now Coker's hate and tears made the scenery a blur.

Off the mountain into Poudre Canyon the mules went with Coker kicking Thunder Red every few steps urging him to go faster. Unaware of the time or the miles, he rode through the canyon, the black cloud of fury suspending his consciousness until he saw a huge boulder blocking the trail. Mystified, he stopped Thunder Red, stared and mumbled, "New rock fell off the hill, I reckon. How am I gonna get around that thing?"

He reined Thunder Red to his right and saw a wagon trail leading into the bushes around the boulder. "Is that Ambush Rock? Naw, I couldn't have come that far."

He turned his mule around to see if he could pick out another landmark which would tell him where he was. A lone ponderosa tree with long scratch marks down its side stood out from the foot of the canyon wall. Twisting in his saddle, he looked at the surrounding area.

"That's the bear tree all right, but how in hell could I be this far? I'm way down in the narrows or I'm crazy."

Gradually, he realized what he had done. "I musta been clean outa my head to ride like that. What've I done to my mules?"

He got down from Thunder Red and looked at his sweating animals. "If I'da been ridin' horses, I'da killed 'em."

Leading the three under a big spruce, he unsaddled them and wiped the sweat from their sides with a large rag. "I don't guess I was too hard on you, or you woulda quit, but we may have a long way to go, so I'd better take it a might easier from now on."

He turned the mules loose and they grazed in the tall grass along the river for an hour before meandering to the water. Coker watched until they finished drinking, then whistled. They came running to him and he fed them grain from his hands. They nipped at each other as they fought to be the first to get the oats.

Coker laughed. "You'd kill for a bite of oats, wouldn't you. But it always keeps you comin' back to me."

Shadows filled the canyon and the September chill came with them. Coker shivered. Never having spent a night in this particular spot, he studied it carefully before he carried the saddles and packs to a spot under a huge spruce tree and covered them with an elkskin. He laid the buffalo robe he had brought for cover a few feet away on a blanket of needles which had been forming for a hundred years.

Crawling under the skin he lay watching the mules and gnawed on a piece of jerky until it grew too dark to see. Then he rose quietly, slipped his rifle out of its scabbard and, carrying the gun and the buffalo robe, he went down the hill until he could hear the river. Carefully, he felt with his moccasined feet until he detected tall grass some distance from where he had first put his packs. This time he laid the skin with the fur side on top. Lying on the edge he rolled up in the skin holding his arms so that it would be loose around him. When he had found the position with the fewest bumps under him, he pulled the hatchet and big knife from his belt and the throwing knife from its scabbard behind his neck. Then he put them by his waist with the rifle. He lay on his back and pulled the robe down from his head far enough to see the sky and hear the river.

"Old river, you make a mighty purty sound. Am I layin' by your side for the last time?"

He explored the stars over the canyon and pondered the vastness of the sky. After a time he focused on the north star.

"Lonesome star, You've guided me to Misty Valley many a time. Someday, maybe I'll follow you there again. But I don't know. I wish I knowed where I was goin'."

The rhythm of the running water gradually dulled his senses, and he drifted into a troubled dream:

> Bonnie ran along the bank of the pond at the end of Misty Valley   snake,   snake with a human head   Trissy's aunt   out of the water   long, ugly, green   biting Bonnie's leg   poison   Trissy floating from above   trying to pull Bonnie from its mouth   both running   snake grabs Trissy   slimy, filthy teeth   by the neck and pulls her into the pond   Bonnie screaming, trying to help her mother   Coker yells, "Wait, Bonnie, wait!" feet won't move reach, reach   Bonnie slipping away into lake   "Cain't reach her!"   "Cain't reach her!"

His own yells roused him a number of times. Sweat from his exertion forced him to unroll the buffalo skin. Each time he shook his head and tried to force the images out of his mind, but to no avail. Every time he dozed, the dream returned, and he would strain with all his might to save Bonnie from the demon of the pond. But he could never touch her. Always just out of his reach, she slid into the dark water.

Dawn seeped into the canyon changing the black of the night to a dull gray, but to Coker it was a welcome, bright light which temporarily ended the horrors of his dreams. When he saw the lightening sky, he wrestled out of the buffalo skin, headed for the river and knelt in the long grass to wash his hands.

The dream! He cupped his hands and pushed them full of icy water against his face again and again trying to rid himself of the gloom that soared over him like a hungry buzzard.

Splashing the water wasn't enough. He stood and jerked off the leather shirt and pants. Throwing them on the ground, he waded into the river until he found a hole nearly waist deep. Diving into the water he rolled over and over until the current carried him into the shallows. His teeth chattered and a violent chill shook his body. Like an ascetic torturing the flesh, he relished the pain and lay in the water until he turned blue. When his body quit aching and became numb, he went back on shore.

A stiff breeze evaporated the water on his skin making the cold more unbearable. But Coker had plunged into many icy streams and cold lakes after Trissy had died and Bonnie Thankful had been taken from him. Countering the pain of losing his wife and child with the pain of the freezing water had enabled him to retain his sanity until he had found Rufe and they had built their cabin. Rufe had given him an escape and had helped him bear the pain for thirty years. Now with Bonnie's letter all the anguish had returned, and once more he had resorted to the old remedy.

As soon as he was dry, he pulled on his clothes and looked around for the mules. Standing just a few yards away, they eyed him, their ears pointed in his direction.

"Yeah, I know you cain't figger it out. It must look awful dumb to mules which don't like any kind of water. I cain't figger it out neither, but it keeps me from goin' crazy. Go on and eat some more grass while I get me some breakfast."

His senses restored, Coker surveyed the area before he moved again. He scooped his hatchet and knife off the ground and put them in his belt. Carrying the robe over his shoulder, he trotted up the hill, took matches from a saddlebag and started a small fire. As soon as it was burning well, he ran to the river and filled a kettle with water. He drank some, poured ground corn into what was left, added salt and set it on the fire.

"Don't know how them Injuns ever et corn without cookin' it. Never could get the stuff to go down."

In a few minutes, the kernels softened in the boiling water. Coker ate, wiped out his pan with grass and put it back in his pack. Then he whistled for the mules and they came running for another handful of grain.

By the time the sun touched the grass on the ridges, he had the packs on Thunder Red and Stranger and the riding saddle on Switchback. They were headed down the Poudre River Trail once more. To keep from descending into that morbid mood again, he talked to his mules constantly.

"Why ain't you actin' up this mornin', Stranger?" he asked the big, black mule. "Did we come too many miles yesterday? Maybe I oughta do that ever' time afore I ride you, and I wouldn't get throwed so much. Come on, Thunder Red, or I'll ride you again and wear your legs down to your knees. Switchback, you goin' to let these lazy critters outwalk you? Quit eatin' that bush and get on down the trail."

The continual patter served his purpose for many miles, but finally he ran out of anything to chide his mules about and lapsed into silence. As soon as he quit talking, images of the dream returned and the black mood threatened to overpower him. Immediately, he got off Switchback and walked in front of the animals. Paying attention to the trail as he led the mules forced him to keep his mind occupied.

24

He walked for a mile or two and then trotted for several more. Whatever pace the tormented man set, the mules matched.

Late in the afternoon he reached Fort Collins and proceeded down the dusty main street without looking to either side, making his way to a stable. After he had given instructions to Roger, the livery boy, he looked up and down the line of buildings trying to decide where to get his letter read. He saw the hardware store where he had bought cartridges. "Well, I guess I'll go to there. Don't care much for Carl, but I reckon he can read."

Pushing his way through the wide door, he paused just inside to let his eyes adjust to the dim light and looked around to see if he recognized anyone.

"Why, hello Coker," the proprietor of the store greeted him with a false heartiness. "Haven't seen you in a long time. What do you need today?"

"Don't know for sure, Carl. I won't know until I get someone to read a letter for me."

Carl Mann looked at him, but made no reply. Coker edged closer to the counter. He was reluctant to ask Carl to read his letter because he didn't particularly like him, but he needed to know what was in it right away.

"You can read cain't you, Carl?" he asked and looked directly at the man.

"Yes, I can read, but I'm busy right now. Why don't you take it to the postmaster . . . oh, there's our schoolteacher, Miss Caton, coming in. Maybe she'll read it to you."

Coker looked at the woman who had entered the store. The apprehension he had felt about asking Carl Mann to read the letter paled by comparison with the fear he felt for any strange woman. Someone had pointed the schoolteacher out to him once, and Coker had vowed to avoid one so intelligent forever. But the afternoon was slipping into darkness and Coker needed to know what was in the letter immediately. Desperation pushed him to approach her. Worse than facing a grizzly bear, he thought.

Like a first grade boy completely awed by his teacher, Coker shuffled up to the woman. "Miz Ca . . . Miz Caton," he said.

"Yes," she said as she turned to face him.

Although he was a foot taller, Coker felt that the young woman was looking down at his head. "Miz Caton," he said, "I got a letter that I need someone to read to me purty bad. Would you read it for m-me?"

"Why surely I'll read it for you," she said in such a pleasant voice that Coker couldn't hide his surprise. He had expected a teacher to be stern.

He pulled the paper from his pocket and handed it to her. By now the letter was wrinkled badly and looked like an assignment some student had wadded up and thrown away. Miss Caton unfolded it carefully.

"Let's move over here by the window where the light is better," she said.

Coker was happy to get out of the hearing of Carl Mann. The teacher smoothed the paper on the window to remove as many wrinkles as possible. With the light behind her, she read the letter:

"My Dearest Father,

"I pray that somehow this letter will reach you. I have very little hope that it will because it has been so many years since I have heard about you.

"I have written to you a number of times over the years, but I sent the letters to Denver and they all came back.

"Just a few days ago I was thinking about Misty Valley. For some reason, I remembered the trail led to Fort Collins and Mother picked up mail there. I thought perhaps you might still get your mail there instead of at

Denver. It is a slender hope, but you are the only one I know who might keep my babies from being taken from me."

"How horrible!" Miss Caton said before she continued:

"It is extremely painful for me to realize you may not know that I have children. I have two, a girl named Misty Cherie after the valley where we lived, and a boy named Richard Lincoln. My husband died four months ago very mysteriously. His sister and her husband have started court proceedings to take my boy and girl.

"My husband was wealthy. He told his sister he left a will, but she can't find it. They have a court order to keep me from spending any of his money. I can't hire a lawyer, so I am desperately afraid the judge will award my children to them because I am in such poor health. They have great influence in this county. They are keeping me a virtual prisoner in their house. I have been ill for some time and although a doctor is giving me medicine, I seem to be getting weaker every day. I am writing this letter in my room while they think I'm asleep. Must hurry and finish and somehow I will get it to the post office. One of the servants is my friend. Perhaps by some quirk of fate you will get this."

Miss Caton dropped her hands. "Why, that's an outrage," she said and held her hand to her head. She fought her own tears, but regained her composure and went on:

"The years I spent with you and Mother roaming through the trees and looking down from those high mountain peaks will always be my fondest memory. I still see you as a strong man. I have never quit loving you even though I have not seen you in over thirty years. Come and take me and your grandchildren back to Misty Valley. I hear someone coming up the stairs so I must hide this letter. I am writing from Freeda, Oklahoma. My last name is Cook. With all my love, Bonnie."

Thirty years of anguish reinforced by the words of the letter rendered Coker immobile and speechless. His face contorted like a trapped wolf; he stared helplessly at Miss Caton. While she looked on in surprise, he paced from one end of the store to the other, then stopped in front of Miss Caton, his eyes glazed and unseeing. The young woman put her hand on his arm.

"I had no idea it would be so bad. Your poor daughter. I feel so helpless."

Coker extended a hand for the letter and said, "Thanks, Miz Caton."

"I wish there was something I could do for you." She handed the paper to him.

He pushed it into his pocket. Without seeing her, he walked outside, slumped on the boardwalk against the building and shut his eyes. Darkness covered him with dreams and the pond from the lower end of Misty Valley submerged him in its filthy, black water.

4

Long Trail

"Godamighty! Oklahoma!" Coker said as the first rays of sun splashed light in his face causing him to squeeze his eyes tight and then open them. "How'd Bonnie ever end up in Oklahoma? Why'd she want to go to the end of the world?"

He struggled to his feet. Feeling the chill for the first time, he shivered, rubbing arms and shoulders with his hands. "Well, if Bonnie's in Oklahoma, then I've gotta go to Oklahoma. I've been from the east coast to the west. Don't know why it hit me so hard. Daylight makes it sound better'n it did last night, but it's still a hell of a fur piece. Gotta hit the trail soon's I can."

He looked at the sun to judge the time. "Reckon the rest'runt is open. Guess I better eat there and save my jerky. Gotta stop by the stable and tell Roger to tie my mules out front."

The livery lay between him and the cafe. It only took a minute for Coker to tell Roger what he wanted. Jack Leady was just opening the restaurant door and recognized him.

"Well, Coker, don't tell me you're gonna eat some good food for once." Leady was a pleasant man. Coker had always liked him.

"Yeah, I reckon I have to eat your grub that don't have no taste 'cause I gotta save my good jerky for the trail."

"You going to Denver?" Leady asked. "If you are I'd like to get you to bring me back some silverware I've

29

paid for down there. Waiting for them to send it is too damned slow."

"I wish I could help," Coker told him, "but I'm gonna miss Denver by forty miles. And, anyways, I ain't comin' back any time soon. What do you know about Oklahoma?"

Leady gave him a questioning look, "Why do you want to know about Oklahoma? I thought you'd been over all those trails on the plains."

Ignoring Leady's question, Coker nodded his head, "Reckon I have, but it's been over thirty year since I been out there. Knowin' the prairie I don't reckon it's changed none."

"There's a lot more barbed wire. Most everybody is fencing their land and it's getting more difficult to go as the crow flies."

Coker considered Leady's statement and said, "Damned bobwire. I'll have to remember to get some pliers when I go back to the hardware to get shells."

Taking a table by a window he sat staring into the street, muttering about the "bobwire" until his breakfast arrived. Lord almighty, he was hungry. He had gone without food the night before. He ate the steak, eggs, biscuits and gravy in huge bites, commenting about the meal as he chewed. "Eggs and gravy is good, better'n Rufe makes. Biscuits ain't bad, but don't see how anybody eats beef. Ain't got no taste."

Gulping down his last bite, he went to the counter and dropped a twenty-dollar bill by the cash register. Leady picked up the bill, started to put it in the till then stopped. "I don't have change for a twenty this early in the morning. Do you have anything else?"

"I got another twenty, but that don't help none," Coker told him as he tried to think of a solution.

"If you're going to be in town for a while, I'll get some change when the bank opens," Leady suggested.

"Naw, I gotta be on the trail a long time afore the bank opens," Coker said as he rubbed his chin. "I'll tell you. I gotta get some things at the hardware, and maybe Mann will have some change. I'll have 'im give it to you."

Leady hesitated. "Well, Mann doesn't always . . . Okay, I guess that will be all right."

Leaving quickly, Coker went directly to the hardware store. Instead of looking for what he wanted, he went straight to the counter where Mann was standing and spoke brusquely to the proprietor.

"I need some things, Carl." Not waiting for a reply, he went on, "Give me four boxes of twelve-gauge shotgun shells with double-ought buck, four boxes of 38-56 cartridges and your biggest pair of wire cutters."

Without a word, Mann got the ammunition, but when he brought the pliers he asked, "Going to be cutting someone's fences, Coker?"

Coker bridled at the implied accusation, moved closer and his piercing eyes stabbed at Mann, "No," he sneered. "I need 'em to pull quills out of my pet porkypine so I can sleep with 'im."

"Okay, okay," Mann said as he dropped the pliers and quickly put everything in a large sack. "Just making conversation. No need to get huffy."

Coker continued to look through him, but handed him the twenty. Mann took the bill, then paused. "Your pliers and shells come to eight-fifty. I don't have enough change this early in the morning."

"He's lyin'," Coker thought, but he had no way of establishing that without forcefully looking into the cash register. "Okay, tell you what. I owe Jack Leady for my breakfast, and I'm gonna owe Roger for keepin' my mules last night. I gotta leave. You git some change and I'll send 'em here so you can pay 'em. I'll be through sometime to get what's left."

31

Mann's eyes shifted from side to side. "All right, I'll pay them if I don't forget."

Coker leaned down until his nose was only two inches from Mann's. "No," he said, "you won't forget. 'Cause iffen you forget, Coker will come back and get his change outta your hide."

Mann gulped and blinked nervously. "I'll, I'll see to it that they get their money, and I'll keep your change for you."

Coker continued to stare into his eyes as he slowly turned and then left the store. Mann shivered and let out a long sigh of relief when the door closed behind him. Immediately, hands trembling, he fished the necessary change from a sack underneath the counter and put it aside for Roger and Jack.

Coker headed for the stable where his mules were tied at the hitching rail. Roger saw him approaching and came out to help Coker put on the packs.

"Roger," Coker explained to him, "I couldn't get a twenty changed so I left it with Mann. He's s'pozed to get the change and pay you and Leady. I done told Jack."

"Sure thing, I'll try to collect from Mann, but we may have trouble gettin' money out of that shifty cuss."

"Don't think you will," Coker said as he remembered Mann's frightened look, "but if he don't pay you, I'll take care of it next time through. If he tries to keep your money, he won't never hold out on nobody else."

Knowing Coker, Roger said, "I'll bet he won't."

Mounting Thunder Red he raised his hand head high to Roger and trotted his mules east out of Fort Collins talking to himself and his animals as he went.

"Guess goin' by Greeley and driftin' toward Kit Carson and Lamar'll be the shortest way to Oklahoma, and maybe somebody along the way can tell me where

Freeda is. Hafta cross the Platte somewhere. Maybe they've got a bridge crost it by now."

Setting a course southeast he rode for ten miles away from the foothills on the road to Greeley and then pulled Switchback to a sudden stop. Surprised by the quick halt, Thunder Red bumped into Switchback's rump slightly which caused the bay mule to back his ears and threaten to kick, but Coker jerked his head up, "Here! Here! You damned mules better not git to fightin' or we'll go so fast you won't have 'nough strength to kick at a dog."

For a time he sat looking east across the flatland. Furrows cut across his forehead and he rubbed his chin as he deliberated. The mountains made him twist him in his saddle and he considered their peaks and canyons.

After some time he spoke. "Y'know, Switchback, it's bound to be shorter cuttin' crost them plains, but iffen I recollect right, water is mighty hard to find out there. Not much to eat on that prairie but jackrabbits and antelopes. Jackrabbits is tough and antelope ain't much better'n beef. Maybe we better stay by the mountains long as we can. At least we'll have plenty of water, and deer'll be along the way."

He looked east and south while he considered his argument. "Yeah, deer's a hell of a lot better than antelopes. Besides, it'd prob'ly take me longer to hunt meat for me and find grass and water for you critters out there."

But the shortage of grass or the quality of the game did not turn his head south. The mountains and the unconscious need to look at a certain house in the big city changed his course. So south he rode always in sight of the comforting purple ranges.

Staying just far enough east to avoid the gulches and rocks of the foothills, Coker continually exhorted his mules to walk faster.

33

"Come on, Thunder Red," he would say, "we've got a hell of a long way to go. Keep pickin' them feet up and down. I'll give you the whole winter off when we get back if you don't quit on me."

The deep malaise he had felt earlier got the best of him after several miles, and he climbed off Switchback without stopping and jogged down the trail ahead of the mules, forcing them to trot. Repeating this pattern every time gloom overtook him, Coker pressed on for thirty miles before he found a camping place that suited him.

"Plenty a grass and water here for you critters," he told them. "I've stopped here afore. Soft under that big cottonwood."

Swiftly removing the packs, he let the mules go. Next, he took out the bedroll and laid it down. Following the same procedure as always, he pretended that he was going to sleep by his packs, but after dark he moved his robe under the big cottonwood where the tall grass made a softer bed and where he could hear the creek running nearby.

"Don't wanna go to sleep until I have to," he muttered as he lay gazing at the stars. But fatigue and the steady whispering of the stream soon carried him to face the snake carrying Trissy and Bonnie into the bottomless lake while he struggled in vain to go after them.

5

Through Denver and On South

By the time the sun reflected off patches of snow left on the high peaks, Coker had taken a plunge in the creek, eaten breakfast and ridden for ten miles trying to grind the anguish of the night under the pounding hooves of his tireless mules. Ahead of him lay Denver. He had tried to convince himself to ride around it, but, like a nail yielding to a magnet, he was drawn as helplessly toward the town as he had been when he returned to get Trissy.

At noon he reached the western edge of the city and stood across the street from the house where Trissy had lived with her aunt.

"Right here's where I was when Trissy come tearin' out to go with me. Maybe me and her woulda' been better off if I had stayed in the mountains," he said.

Gradually, his eyes dimmed and he was back in time to the day it happened:

Trissy came racing across the street smiling happily, her big, blue eyes sparkling and eager. Coker felt a warm soft glow as he watched the long black hair bouncing on her shoulders. She hurried to him, carrying a small carpetbag. He admired her little nose, the gleaming white teeth and rosy pink cheeks. He opened his arms and she leaped into them, laughing with delight. He hugged her, then held her out and looked into her eyes. Immediately she pulled his head to hers and kissed him softly on the lips and said, "We better hurry. Aunt Tilda went to visit, but I don't know how long she'll be gone."

Coker tied her bundle behind the saddle on the horse and they rode out of Denver with Coker trying to subdue his throbbing heart. They headed straight for the mountains instead of going to Fort Collins, Coker's usual route. Longer and more hazardous, the trail led past crystal blue lakes and there were breathtaking views from the ridges. Coker's ecstasy increased each time Trissy cried out in delight when she gazed at the scenery.

They rode until the sun set behind Long's Peak. Coker laid down two buffalo robes he had brought for them to sleep between and stood, not knowing what to do as Trissy smiled and took off her shoes. His heart pounded as he tried to decide. He looked at her and said, "Trissy . . . Trissy . . . what . . are we going . . ."

Stranger reared, jerked the reins out of Coker's limp hand and tore off, running away from a horseless carriage clattering down the street. Switchback and Thunder Red, snorting and bucking, followed hard on his heels.

"What in the hell?" Coker looked to see what had spooked his mules and ended his reverie. "One of them goddam things. I'll put a bullet in the sonuvabitch." But his rifle hung on Stranger's saddle. He jerked his hatchet out of his belt and ran a few steps after the offending automobile as it disappeared out of sight around a corner leaving a cloud of dust.

Continuing to swear, he ran down the street to find his mules. "Prob'ly run all the way to Aspen Hill. Iffen they do, I'll track that guy down and nail his ears to the back of his damned buggy."

For three blocks he followed the trail of his mules in the dust of the street. Finally, he spotted Thunder Red and Switchback tiptoeing toward him with their noses high. Coker whistled and they came stiff-legged. Talking to them softly, he got close enough to Switchback to grab his lead rope. Leading him and letting Thunder Red follow, he searched for Stranger. The black mule stood in a yard, a half-block down a side street, afraid to come back. Coker walked to him slowly and coaxed him into letting him pick up the reins. "Let's see how fast we can get out of this place. It's sure 'nough goin' to be bad."

Away from Denver he led the animals in a fast trot. He tried to get on Stranger, but the mule spooked and jerked at the reins. Furious, Coker swore. "Stand still, you sonuvabitch, or I'll beat your wild head off."

Jerking the reins Coker looked for a stick. The mule reared and snorted, and the whites of his eyes showed above the irises. Coker couldn't keep hold of the mule and get a club, so in his fury he jerked his hatchet from his belt. He had raised his arm to drive the hatchet into Stranger's head when he regained his sanity.

"What the hell am I doin'? I've gone plumb loco."

With trembling hands, he put the hatchet back in his belt and talked to Stranger. "All right, black mule, I kinda went off my rocker. Settle down, now. I don't blame you none for bein' scared of that thing in Denver. I ain't never hit you afore, and I ain't agonna do it now. What I been through these last two days just built up, and I was about to do somethin' real crazy. But don't worry old mule, somethin' just went out of me, and I'm limp as a old rope."

As he calmed down, Stranger did too and in a few minutes he mounted him with no trouble. Anger still drove him on, but with his hatchet he had tucked away the white-hot fire driving him to almost madness.

"I got to get to Bonnie no matter what, but iffen I'd killed my mule, it would have killed me too."

Along the mountains he rode letting his mind wander among the trees and the peaks:

Big, brown rock. Got that green stuff on it. Kinda like the one old Featherfoot's got his hole under. He's been there a long time. Wonder how old that coyote is. Why'd he stay there all

37

these years? Cain't recollect when he first come. Maybe Rufe can 'member. Wonder how Rufe's doin'. Hope he don't fall and break another leg. Sure hated to leave him there by hisself. Ain't been by hisself since I went to Lar'mie t'git a mare Roger told me about. Wonder if Roger's got his money from Mann. Hope so. Hate to kill old Mann over a few dollars. Somethin' shinin' over there. Hope Mann pays Jack too. See that shinin' agin up off the ground. Looks like bobwire. Jack said there'd be more of that stuff.

"Bobwire!" he bellowed. "All along the trail as far as I can see. He said there'd be more of it on the plains, but I didn't think I'd run into it here. Hope there ain't none in my way."

Coker watched ahead on the trail for the hated fences as he rode the main road between Denver and Colorado Springs. Too many horses and carriages used the route for it to be blocked. Swearing at the barbed wire every step, Coker covered ten miles before finding a spring where he had stayed years before.

"It's a little early, but I better let you critters eat a while longer than I have been."

As he walked around a huge tree toward the water, he almost ran into barbed wire nailed to the pine. "Goddamn," he said. "Even usin' trees for posts."

Without hesitation Coker pulled the pliers from his saddlebag and, chuckling at the thought of the rancher having to fix his fence, cut the three strands.

Following his custom, he put the packs together under a large spruce and pretended to make his bed by them. For some time he sat on the buffalo robe with the rifle across his lap and gazed at the mountains west of him. "Pikes Peak is a big 'un. Never rode it but oncet, and it was rugged."

Something moved to his left and without turning his head he looked at the spot. A young deer tiptoed through the grass to get a drink at the spring. Slowly, Coker raised his rifle and shot it through the neck. "Good meat!" he said as he approached the dead animal. "I can save my jerky for when I really need it."

Leaning the gun against a tree, he looked carefully around him and cleaned the deer. He was skinning the animal when he saw a rider leading another horse. He was trotting through the timber. Coker stopped working and eyed the man as he approached. "Maybe I oughta get my rifle. Naw, he ain't wearin' no gun. Don't look too mean. Prob'ly just wants to talk."

The man rode straight at Coker as if he were going to run him down, but stopped just short and swung his horse so his left side was toward him, and his right hand hung down out of sight. "Howdy," Coker said. "Get down and rest a spell. I'll have some good venison cookin' afore long."

A young cowhand, clean shaven and muscular, that's what he was, Coker decided and noticed that the fellow's dark eyes didn't look very mean.

The man stared and said, "Mister, you're on private property. How'd you get in here?"

Coker met his gaze, but showed no anger. "Well, sir, I come through over there where it looks like a bull elk done run through the fence. Broke 'em all down looks like. Big hole there by that big tree, so I didn't see nothin' wrong with campin' here tonight."

"I rode that fence yesterday and there wasn't no hole in it. I thought you damned mountain men had quit cuttin' fences, but I bet you've got a pair of pliers in your saddlebag."

"Cain't recollect whether I do or not. I don't usually have none, but I could look and see."

"All you're gonna do is get off this land before I take you to the man who owns this property. If I do you'll wind up in jail for cuttin' his fence. Now pick up your stuff and get. Leave the deer hanging where it is."

"Ain't you a little young to be orderin' a old man like me around? I've done settled down for the night so I reckon I'll stay. Won't hurt none for me to drink spring water for a night. I don't 'magine you or the guy who claims this is his'n made the water in this spring." Coker's face showed no anger, but his steely eyes made the man squirm in his saddle. "How do you 'spect to take me anywheres iffen I don't wanna go?"

"This forty-five will make you go anywhere I want you to go," the man said as he pointed a pistol he had kept out of sight. "Now I'll let you get your gear, but that's all."

"Damn. Never get old enough to misjudge a man. So you had your gun hangin' from your saddlehorn. Reckon they ain't nothin' for me to do but get outta here. Could you tell me where there's a place on the road where I can camp?" As Coker spoke he took an imperceptible half step toward the man.

"I don't give a damn whether you find a place to camp or if you ride all night. Just get on down the road."

"It won't hurt you none to help a pore old man. Couldn't you just tell me iffen there's a spot down the road." Shifting as if to look past the horse's rump down the trail, Coker took another half step and pointed behind the man.

Turning in his saddle the man pointed in the same direction with his gun. "There may be somethin'...wup!"

Quick as an attacking cougar, Coker caught the man's right wrist with his left hand and jerked him off the horse. As he hit the ground, Coker's knee ground into his chest and he pressed the point of his throwing knife against his throat. "Unless you wanna swaller this knife without openin' your mouth, you better drop that gun."

The man's fingers let the revolver fall to the ground as he croaked, "Don't kill me! Don't kill me! I was just doin' my job."

Coker lessened the pressure on the knife slightly. "Iffen Coker had wanted to kill you, Coker could have put a knife through your heart any time."

The man's face took on the color of cold ashes. "Not . . . Not Coker Ford," he said.

"Nope, not Coker Ford. Coker Owen Ford."

Squirming on the ground, the man shuddered as he said, "Damn, I nearly committed suicide. If I'd known who you was, I sure wouldn't have come within a mile of you."

"You know me?"

"No, but my daddy has told me stories about you and a guy named Rufe something or other." He shook again. "Man alive, I thought you guys would've been dead by now."

Picking up the man's gun, Coker stepped back and unloaded it. "You're gonna have to spend a night with me so you might as well get up and help me cut up this deer. What's your name?"

"Randy Stevens. But I can't stay here tonight. I have to be at cow camp tonight and report back to the boss tomorrow. Thanks for the offer, anyway."

Coker's steel eyes caused goosebumps to pop out up and down Stevens' arms. "I didn't offer nothin'. I cain't have you runnin' to your boss and bringin' a bunch a guys to run me off or havin' me throwed in jail. I ain't lookin' for no trouble, and I sure as hell don't aim to spend no time in the calaboose. I got some elkskin you can wrap up in, and we got plenty to eat. I'd like to hear some of your old man's stories anyway. Sometimes they

41

git confusin' when they're told a bunch a times."

As Coker spoke a dark shadow crossed Stevens' face, then interest in Coker pushed it away. "All right. I'll stay. Gettin' tired of my sorry boss and this job anyway."

"Son, if you're honest, I won't tie you up. My mules'll let me know iffen you try to leave with your horse. I'm in kind of a hurry, but if you run away tonight and I don't ketch you, someday I will and you won't run anywheres no more."

"No, sir, I'm not goin' to run away. I won't run out on you. I'd like to talk to you."

"Right, well put your saddle over there by my stuff, and let's get some grub."

Stevens unsaddled his horse and then gathered wood while Coker cut up the deer. Before long he had a fire going good and hot. Coker shoved the venison on spits and started roasting it methodically.

The meat had barely warmed up when Coker speared a piece on his knife and ate it in huge gulps, blood dripping to the ground as he chewed. Stevens watched and shook his head in wonder.

"I never dreamed I'd ever be settin' by a fire with one of the last wild mountain men. Boy, I'm lucky I'm alive and lucky to get to talk to you."

Finally, the meat was done enough to suit him and he started in.

"Well," Coker said through a mouthful, "I needed someone to talk to, but we ain't got long afore we got to turn in. Get your stories told if you're goin to."

Stevens wiped his hands on his pants, leaned back against a large tree to get the most heat from the fire and raised his head to look at Coker, but he saw nothing. He jerked his head from one side to the other looking for the old mountain man. Then he heard him say from the shadows, "Are you gonna talk or set there all night lookin' like a nut?"

42

Stevens squinted his eyes and looked in the direction of the voice. Finally, he made out Coker's form beside a willow bush which blotted out the light from the fire. "I didn't see you move. What are you doin' over there? Do you think someone will come lookin for me?"

"Naw. I think you're tellin' me the truth. It just don't pay to set out in the light where you make an easy target."

"Are you scared?"

"Don't know whether bein' careful is the same as bein scared, but I'm alive. And I know of a bunch of white men and Injuns both which liked to set in the light of their fires which ain't."

Impenetrable blackness circled the fire; Stevens stiffened. "Well, I don't reckon any Indians are skulkin' around out there so I'll stay here where it's warm."

Nonetheless, he scooted slightly toward the shadows and began his first story.

"Daddy told me you and . . . what's your pardner's name?"

"Rufe Cantrell."

"Oh, yeah, Rufe Cantrell. Well, he told me about the time ten guys stole a couple of your horses and you cornered them in a bar in Fort Collins and whipped 'em all. He said you beat on 'em until they was happy to give you their horses as well as yours. I understand the sheriff found something to do on the other side of town to keep away from you. Is that true?"

"Part of it is. Rufe used to be the fightenist man which ever lived. When he was riled, he was turrible. A bobcat couldn't move any quicker. He'd kick and bite and scratch if he had to. With a twelve-inch knife in one hand and a tomahawk in the other, he was a frightful sight.

"But we didn't go in no bar. We wouldn't go in there to drink, and we sure as hell never went in no bar to fight anyone. Sure way to get killed because you don't

43

ever know what's ahind the side doors. No, we waited for 'em to come outside. Wasn't ten of 'em neither. Cain't no two men whip ten. Wasn't but eight. Didn't exactly whip 'em. Cut 'em and chopped 'em some. Didn't last long. They quit quick when one of 'em spilt his guts on the sidewalk and another'n scattered his brains on the side of the saloon. The others didn't have but a cut or two apiece, but they was real glad to tell us where our horses was. Only thing, we had to wait 'til they stopped blubberin' afore we could tell what they was sayin. Don't know 'bout the sheriff. We just found our horses and lit out. S'funny. Nobody never stole no more of our horses."

Stevens shuddered, slid around the tree into the shadow and said, "And I rode up and told him to get off this land." A sudden chill ran through his body, but he stayed in the shadow.

"What did you say?"

"Oh, I was thinkin' about something else my Daddy told me. He said you and Rufe fought fifty men in Poudre Canyon and killed them all. How did you do that?"

"Them stories get stretched awful bad over the years. They wasn't much law in the eighties and nineties. You had to take care of yourself. Them guys heard me and Rufe had found a rich vein of gold. Wasn't true. We panned up and down the cricks and had a lot of gold dust, but we didn't have no mine atall. Anyways, they was a follerin' us up the Poudre. We saw 'em behind us and was gettin' away from 'em, but what we didn't know was some more renegades in cahoots with them guys was already waitin' up the canyon. They ambushed us. Shot Rufe in the leg, but we didn't know it was broke 'til we got back to Aspen Hill. We hid out in the rocks and shot it out with 'em."

Stevens stared at the shadow behind the bush. "It's hard to believe you killed fifty? How'd you do that?"

Coker snorted. "No, we didn't kill fifty. Wasn't more'n thirty or forty to begin with. They throwed a lotta lead, but me'n Rufe don't never shoot 'less we know we're gonna hit somethin'. Ever' time we shot, one of those bastards died. Prob'ly didn't kill more'n a dozen 'fore they give it up and sneaked off. Me'n Rufe knowed the trail good 'nough to foller it in the dark, so we stayed there 'til night and then we went home. Next mornin' we found Rufe's leg was broke. Bullet went clean through though. Rufe's all right, but couldn't walk good no more."

Stevens sat in silence overwhelmed by the story Coker had told him. Perhaps his father had exaggerated in a way, he thought, and Coker had undoubtedly stretched the truth. Even at that he knew he camped with a man more deadly and fearsome than he had imagined. He asked, "Did they try to follow you to Aspen Hill?"

"No, I went down and hid on the trail and watched for 'em ever' day fer a month, but they never showed."

"Didn't the sheriff ever ask any questions?"

"Well, we didn't break no law neither one of the times you talked about. We was just gittin' our horses back and protectin' ourselves. Besides, we didn't go anywheres and tell we done it. And no one is gonna come up to Aspen Hill and ask us nothin'.."

"Where is Aspen Hill?"

"In the mountains."

"Where is it in the mountains?"

"'Tween Fort Collins and Grand Junction."

"Where are you going now?"

"South."

Stevens imagined he could feel Coker's eyes piercing the darkness and penetrating his body. He thought about some more stories his father had told, but decided the session had gone far enough. "Well, that's all I remember. I'm ready to hit the hay."

He paused and then asked, "Don't you ever have a hard time gettin' around in the winter in the deep snow?

"Yep, the snow gits deep, but we got snowshoes and we go all over."

"Do you ever get lost?"

"No, sir. There's always somethin' you can see to tell where you are. Cain't git lost if you know your mountains." Coker waved his hand toward the east and said, "It's them damn plains where you're gonna get lost and die. When you git ketched in a blizzard, you cain't see nothin' and iffen you could it all looks the same. Ain't nobody can find his way out there. Only thing you can do is try to find a rock or somethin' to get ahind and let the snow cover you up to keep warm. Many a good man's died in a blizzard on them plains."

The old mountain man handed him an elkskin. Then he put his own buffalo robe a few feet from Stevens. Randy lay on his back, looked at the sky and asked, "Ever wonder how all those stars got up there?"

No answer came, so he continued. "I've thought many a time about whether there was a God powerful enough to make all those lights up there. What do you think, Coker?" No reply. "Coker? Coker what do you think?"

Raising his head he looked where Coker had been. He saw nothing so he got up and crawled the few feet to where Coker had put his bed. Nothing there.

"I'll be damned," he whispered. "I didn't hear anything. How'd he do that?" He felt around the pine needles, but Coker was gone.

Looking up at the stars once more, he said, "Coker Owen Ford. Mysterious as the universe, and a hell of a lot more scary. Where are you going, and what are you up to? I'll probably never know, but I hope you're always on my side."

6

Weary Ride

Awakened by a hard poke in the ribs, Randy Stevens whipped the elkskin from his face to see what was going on with that old man. Pitch blackness greeted him. He froze, heart throbbing. He just knew Coker was going to kill him before he left.

"Git up and let's eat some breakfast," Coker said. It's near dawn, and I've got to git rollin'."

Stevens sighed and unrolled the skin cover. "How'd you know where I was? I moved my bed after you moved yours."

"Yeah, I heard you thrashin' 'round like a crippled buff'lo. Thought maybe you was trying to run away, but then I heard you rollin' up agin. Sure was glad 'cause I kinda got to likin' you, and I didn't want to cut your throat. But if I was hidin' from Injuns I wouldn't want you makin' all that racket. I got the fire goin', so let's eat and light out."

Stevens followed Coker over to where spits of venison were sizzling. He squatted, warming his hands, and, without looking at the mountain man, asked. "Is it all right if I go with you?"

Coker stared at him across the fire. "Why do you wanna go with me?"

"Well I thought about it last night. My boss is mean, and I know he'll fire me for not showin' up at the camp. I get the feelin' you're headin' toward somethin' dangerous, and I'd like to help you if I can."

Coker continued to look at Stevens for a minute before he spoke. "I don't know what I'm headin' for. It's

47

prob'ly gonna end up in killin' or gittin' kilt. You can foller along, but your horses cain't keep up with my mules as far as I'm goin."

"I've got good horses. Is it all right if I try?"

"Yeah, you can try. I can stand some company for a ways. Get your meat et iffen you're goin' with me."

Coker chomped down four fist-sized chunks of venison more raw than cooked before Randy could get one roasted. By the time he had finished his first piece, Coker had the mules loaded and stood glaring at him. He took huge bites off his second hunk of venison, chewed two or three times and swallowed, choking on the bloody lumps. While he saddled his horse, he struggled to keep the meat from coming back up.

Dawn gave a fuzzy light as Coker led his mules to the tree where he had come through the fence. Stevens stopped and examined the wire. "Yep," he said, "an elk sure went through here. He didn't run through the wire though. He cut it off with his antlers clean as a whistle."

Coker said, "Yeah, elkhorns is sharp. Seems them onnery critters cut ever' fence that gits put up."

Surprised at the light response, Stevens relaxed and before long they were kidding each other and Coker was enjoying it almost as much as when he and Rufe shot the breeze. A couple of loudmouth critters. Some of the remarks might have gotten Randy a knife in his chest the previous night, but now they were welcome relief for Coker.

Stevens fell silent as he watched Coker ride for miles and trot for almost as many more. Awed by Coker's determination and stamina, he did little but watch and wonder.

"How can that old codger keep goin' like this?" he murmured. "Surely he's got to stop and rest sometime."

After two more hours of the constant trot, he mumbled, "He ain't human. No man any age can go this long. Hell, there ain't no animal can go this long neither. If he keeps goin' like this, he's sure right about my horses. They'll be plumb wore out in two or three days. Maybe he'll wear down in a day or so."

Randy took heart when Coker pulled his mules off the trail and hollered at him, "You hungry?"

"A little I guess."

Coker reached under the elkskin into the pack and brought out a large slice of venison left from the deer, cut it in half and handed one piece to Randy. "Ain't got time to cook it, but it'll keep you goin'."

Stevens took the meat, held it in his hand trying to decide whether to eat it or throw it away. A quick look at Coker was enough. He bit off a chunk with feigned relish. A little blood dribbled down his lip and he wiped it away with the back of his hand.

"Hey, this ain't bad." He tried to sound normal. This was his first taste of raw meat, and damn, he would survive it somehow. "So maybe it's just because I'm hungry, but this tastes pretty good."

"This'ns a young, tender deer," Coker said. "A old buck or a old bull elk ain't near as good. Less you make it into jerky you cain't hardly eat it atall."

To Randy's dismay Coker trotted off down the trail forcing him to eat the rest of his venison while he was riding. "Tarnation," he said. "I was hopin' he'd rest a while. I thought I was tough, and here he's makin' me feel like a rank tenderfoot."

Watching Coker run mile after mile became more than he could endure. He swung off his horse and trotted after the mules, but in a half mile his boots slipped on his feet making him stumble every few steps. His toes lapped over each other, starting blisters. Angry and frustrated, he got back on his horse.

"He's got to be some kind of devil, or maybe the devil's after him. I know he ain't a natural human being."

49

Not slowing or missing a step, they guided the animals down the main street of Colorado Springs and on through the rest of town moving like a small whirlwind that appears suddenly and is gone. Some people stared at them, but they were soon out of sight. Coker kept his pace until the houses had faded in the distance.

The sun was setting behind Pike's Peak before he found a place to camp.

"Man, I thought I could fork a nag as long as anybody," Stevens grumbled as he stepped down, "but damned if I ever rode one until I was numb before."

"Got troubles, son?" Coker asked him. "I ain't a makin' you come you know."

"Yeah, I know. I asked you to let me come so I'll hang in." He loosened the cinch straps. By the time he pulled his saddle off, Coker already had removed both packs from the mules and had placed them over a nearby log.

"How'd you do . . . " he began but, realizing how he had asked the question over and over, he broke off and set his saddle on the same log.

They watered the animals in a foot-wide stream. By the time Randy found some good grass and staked his horse, Coker had a fire going and venison cooking. He walked up to him and scowled. "How many times are we goin' to eat venison before we try somethin' else?"

"'Til it's gone," Coker said.

Stevens coughed as he inhaled smoke and the scent of scorching venison. Not trying to conceal his disgust, he said, "I hope it runs out real soon."

Focusing his attention on the spit of cooking meat, Coker slid a chunk off on his knife. Just before he bit into it, he said, "Sure as hell don't hafta eat it. If you wanna do without, just gripe one more time."

Randy knew he had stepped onto dangerous ground. "I wasn't gripin' actually, sort of just tryin' to be funny."

There was no reply so he took some meat and ate it with mock relish, commenting frequently as to how good it was. When he finished eating, he rolled up in the elkskin, and the forty miles of hard riding made sleep come easy.

Morning and the kick in the ribs came too soon for Randy Stevens, but he struggled up, ate venison again and got his horse saddled. Repeating the procedure of the day before, Coker swept along the trail gazing at his beloved mountains as he went. He trotted at his usual speed, but Randy thought he was going twice as fast as when they started.

When Coker finally stopped for the night, Stevens almost fell off his horse. Determined to maintain his image as a rugged cowboy, he unsaddled and tried to conceal his fatigue by talking constantly.

"This is a good spot," he said without examining the area. "I bet we must have covered more ground today than we did yesterday. We came right on through Pueblo in a hurry. That grub's gonna taste good tonight."

Too tired to eat more than a little, he dozed off while he was chewing a bite of venison. He woke with a start and got the elkskin. He rolled halfway into it and fell asleep. Cold October air caused him to pull the cover over him the rest of the way before the night was over.

Three more days he clung to his horse following the indefatigable old mountain man and his mules. He remembered blurs of Walsenburg, Aguilar and Trinidad. Where the hell were they going anyway?

By the time Coker went over the pass and dropped into the town of Raton, Randy was near collapse. He was barely aware when they stopped at a livery stable.

"Let's put our animals up here for the night," Coker told him. "I've got to find out where Freeda, Oklahoma, is iffen I can, so get your saddlebags and let's find a hotel."

A more welcome statement Randy had never heard. He told the livery man to unsaddle his horse and put him in a stall. Coker fished a leather sack out of the pack that contained his moneybags, put his shotguns in with them and slung the carrier over his shoulder. Carrying his rifle he headed down the board sidewalk where the livery man had told him to go. Randy swayed along behind until they reached a small boarding house. They stashed their gear in the room, locked it and went down to the cafe.

"What you want to eat?" Coker asked as they sat down.

Randy studied the tattered menu looking for something cheap. "Get what you want," Coker told him. "I know cowboys don't never have no money so I'll pay for it. Tryin' to keep up with my mules is mighty tirin'. I know you're hungry."

Surprised at the generosity and too hungry to spurn the offer, Randy looked at the menu again and said, "I think I'll have the fried chicken."

"Chicken! You must've got godawful tired of that deer meat," Coker said. "Well, the beef ain't got no taste so I reckon as how I'll try the chicken too. It ain't near as good as grouse, but it's better'n the beef."

Both of them wolfed down the roasted chicken in short order.

"I'm gonna walk around and see iffen I can find somebody which knows where Freeda, Oklahoma is," Coker said. "The guy here at the cafe don't know, and I've gotta find someone which does."

"I think I'll go to bed right now," Stevens told him. "I'm mighty tired."

Coker paid the bill and headed out while Randy made his way upstairs. The street was almost deserted. Coker searched in vain for anyone who could tell him the best way to Oklahoma. Finally, he found a man who told him to go to Amarillo.

"That place is right on the way to anywhere you want to go in Oklahoma."

Coker thanked him and made his way back to the room where Randy was already snoring. He took one of the blankets, rolled up in the corner with his head on the saddlebag and was soon asleep.

By the time the cafe was opened early next morning, Coker and Randy had the animals tied to the hitching rail out front. They ate two orders of biscuits, eggs and gravy and headed out into the crisp air. Randy unhitched his horses and walked them around preparing to mount. "Man, these fellows are stiff this mornin'," he said as he led them a few more steps.

Coker looked closely at the man holding one horse. "Gone as far as you can." he stated more than asked.

"I'm afraid so. I don't think my horses can keep up any more."

"What you gonna do?"

"Well, I've heard a big rancher south of town here needs some hands, so I reckon I'll look him up and see if I can get a job."

Coker nodded his head in approval. "Any rancher oughtta be lookin' for a good hand. 'Specially one as tough as a elkhide which ain't been tanned."

"I'm sorry I wasn't tough enough to hang in and help you out. If you come back this way, look me up. I'll be around here somewhere. If you need any help, send for me, and I'll come runnin'."

"You're tough enough, but you didn't have no mules and you ain't run near as many years as this old coot," Coker said, then looked at Randy and smiled.

53

"What are you grinnin' at, you old codger? That's the first time I ever saw you laugh at anything."

"I was just thinkin' it'd be a good idea iffen you don't try to run nobody off with that old hogleg you got in your saddlebag. Next guy'll prob'ly kill you."

Randy smiled and then laughed. "For sure I won't point it at a renegade-of-a-mountain man. I'll use it just to shoot at coyotes."

Coker's lips curled into a snarl and he pushed his face close to Stevens'. "Don't never shoot no coyote!" His anger caused Randy to stumble backward.

"I . . . I . . . don't know . . . what's wrong with killin' coyotes?" he stammered. "Every cowboy hates coyotes because they kill cattle. I would've thought you'd want to kill coyotes."

Coker's eyes flamed. "Coyotes ain't big enough to kill cows. That's a big lie some cowboy done told to hide the steers he rustled. Coyotes is a friend to anyone who'll let'm be. Iffen you're gonna go around shootin' coyotes, maybe you don't want me to find you again."

Randy shook as he tried to placate the old man. "No, no, I mean I didn't know you liked coyotes so much. I want to be your friend so I won't ever kill a coyote or let anyone else kill one."

Coker's face softened and he extended his hand. "Reckon I got a little het up so let's part friends. But I hope you mean what you said about not killin' coyotes. It'd hurt me awful bad if I thought you'd lie to me."

Randy took his hand, squeezed it hard and said, "I wouldn't lie to you, and I'm sure glad we're still friends. Don't forget what I said. I'll be here if you need me."

Coker shook his hand and put one hand on his shoulder.

"Never know when I'll need a friend. Don't know if I'll ever be back this way so don't waste no time lookin' for me, but iffen I ever do I'll find you. I gotta say so long now, Randy, 'cause I cain't look back at the mountains or I'd never get away from 'em."

"He called me Randy," Stevens murmured as he watched Coker swing onto Thunder Red and trot out of Raton. He mounted his own horse and followed Coker to the edge of town.

The man and his mules slowly disappeared around a small hill in the curve of the roadway.

"Good luck Coker Owen Ford," Randy whispered.

Then he shivered as he said, "Maybe you don't need the luck as much as whoever you're after. I'm sure as hell glad we parted friends, and you're not after me."

He turned his horse around slowly and headed south of Raton to look for a job.

7

Amarillo and Freeda

Down from the mountains holding his spirit, Coker rode, his eyes riveted on the endless horizon. He saw Misty Valley and the creek, running out of the big pond at the head of the valley, murmured in his ears. He could see Trissy and hear her laugh as she watched Bonnie Thankful dashing happily through the knee-high grass in the meadow. He listened to them playing their guitars and singing. The vision urged him to go back to Misty Valley and spend his days reliving his memories.

Another image, Bonnie's tearful eyes looking at him as Trissy's aunt led her from the courtroom while four deputies restrained him. "Bonnie's eyes. I gotta see her, Switchback. Thirty years is too damned long. I gotta see my little girl."

Changing his thoughts, he concentrated on what lay ahead. "Been acrost here one time back, Switchback. Snakes oughta be in this time of year, but you cain't trust them. Might hafta to do without water for a couple of days. Looks kinda dry. Too bad that young feller couldn't have come along. Kinda green, but he'da been good to talk to. Gets mighty lonesome on these damned plains. Still he ain't got no business gittin' mixed up in my fight."

Coker rode away from the pines through the juniper in the rolling hills heading east. To his left the crumbly, black lava from an extinct volcano tapered to the plains. Lava rocks cut at his moccasins and the mule's feet, forcing him to pick his way. To his right the flat land sprawled into infinity.

As he trotted on, he studied the prairie. Gramma grass grew among the sagebrush. Grasshoppers made a constant wave in front of him, and occasionally a jackrabbit would hop away from the trail, stand up and look at the mules. Coker said, "I guess I can eat grasshoppers and jackrabbits. At least I won't die iffen I can find some water."

Gloom caught up with him and he resorted to running ahead of his mules, driven forward by his great love for his daughter, but tormented by his passion for the high mountains. This mission was pulling him farther away from Rufe, farther away from Aspen Hill.

Refusing to look back, he drifted out of the cedars in the foothills and swore at the beargrass and sagebrush of the prairie. Now that he was far away from the mountains, his burning desire to help Bonnie drove him mile after dusty mile. Only darkness forced him to a reluctant stop. Not bothering to build a fire, he ate some of his jerky and rolled into his buffalo robe for the night. Restless sleep came quickly:

<u>Soft autumn snowflakes Cool breeze blowing down</u> toward Misty Valley. <u>Porch of cabin. Golden aspen leaves slipping back and forth to the ground. Smoke from stove drifting down canyon. Watch last switchback. Rufe shoulda been back. Where's Rufe? Coyote howls. Featherfoot? Horse neighs. Blackie? Shadows at end of switchback holding somethin'. Blackie? Rufe? Come on, Rufe. Rufe won't come Rufe's got to get out of the shadows. Run and help him. Cain't move. Rufe! Rufe!</u>

Shouting his partner's name shook Coker from his fitful rest. He unrolled the robe and looked at the stars. "Light not far away. Ain't no reason to try to sleep. Why'd I dream about old Rufe? Hope he's all right. Dream don't make no sense. Maybe Rufe's in trouble.

57

Naw, Rufe can take care of hisself. Cain't let this crazy dream slow me down. Just wait for light and move on."

Not like the soft and whispering dawn of the mountains, light sprang from the horizon and swooped like a diving hawk across the prairie shoving the darkness back in a few moments. Shortly after the sun exploded over the treeless horizon, Coker hit the trail, trotting tirelessly across the plains.

At Clayton, New Mexico, he looked back. The tips of the mountains had disappeared beneath the horizon behind him. Not being able to see them reduced their pull, so he plunged on toward Amarillo, more determined than ever.

As the sun reached its zenith, the great prairie swallowed the specks of man and mules in its endless mirages.

He saw the tip of the tower while he was riding Stranger. He stopped the mule, looked again and made out the wheel on top. "I'll be damned," he said. "It's a windmill. That means there's gonna be water." For a short time he felt a slight twinge of happiness.

But the barbed wire stretched everywhere. Time after time Coker cut the wire to water his mules in a stock tank. Nor did he bother to go out the way he came in but cut a different set of wires each time as he left.

"They ain't got no right to put up bobwire," he would say. "Don't reckon it'll do no good to cut'em, but maybe they'll know somebody don't like it."

How long he took to cross the plains, he didn't know. Cactus grew thicker and the plains turned into rolling hills, so he knew he was nearing Amarillo. One day early in the afternoon he came to the crest of a small hill and saw a town visible in the distance. He looked around the area to get his bearings.

"Well, it's some bigger, but it's got to be Amarilla. Maybe I oughta buy some duds here to look more like people do nowadays. Ain't nothin' as good as buckskin, but don't wanna look too differ'nt 'cause people think you're crazy."

He found a livery stable at the edge of town. The proprietor turned away from a hard-looking man he was talking to and stood squarely in the door leading to the stalls of the big barn. He crossed burly arms in front of him and said, "What can I do for you?"

"I'd like to rest my mules and get some grain in 'em."

He eyed Coker and spit on the ground by his feet. "Cost six bits a mule for the night. You got any money?"

Coker looked straight into the man's eyes until he began to fidget. "Got enough for tonight," and dug in his jacket pocket for the change left from his stay in Raton. He reached into the wrong pocket and pulled on the end of a bill. As he did, ten twenty-dollar bills fell to the ground.

The proprietor gasped and the man at the edge of the door took two steps for a better look. Coker scooped up the bills and got the correct change out of his other pocket. He paid the man and started to take the packs off the mules. He was lifting one from Stranger when the livery owner reached up to take the pack off the other side. When he did, Stranger jumped into Coker and knocked the pack to the barn floor. All the contents spilled. One of the moneybags opened slightly, exposing several bills.

The other man stooped to pick up the bags, but Coker yanked them away from him. "I'll take care of my own property."

The man continued to stare at the bags. "I was just tryin' to help. Don't get so huffy."

Coker turned to the proprietor. "Where can I find a dry goods store?"

"Straight down the street about three blocks."

59

Coker tied the bags together, slung them over his shoulder and went up the street in the direction the man had indicated.

The store owner started to say something when he saw Coker armed with a knife and rifle, but Coker's icy stare convinced him it was better to take a chance on what looked like one tough customer.

"Need myself some clothes," Coker said. "You fix me up good, hear?"

With trembling fingers the man managed to do some measuring and got him fitted with blue work pants. Coker asked for two pairs of them and two shirts.

As the store owner laid the clothes on the counter, Coker pointed to the window. "Got a hat like those guys outside is wearin'?"

"Yes, sir. What size?"

"Don't know. Just give me some to try on."

The man put three hats on the counter. Coker set one on his head and asked, "Got any boots?"

"You bet. What size . . . never mind I'll bring several pair."

Coker found a comfortable hat, but he tried on five different pairs of boots before he found a reasonable fit. When he had all of his purchases in a pile, he asked, "How much?"

The man toted up and said, "Nine sixty."

When Coker gave him ten dollars and told him to keep the change, the fellow beamed with joy. He fumbled three times trying to tie a string around the packages.

Coker watched patiently until he finished. "Could you tell me where there's a hotel?"

The man was so happy he had not been stabbed or shot, he went out on the sidewalk and pointed down the street. "There's the hotel, and there's a restaurant right by it."

Coker thanked him and went along to the hotel two blocks away. There he paid the clerk, took the key and searched out his room.

He put the moneybags, rifle, Bowie knife and hatchet between the mattress and springs of the bed. Then he changed into the new clothes.

"Fit toler'bly well, I reckon," he said as he wrestled with the buttons, "though my throwin' knife might show through this thin shirt."

He thought about leaving it, but decided he didn't want to be unarmed. Last thing, he slung the moneybags over his shoulder.

"Gotta get going to Freeda and can't waste any time so best be asking around."

He went outside the hotel intending to stop every man who came by until he found one who could tell him how to get there. The first two had no idea of where Amarillo was, but the third man he stopped had lived in Memphis, Texas, so he knew something about western Oklahoma.

"Go straight on east through Memphis," he told Coker. "The first town you'll get to in Oklahoma is Hollis. Freeda is southeast, but you'd better stop in Hollis and ask just how's the best way."

Coker thanked him and went to eat. Trouble! Three men who appeared to be lounging against the side of a hardware store building were watching his every move. Coker did not change expression or look their way. As he ate he thought about the situation.

"Don't know why them guys was so innersted in me. Maybe I do. One of 'em might be the guy standin' at the livery when I dropped the money. Reckon I better watch my back."

When he left the restaurant, only one man stood by the hardware store. Coker seemed not to notice him and went into the hotel. Standing back from the window so he could not be seen, he looked the man over. "Yeah, he's the same man which was at the livery. Wonder if the other two are waitin' in my room."

Quietly he went down the hall, stood outside and listened. Nothing. He opened the door. Holding the throwing knife in his teeth, he got down on his hands and knees and, like a bobcat stalking its prey, inched his way into the room. Nothing moved. "Reckon they're gonna wait 'til later."

The corner room had windows on two sides. "Bad spot. Be hard to watch those windas and the door."

A lamp stood on a small table, but Coker ignored it. Waiting until it was dark, he gathered up his weapons and put his leather clothes in the bag. Then he slowly raised a window and stepped to the ground holding his rifle ready to shoot. He went to the alley behind the hotel and followed it until he was across the street from the livery.

A lamp light down the block made it possible for him to make out the dim outline of the livery barn. Seeing no one, he ran across the street and stood in the shadows just inside the barn. He heard horses stomping around but no voices. He had seen a ladder near the front of the barn. He felt around until he found it and climbed to the loft. Placing his weapons in front of him, he went to sleep in the hay.

"Do you really think he has that much money with him?" Uvie Tigert asked.

"Hell, yes," Leonard Swink nodded. "I'm tellin' you I saw a roll of bills that you couldn't get in your pocket and two bags full of money fell out of his pack."

Larnce Laseman was listening to the two men. "You say all you saw was twenties?"

"Yeah, and from the size of the bags, he's got to be carryin' seven or eight thousand dollars."

"If he's got that much money, I think we'd better pay him a visit at the hotel."

"Okay," Swink said. "You guys can watch outside, and I'll go in and take care of him. He acted tough today, so I want him all by myself."

Tigert and Laseman sat in the dark watching the windows while Swink kicked in the door. He waited several hours in the room before he decided Coker had fled. He went out through a window and found his partners.

"I guess he ain't comin' back here tonight."

"Yeah," Laseman said, "he must have been suspicious. Uvie can find those mule tracks easy in the mornin' if you think it's worth givin' up reward money on Jack Arnold to go after him."

"Dammit, I told you I saw the money. He's got more money in them bags than we could make catchin' ten wanted men."

"Okay, I believe you. We'll get on his trail early. "

Before the owner of the livery showed up, Coker had packed his gear and left town. Twenty miles out he found a windmill and stopped to water the mules. As they drank he studied the trail. Behind him he saw dust rising slowly.

"Looks like three or four horses travelin' pretty fast. Don't s'poze they got nothin' to do with me, but I reckon I'd better keep a eye out."

For miles he watched the dust. "They're gittin' closer, Thunder Red. Guess we'd better pull off the trail and wait for 'em."

He spotted a clump of mesquite and tied his mules short, so they could not move around. He leaned his rifle against a tree standing by the trail and waited. Not as much dust rose from the trail as before.

"Uh, oh," he said. "Looks like just one of 'em still on the trail. Wonder where the rest of 'em got to."

He stood by the tree, almost out of sight. The rider was only twenty feet away when he saw him. Startled, he jerked his horse to a stop.

Coker looked up at the man several seconds before he spoke. "Howdy. Where you headed in such a hurry?"

With a lightning flick of his wrist, Swink pulled his pistol. "I'm goin' right here. Now just find all that money I saw you with and throw it on the ground."

Coker managed to look frightened. "Don't shoot. Don't shoot. I'll get it."

He reached in one pants pocket and pulled out two bills and dropped them to the ground.

"You've got a helluva lot more money than that, and I want those two bags out of your pack. Now find it fast."

Coker felt in one pocket and pulled out three more bills. He dropped them and scratched his left ear. "I got some more, but I got this new shirt, and I don't know where all the pockets are in this damned thing."

He checked the left shirt pocket with his right hand and then reached with his left hand to the right pocket. The man motioned with his gun and said, "I'm gettin' tired of waitin'. Figure it out damned quick."

Coker frowned and scratched the back of his head with his right hand. The knife flashed in the sun, but the man had no time to react. Blood gushed from his chest and he slid from his horse.

Like a darting weasel, Coker picked up his money and dragged the dead man into the mesquite off the trail. Before he did anything else, he took a quick look at the back trail.

With his hatchet he cut a large branch from a mesquite bush and swept the tracks he had made dragging the body. He tied the man's horse behind Switchback and took Thunder Red's lead rope in his hand. One more hasty look at the trail, and he trotted away from the scene.

"Guess I'd better stay on the ground for a while, Thunder Red. That way I can get out of sight a mite faster."

An hour later Laseman and Tigert trotted their horses past the spot where Coker had killed their partner. In their eagerness to catch up, they were looking at the dust in the far distance and failed to see where Coker had swept the trail. For five miles they trotted their horses trying to catch sight of their intended prey.

They slowed again to take a closer look at the tracks. Tigert leaned down.

"Leonard's not ridin' his horse. Somethin' funny goin' on. I knowed we shouldn't have let him talk us into lettin' him try to handle that mountain man by hisself."

Laseman stopped and looked more closely at the tracks. "Goddamn, you're right. Come on, we've got to catch up."

Spurring their horses into a lope, they charged up the trail. For two miles they maintained their pace. When they saw Leonard's horse grazing at the side of the trail, they skidded to a stop and turned their horses aside into the mesquite. For some time they looked at the area trying to detect any movement or sound.

"What do you think, Uvie? See any sign of anybody?"

"Nope, I don't, but somethin's bad wrong. That's Leonard's horse and he sure as hell didn't fall off."

"That's for damn sure."

They dismounted and circled through the mesquite with guns drawn. Thirty minutes later they approached the horse. "Cover me," Tigert said. "I'm gonna take a look."

As he stepped into the trail, he peered in every direction before he went on to the horse. "Hey! There's blood on the saddle. I'm afraid that son of a bitch killed Leonard."

"How in the hell could he have done that? Leonard's the fastest gun I ever saw."

Uvie studied the trail. "He stopped here and let the horse loose. If Leonard ain't dead he's back yonder hurt and maybe tied up."

By the time they backtracked the seven miles, the sun was going down. Uvie spotted where Coker had brushed the tracks with the mesquite branches.

"Hell's bells!" he said. "We was goin' too fast. His mules stood here, and there's where Leonard's horse stopped in the trail. Somebody drug somethin' into the bushes."

He soon found Leonard's body. "Sure enough," he shouted. "Looks like he's been stabbed."

Larnce ran to the bush. "That dirty bastard. Leonard's been my friend for twenty years. I'll get him and that money if it's the last thing I ever do."

"Especially that money."

By the time they buried Leonard in a shallow grave, darkness had settled over the region.

"Well, there ain't no moon," Tigert said. "We'll have to wait 'til mornin' to get on his trail."

They had not intended to camp that night, so they huddled together under the one blanket Larnce had rolled behind his saddle. Through the long hours they sipped whisky and swore they would catch the mountain man, take his money and kill him a little at a time.

Coker hit the trail at daylight, constantly looking back for telltale dust. At the edge of Clarendon, a man leading six mules came on to the trail just in front of him.

"I'll be damned!" Coker said. "I was havin' a hard time figgerin' how I was goin'ta hide my mule's tracks."

He followed the man and the mules into Clarendon where they went down a side street. At the end dozens of mules and horses milled around in small corrals. Coker saw a man standing by one of the gates.

"What's goin' on here?" he asked.

"A county fair is what's goin' on. We're havin' a horse and mule pull tomorra. Wanna enter your mules?"

"No, reckon I better not. Thanks anyway," Coker said.

He rode Switchback around the corrals so the tracks would be mixed up with those of his own animals and then went out into the mesquite instead of going back to the main trail.

For two days he rode through the mesquite close enough to the main trail to keep an eye on it. It slowed him to work his way through the thorny trees, but he knew the men would find his tracks if he went back to the main road. At Memphis he returned to the trail and rode toward Oklahoma.

Just about sundown, ten days after he had left Amarillo, he peered through a misty rain at Freeda.

8

The Black Pond

Coker looked up into the drizzling rain. "Smooth cloudy. Miser'ble. Ever'thing's been cloudy since I got Bonnie's letter." Shifting his attention to the trees, he studied the overhanging branches and shook his head.

"Ever' branch is black. Like buzzards spreadin' their wings to shed the rain whilst they wait for me to die. Maybe I'll fool 'em." Looking at the trees again he shuddered and sighed. "Then again, maybe I won't."

Sitting on his heels with his back against a big cottonwood, he studied the town, talking all the while. "Ain't very big. Come in from the west. Looks peaceful. Sometimes looks can be mighty deceivin'. Cain't mess up for me and Bonnie too. Guess I'd better stay here and scout around for a couple o' days."

He went deeper in the trees and found a small creek to water the mules. He put them on picket ropes to minimize the likelihood that somebody would find them and hid the bags and other gear in a mound of leaves and branches. He decided to sleep nearby in a clump of berry bushes.

Just after dark he lay on the buffalo skin for a short while, then crept into the bushes. Pulling the elkskin over him, he closed his eyes. Yeah, he was tired. The journey, almost over, this part anyway. He awakened after many hours. The best night's sleep since he had left Aspen Hill.

Drizzling rain continued into the next morning. He avoided building a fire and instead chewed on a piece of squirrel he had killed while walking around the adjacent woodlands, looking for all the hazards he might encounter if he took off suddenly. He found a good vantage point behind a huge mesquite and again studied the town, noting the pattern of the streets.

"Looks like one main road comin' in from the west where I am," he said, "and one runnin' northeast and southwest. Looks like side streets don't go nowhere."

He spent an hour fixing the image of the place in his mind. "Seems like a right friendly little town," he said. Then he started north, intending to circle the outskirts.

By noon he had covered the eastern part and was headed along the south side. As he ran through a small opening in the scrub oak, he saw a large house. It stood at the southwest edge of town. Coker walked closer to get a better look.

"Somethin' 'bout that place is bad. Gives me the shivers."

The square building loomed two stories tall. Several windows broke the surface of the bare, dark gray plaster walls. Rain trickled down somber green shingles. The four sides of the roof came to a point. There were no gables.

"Never saw such a mean lookin' house," Coker said. "That door looks like it'd take a skinny weasel to git through it. Them windas is all too little to let in any light. Must be awful dark inside. Hate to live in that hell hole."

About the middle of the afternoon the rain ceased. Coker looked at the sun breaking through the clouds. "Well, what about that. Didn't figger I'd see the sun for a while. Hope it means it's gonna shine on me and Bonnie."

He finished the circuit of the town and went back to the camp where he got out the small amount of grain left and gave each mule a double handful. "This'll keep you happy tonight, and I'll get some more tomorra," he said.

Coker watched the sun set behind the black trees, and shivered as the shadows brought a chill. "Guess I'd better get the lay of the land around here."

He rambled through the area memorizing every trail running through the forest before darkness fell.

Silent as a nighthawk he returned to the campsite and chewed on some jerky. "Guess I'd better git me some water to wash this down," he said, and went to the creek to fill the canteen.

As he held the container under the surface, he found himself staring at the stream. Water filled his canteen and ran over his hand, but Coker felt nothing. He whispered, "Somethin' down that crick. Feels like it's somethin' bad. Somethin' I'd oughta leave alone."

Transfixed for a time he pulled himself to his feet and went back to his jerky, but he continued to look down the creek. Finally, he succumbed to the draw of the unknown, rose and followed the waterway through the bushes. He traced it easily. "Doesn't look like much. Maybe I was wrong about it bein' bad, but I feel like a fawn lookin' into a cougar's eyes."

The stream ran into bushes too thick to see through. He stopped and sniffed the air. "Smells rotten like the courthouse where they took Bonnie away."

As he worked his way around the bushes, he saw that the creek ran over a sharp ledge. Hurrying through the undergrowth, he almost stepped off a steep bank. He caught hold of a small tree and peered over the edge. A stagnant pond with blue-black mud around the edges lay in the hollow of a natural dam. Their tips almost touching, forty-foot trees hung over the pond forming what looked like a giant spider web that cut out the light.

He could see the head of a water moccasin swimming away from the bank. The snake circled, then slid under in the center of the pond. Hypnotized, Coker stared into the glassy blackness of the pond:

70

Snake! Bigger. Closer and filthier. Bonnie walkin' by the edge. Pale and weak. She's sick. 'Bout to fall. Trissy has her hand. She's safe. No! No! Snake has her foot. Cain't jerk away. Snake coiled 'round 'em. Swimmin' into the black. Goin' down, down deeper. Pull, Trissy, pull! Gittin' farther away! Gittin' smaller! Gone! Both gone! Trissy and Bonnie's gone! I've got to go after 'em.

Coker leaned to jump into the pond. A flock of ducks splashing onto the water broke the spell. Numb from the vision, he stumbled back to the campsite and, not bothering to roll out his bed, leaned against a tree and pulled an elkskin over his head. "Why'd I go down there? Damned, stupid dreams and pitchers in ponds don't mean nothin'. Iffen they don't, then Bonnie's all right."

He thought again of the vision and pushed on his temples with his hands. "What if they do mean somethin'? Got a feelin' somethin' must be awful wrong with Bonnie. I was gonna take two or three days to git ever'thing worked out, but I guess I'd better git goin' in the mornin'."

He leaned his head on his knees and tried to plan a course of action, but he kept seeing the tail of the snake writhing deeper and deeper in the foul-smelling, ebon pond.

71

9

Toward Misty Valley

Drops from the canopy of the trees rained on Coker's shoulders and soaked his leather shirt as he looked after the mules. Trying to shake his depression, he paid no attention.

Might as well put on those clothes he had bought in Amarillo. Danged things were stiff as some old board. Hard to handle all right. Newfangled ideas, weren't worth a hoot. He fumbled with the front a long time.

"Damned buttons. Why cain't they make clothes like they oughta be made? No damned sense in splittin' a shirt down the front and puttin' buttons on pants. One good thing though, at least it'll let me put my Bowie knife under the shirt."

He pulled on the boots and continued his tirade. "This fool leather's stiff as rawhide dried in the sun. Damned bootmakers don't know how to tan leather. Why in the hell they use wood fer soles, I don't know."

Still fuming he limped around in the boots trying to get used to the tightness. "Two miles into town. Be crippled by the time I walk that fur in these damned foot caskets."

A thought entered his mind and he stopped. "People in Freeda would think it was mighty funny iffen a man walked in without no horse or buggy. Reckon I'd better ride so they won't be too s'picious."

Solving that problem lifted his spirits and Coker hustled to get Switchback. When he got into the saddle, he swore again. "Cain't get nothin' but my toes in the stirrups. Hate to try to ride a long ways in the damned things, but maybe I can make it two miles."

Riding through the woods until he got away from the camp, he eased Switchback to the main road. He stopped and looked up and down to make sure nobody would see him come out of the trees, then went at a trot toward Freeda. At the edge of town he alighted and started walking the mule down the main street.

Faded wooden buildings with shiplap siding sat almost against each other on each side of the dirt road.

At the end of one block, two stores with swinging doors faced each other. "Look like saloons, Switchback, but I wonder why they're acrost the street from each other."

Two blocks away on the north side of the street, he saw a red and white barber pole. "Well, old mule, that's the only place I can learn as much about a town as I can in a saloon and it's a whole lot safer. Reckon I'm kinda shaggy, so I'll git a shave and a haircut."

He tied Switchback to the hitching rail and tried to walk naturally in the damned boots. The dozing barber roused from his nap when Coker came into the shop. He stretched and placed one foot on the floor, but waited a full minute before getting to his feet.

"What'll you have today, mister?"

"I need a shave and a haircut."

"Well, you came to the right place." The barber motioned toward the chair he had just vacated. "Climb up here, and I'll see what I can do."

As he pinned a cloth around Coker's neck, he said, "You're a stranger in these parts, aren't you?"

"Reckon I am."

"Dan Livingston is my name." The barber extended his hand and Coker took it.

He said, "I'm Samuel Brown. You can call me Sam."

"Where you from?"

"Up north."

"Where, up north?"

"Colorado."

"What brings you to these parts?"

Coker thought for some time before he answered, but he knew he had to find where Bonnie lived. He said, "Got some kinfolks here named Cook. Thought maybe you could tell me where I could find 'em."

Livingston dropped his hands and stepped back from the chair. "Marshall Cook is your relative?"

"No, not him. His wife."

The barber regained his composure and started cutting Coker's hair again. "That's a little better, I guess. You knew Marshall died here while back?"

"Yeah, I heered about it. How'd he die?

The barber stopped cutting hair. "Awful strange how he died. He started on a trip to Altus in a buggy. Healthy as he could be, but they found him dead the other side of Olustee. Those Speights hushed everything up, so nobody knows what killed him."

"Who's the Speights?"

"Vester Speight is Marshall's sister." The barber looked to be sure no one was coming in the door. "She married a guy named Albert Speight. They seem to have some money and want a lot more. They've got a lot of influence in Altus, but they're two of the meanest people I've ever known. Better stay away from those two."

Coker gripped the arms of the chair. "Where's Bonnie Cook? How's she doin'?"

Livingston shook his head. "Don't know for sure. The Speights say she's sick, but they keep her and the kids inside the house all the time. I guess it's been over a month since I've seen her. You say she's kin to you?"

"She's my girl."

"She told everyone her maiden name was Ford. You say your name is Brown?"

"Well," Coker paused to think of an answer. "My whole name's Samuel Ford Brown. Bonnie always liked Ford best, so she'd claim her name was Ford a lot of times."

Livingston chuckled. "Yeah, kids are like that sometimes. Mine don't want to claim me at all when other kids are around."

"Could you tell me where Bonnie lives?"

"Oh, yes. She's four blocks down this next street that runs south. In a big two-story house. About the only house in town with stucco on the walls."

Coker muttered, "Mighta knowed it would be that mean lookin' house."

"What did you say?"

"Nothin'. Just talkin' to m'self. Seems kinda quiet today. Is it usually this way?"

"Oh, no. Everyone's out picking cotton. Come Saturday the town will be hopping. They'll all come in to get drunk on Saturday."

"Oh, yeah?" Coker said. "Noticed two saloons up the street. Guess they need 'em to slosh ever'body, huh?"

"Well, yes. Gets busy here when folks have some money after working."

Coker didn't respond. Livingston continued to talk about the crops and the weather until he finished. Then he whipped off the cloth. Coker climbed out of the chair and asked, "How much?"

"Umm, you had a lot of hair. Guess that will be four bits."

Coker gave him a dollar, got his change and said, "Thanks for tellin' me where my girl lives. Sounds like I better go see about her."

"You bet. I hope she's all right, but somebody needs to see about her."

Coker started to fume as he took one slow step after another. He untied the mule and said, "Switchback, we'd better find our girl."

Standing with his hand on the saddlehorn, he said, "Come to think of it, Bonnie won't know me in these duds. She never saw me in nothin' but buckskin and a beaver hat. Guess I'd better get back out in the woods and change."

He walked Switchback until he cleared the last house, then prodded him into a lope for the last mile to camp. He donned the buckskins and was starting to mount again when he stopped and looked at his packs.

"You know, Switchback, after what that barber said, I got a feelin' I better look as mean as I can. Them Speights sound like bad medicine."

He already had the throwing knife, but he got the Bowie knife and hatchet and buckled them around his waist.

"Let's go see about my gal."

Coker rode slowly up the rail fence bordering the yard in front of the gray house. He looked it over and mumbled, "There's a bigger door in front than there is in back. Don't seem to make it any happier." He dismounted and tied Switchback to the top rail.

As he reached to open the latch to the gate, a man carrying a rifle came around the corner of the house and said, "You can't tie your mule there. What do you want here anyway?"

Coker looked the man up and down and thought, "Hard lookin' cuss." Then he stared into the man's eyes. "It ain't any of your damned bus'ness what I'm doin' here, and the mule's already tied."

The man motioned toward the mule with his rifle. "A smart alec, huh. Move your mule or I'll shoot him."

Coker grabbed the barrel of the rifle with his left hand and, with his right, pushed the point of his Bowie knife against the man's midsection. "Just let the gun go. Cause iffen you shoot my mule, you won't have no guts left."

The knife point in his belly caused the man to drop the rifle. Coker caught it. "I'll just take this inside. Iffen you touch my mule while I'm in the house, I'll shoot you in the belly when I come out."

Coker turned his back on the man and trotted to the door. He started to knock, then saw a brass knocker in the middle of the door. He used the knocker and waited. A trim, young black man opened the door and said, "Yassuh, who's callin'?"

"Coker Owen Ford is callin', that's who. Who wants t'know?"

Surprised at the response the man said, "Jus' a minute," and retreated into the house.

Instead of waiting Coker pushed through the door and followed on his heels. A woman appeared in a doorway. "Why did you let this man in, Jesse?"

The butler stammered and shuffled his feet. "I didn't zakly let him in, Miz Speight. He jus' come on in."

She looked at Coker through narrowed eyelids. "Who are you and what do you want?"

Coker didn't answer but studied the woman. She was tall, nearly five feet nine. A long gray, wool dress emphasized her slender frame. She wore her hair knotted in a bun. Dark eyes and broad cheeks on a face with a sharp nose. Wide lips so thin they could hardly be seen.

Coker thought, "Meanest woman I've ever seen. Looks like a snake."

No emotion showed on her face, but again she said, "Well, who are you?"

"I'm Coker Owen Ford."

"That doesn't mean anything to me. What do you want?"

"I'm gonna talk to Bonnie," Coker said.

"Why do you want to talk to her?"

"I didn't say I want to talk to her. I'm gonna talk to my daughter."

Her grim face showed no surprise. She turned to her butler. "Throw this scroungy man out, Jesse."

The black man looked at the hatchet and knife on Coker's belt and said, "I don' rightly b'lieve he wants to be throwed out, Miz Speight."

Coker pushed past the butler and looked down on Vester Speight. "Tell me where Bonnie is. I'm gonna talk to her."

With ice in her voice she said, "What if I don't?"

Coker drew his Bowie knife, held it three inches from her neck. "Then I'm gonna cut your head off and find her myself."

For the first time a flicker of concern flitted across her face. She said, "All right. Jesse show this man to Bonnie's room."

"Yassuh, Miz Speight," he said and motioned to Coker to follow him up the stairs. At the top, he said, "It's the fust door there on the right." He dropped his voice to a whisper. "The chilluns is right across the hall."

"Thanks, Jesse," Coker said. Gently, he pushed the door open a crack and looked into the room. Enough light filtered through the drawn curtains so he could make out a figure on the bed. He closed the door behind him and tiptoed over. Bonnie lay on her back with her head sunk into a large pillow. Long, black hair framed her very pallid face. Though her cheeks were hollow and sunken and her lips dry and purplish, he could tell that she had been a beautiful woman before this sickness ravaged her.

"My poor Bonnie," he mumbled.

Coker stared at wasted face and cried. He fought his heaving chest to keep the sobs from being audible. After a few minutes he gained enough control to whisper, "Good God, what's happened to my girl? I can see Trissy in her face but Bonnie, Bonnie, Bonnie, what's made you into a ghost?"

Softly he said, "Bonnie," but she did not stir. Raising his voice slightly he tried again. "Bonnie."

She opened her eyelids a tiny crack, then closed them. Coker took her hand and caressed it. She felt his and squeezed softly. "I'm here, Bonnie."

She looked at his hand through half open eyes. "Who is holding . . . " Then she opened her eyes wide and stared at the leather sleeve.

"A mountain man," she whispered, "a mountain man. Only one mountain man would come here. Daddy? You've come. You've come. I knew you'd come."

She raised her hands to reach for him, but they fell back on the blanket. Coker sat on the bed and took her tenderly into his arms. When he hugged her, he could no longer contain himself, and he sobbed uncontrollably. Oh, God, how could he stand to see her this way?

"Don't cry, Daddy. I'm going to be all right. I've just been sick a long time and I'm weak. But I'll be fine."

He laid her back on the bed. "What's wrong with you, Bonnie? How're you sick?"

"I don't know, Daddy. I don't know. I take the medicine Doctor Weeks gives me, but I seem to get worse all the time. Now that you're here, I'll get better, I know."

He looked around the room. A stand, the only furniture in the room, with a small bottle and a wash basin stood by the bed. "This room's like the inside of a mine tunnel," he said. "Couldn't they take you to a doctor somewhere else?"

79

"They won't even let me out of the house. A man guards every door." She looked at him and asked, "How did you get past the man in front? He usually stands there with a rifle."

"Him and my Bowie knife had a understandin'. Didn't seem to have the guts to argee. Is he the only one around?"

"No. There's one at the side door, and at night there's one in the hall between me and the children."

Coker frowned. "Why're they keepin' you locked up in here?"

She pursed her lips and then said, "I think I told you about my husband in my letter. He made a great deal of money buying and selling land. His sister..."

Coker broke in. "You mean that female viper downstairs?"

"Yes. Vester Speight is her name. She wanted Marshall to let her be partners with him, but he wouldn't do it. They had words. The day before he died, he told her he had made a will and she wasn't in it. After he died no one could find the will. They have a lot of influence with the judge in Altus, and they're petitioning the court to get control of his money. They claim I'm unable to conduct my affairs and the children are too young. They intend to take them away from me."

She broke into tears and looked up at Coker. "Daddy, I remember you and Mama in our cabin in the mountains. Those happy days have always been with me. You've got to take us away from here. Take us to Misty Valley."

"Can you ride, Bonnie?"

"Somehow I will. Just say you'll take us back with you."

Coker nodded. "That's why I come. But what about the kids? The man said their room is acrost the hall. Are they in there now?"

"Yes, I'm sure they are because they keep them there nearly all the time. Go and get them. I haven't told them you were coming because I was afraid you hadn't gotten my letter."

Coker opened the door and looked up and down the hall before he stepped across into the children's room. When he entered, a boy and a girl, slightly taller, looked at him with wide eyes.

Coker also stared. "Big, blue eyes. Just like Trissy's."

Yep, they both had them eyes. Girl's hair was curly and dark like Trissy's. She looked about nine, but he wasn't very good at figuring ages of kids. The boy, fair haired and freckled, must have taken after his daddy. He took him to be about seven.

They continued to stare at him without speaking. He looked at the older one and said, "You're Misty, ain't you?"

"Yes," she said. "I'm Misty."

"I'm Richard," the boy said, "but you can call me Pete."

"Who are you?" Misty asked.

"I'm the guy what's gonna take you out of this jail."

They looked at each other and smiled. "When?" Misty asked.

"Let's go and talk to your mama and find out."

They danced and skipped as they followed Coker across the hall. They ran to Bonnie's side bubbling with questions. "Are we really going to get out of here, Mother?" Misty asked.

"I hope so, I hope so," Bonnie said.

"When are we going?" Richard asked.

Bonnie looked at Coker. "When are we going?"

Coker thought for a minute and said, "The town'll be full of people Saturday evenin'. Nobody'll notice us, so

81

we'll leave then. I'll have enough horses for everyone to ride." He looked hopefully at Bonnie. "I may have to tie you on a horse 'til we find a doctor."

Misty asked, "How are we going to get past the guards?"

"I could kill 'em," Coker said. "But then a lot of people would be lookin' for us. I saw a winda in your room. Does it open?"

"Yes, I can get it open," Richard said.

"All right. Saturday evenin' you open it, and I'll throw a rope through it. You tie it to your bed real good. We'll go down the rope. I'll have to make a basket out of rope for Bonnie."

"But there's a guard who stands under our window all night," Misty said.

"Don't worry about the guard. He'll take a vacation. You just put what you wanna take in a sack. We cain't bring much so get what you like best."

Barely able to speak, Bonnie said, "Be careful."

"I'll be careful, but guess I'd better go now afore old snake eyes down there sticks her sharp nose in here. I've got some thinkin' to do to get ready."

"I'm too tired to talk any more," Bonnie said. "I'll see you Saturday."

As Coker closed the door, Misty asked, "Who is that man, Mother?"

"Yeah, who is he?" Richard asked.

No answer came for their mother had fallen asleep.

Pete noticed her closed eyes and said, "Ssh, don't wake her up. Let's go back to our room."

They tiptoed out and whispered back and forth until midnight about what had happened.

Coker watched in front and behind as he went down the stairs. Vester Speight and a man who was obviously her husband stood between him and the door. Short, with thin, black hair and a pointed chin, Speight came only to his wife's eyes. As Coker approached, Vester said, "Do not come back here again or we'll take action against you."

Coker put his hand on his Bowie knife. "Suits me. Do you wanna do it now?"

Vester clamped her thin lips together. Coker eyed her husband. "What's your name?"

"I'm Albert Speight," the man said. "Why do you want to know?"

Coker said, "Just wonderin' what they're gonna put on your tombstone 'cause if you fool with me I'm fixin' to shorten you about a foot. Now get out of my way and stay out. I'm gonna come back here t'see about my daughter when I damn well please. I think you reptiles got somethin' to do with her bein' sick, and I'm gonna bring another doctor to see what's wrong with her."

With that he went between them. He saw the rifle standing by the door where he had left it, so he picked it up and held it ready to shoot. He saw no one as he went to his mule. "Well, I see he didn't do nothin'to you, Switchback."

Before mounting he bent the rifle around a post. "Don't reckon he'll shoot me with that."

A block toward the main street, he saw a man carrying barbed wire, coming out of what looked like a hardware store. He tied up Switchback and went in. Two customers were just leaving. The proprietor said to them, "Y'all come back now."

Then he turned to Coker, "What can I do for you?"

"Need about fifty feet of soft rope."

"What size?"

"An inch I reckon."

The man cut the rope and placed it on the counter. "Anything else?"

"Got any 38-56 shells?"

"Yeah, got two boxes left."

"I'll take both of 'em," Coker said. "Where can you buy a good horse in this town?"

"Follow this street north until you get to a little rock house. There's a corral out back, and Wallace Abner's always got some horses. Got some feed for sale too if you need it."

Coker paid the man and took his rope and cartridges. He tied the rope on Switchback, put the ammo in his saddlebag and rode up the street to the rock house. He saw a man standing by the corral.

"Your name Wallace Abner?" Coker asked.

"Yep, shore is. What do you need?"

"Fellow at the hardware store said you had some horses for sale."

"Yep, got some good ones." He motioned toward the corral.

Coker pointed to a bay and a sorrel. "What are them horses like?"

"You got a good eye. You picked out the best ones. They're good and gentle too."

"How much you want for 'em?"

"Fifteen dollars apiece."

"Kinda high, but I'll take 'em," Coker said. "Iffen they ain't gentle, I'll bring 'em back."

"I don't have no worry. You'll like those horses."

"Got any saddles?" Coker asked.

"Yeah, got a couple, but they ain't big enough for you."

"Let's look at 'em."

He led Coker to a small tack room and showed him the saddles. "Just about right for what I want," Coker said.

84

"They'll be five dollars apiece with the blankets."

Coker haggled until he got him to throw in lead ropes and two fifty-pound sacks of grain. Then he loaded the grain, tied the sorrel to the bay and led that horse from Switchback.

"Pleasure doing business with you," Abner said.

Coker hurried to his camp and found Thunder Red and Stranger. He fed them grain and talked to them. "How do you like the comp'ny I brought you? Prob'ly don't like 'em, but I need 'em for the kids. Bonnie can ride one of you critters, and I'll run along."

He went to bed as soon as it got dark and lay there thinking about the day. "Prob'ly shouldn'a told them Speights I'uz comin' back. They may put more guards around. Haveta be careful. Hope I don't haveta kill none of 'em. Bonnie sure worries me. She seems awful sick. I don't see how she can go, but she sure wants to."

Soon he drifted to sleep. He had seen Bonnie and the kids and knew what he was going to do.

At dawn he checked the animals and cooked a breakfast of cornmeal. He kept talking between bites. "Gotta get some eats for Bonnie and the kids. Gotta fix somethin' to get Bonnie down with. Need some more canteens."

When he finished, he took the rope and fashioned a kind of cradle. He could put Bonnie in it and lower her from the window. Then he saddled Thunder Red and tied the panniers on Stranger who resisted less than he usually did. He rode into town for supplies. By the time he got back, it was mid-afternoon. He oiled the rifle and shotguns and practiced with the throwing knife for an hour. Satisfied he was ready, he hid his guns and walked north to check the side roads and trails. He got back just before dark, looked at his animals and went to sleep.

At sunup Saturday he was set up in the woods behind the Speights' house. All day long he squatted there and watched, familiarizing himself with every aspect of the house and counting the number of guards. Late in the afternoon he calculated his move.

"Sun's 'bout an hour high," he said. "Takes me half an hour to git to camp, so I can get back here just afore dark. Gotta get movin'."

He trotted Thunder Red back, found Switchback and Stranger and led them all to the packs and fed them some grain. He put the pack saddles on Thunder Red and Stranger. "Reckon the kids'll get along a little better with Switchback. He's shorter."

When he went to get the horses, he found only their ropes. "Dammit," he said. "Stupid horses whinnied all the time and someone found 'em." He ran in a big circle to see if they were still in the vicinity, but they were nowhere in sight.

He hung his head and went back to his mules. "Rotten thieves. I could find 'em in the mornin'. Guess I'll just haveta wait. No, I cain't wait. The kids'll have their winda open waitin' for me, and Bonnie's gonna get weaker the longer I wait. Just haveta get 'em tonight and bring 'em here 'til I can git some more horses."

With that he mounted Switchback and rode until he could see the house through the trees. There he tied the mules and crept closer. He spotted the guard leaning against the back of the house. "Yeah, they've got a guy there all right. But he's the only one."

As darkness descended, he crawled on his belly inches at a time until he lay a few feet from the guard. The man looked around the corner of the house and turned to walk to the other corner. Coker stood and walked behind him. When he stopped, he hit him behind the ear with the butt of his Bowie knife. The guard folded and Coker tied his hands and feet. Then he gagged him with a small piece of leather.

He ran back to the mules and got the rope. A faint light shone from the children's room, and he could see they had raised the window. On the second throw the rope went through and immediately it slid upward, and he knew Misty and Pete had been waiting.

With his feet on the wall, he went hand over hand up the rope and slid through the window. The children grabbed his arms to help, but he said, "Never mind. Turn down your light."

Misty went to the kerosene lamp and trimmed the wick until it barely burned. Coker peeked around the edge of the window to see if anyone was below. "No one's there," he said. "Now I gotta get the guy in the hall. Open the door a crack and tell me where he is."

The little girl watched for a time and then said, "He's walking up and down out there."

"Good." He pulled Misty back and peered through the crack until the guard went ambling past, then he stepped into the hall and knocked him unconscious. He dragged him into the room and tied him.

Coker said, "Okay, let's go git your mama."

The three of them tiptoed into her bedroom. A lantern made a faint light so they could see Bonnie's head on the pillow. When they stood beside the bed, she opened her eyes. Coker looked at her and choked. He knew.

Bonnie lifted her head slightly and said, "Misty, Pete, come here."

Obediently, they moved closer. "Kiss me goodbye. I'm just too weak to go, but I'll be ready when you come back for me."

Misty and Pete cried, but Bonnie said, "Don't cry now. I'll be all right. Listen to me." She took Coker's hand. "You do whatever he tells you no matter what you think about it. Do you understand?"

"Yes, Mother, we understand," they said in unison. Then Misty asked, "But who is he?"

"He's, he's your . . ." Bonnie tried to answer, but her head fell back on the pillow. She lay for a few minutes while they watched in fear. Finally, she said, "Kiss me children and go into your room. I need to talk just a little while to . . ." Her voice trailed off again, but Misty and Pete had heard the first part.

Coker said, "Hurry, go get your stuff ready."

They hesitated but obeyed. As soon as they left, Coker knelt by the bed, took Bonnie in his arms and kissed her face. She roused and slowly ran her fingers down his cheek.

"Daddy," she whispered. "Listen. Marshall has another sister in Phoenix, Arizona, who is as good as Vester is bad. She would love Misty and Pete. Her name is Madeline Wright. If you can't take the children to Misty Valley, take them to her. Now hurry. I'll be all right."

"I'll be back for you, Bonnie," he said, but he thought, "I know I'm kissin' my gal for the last time."

She said, "Give me some of my medicine on the stand, and I'll feel better."

He saw the bottle and picked it up, but when he turned she had closed her eyes. The tears started to come as he lifted her to him and kissed her again.

Her lips moved slowly and he could barely hear her say, "Daddy, Daddy." Then the snake took her deep into the black pond.

Coker knew she had gone. He laid her back on the pillow and folded her hands. "Goddamn snakes. Think I'll go kill 'em now. No, the kids is waitin', and nobody's gonna take 'em away from me."

Overwhelmed with grief and rage, he stopped and leaned against the side of the door and tried to get control. "Bonnie, my Bonnie," he said and wiped the tears with the back of his hand. He put the bottle in his pouch and after a few moments, stepped into the hall.

Through his bleary eyes he saw a figure at the head of the stairs. Galvanized into action he drew his Bowie and lunged for the figure. At the last second he saw it was the butler and paused. Jesse held his hands flat in front of him and said softly, "I ain't gonna tell them Speights nothin'. I was the one that mailed the letter to you. Y'all get out of here before they hears yuh."

"Thanks, Jesse. You're a good man."

"I tries to be, suh. But sometimes it's hard when you're workin' for these people."

Coker reached over and squeezed his hand. Jesse smiled and went down the stairs,

Coker hurried into the children's room. "Get your pack," he said to Richard. "Let's git outa here."

"Is Mother coming?" Misty asked.

"No, but she's okay," he said. "I'll come back and get her."

He pulled the rope up and tied it to Richard's waist. "Untie it fast when you get down," he said and lowered him to the ground. When he felt the rope go slack, he pulled it up and tied it around Misty. "Get your pack quick," he said. She picked up a bag from the floor, and Coker started to lower her. Then he saw she had a two-foot long box in one hand. "What in the hell is that?" he asked.

"It's my mandolin."

"Your mandolin! We cain't take that thing."

"Mother taught me to play it and Daddy told me never to let it out of my sight."

"Hell, we'll git anothern."

"No, if I can't take it, I'll stay here with Mother."

Coker hid his tears. "Okay, we'll take it."

He lowered Misty and then untied the rope from the bed. He hooked the end around the bedpost and slid down the long part of the rope to the ground. Then he pulled the rope down and coiled it around his arm.

"One of you take my hand," he said. Pete reached over.

"Now Misty, hold his hand."

Misty did as she was told, and Coker led them slowly through the trees to the mules.

"Have you rode horses afore?"

"One time we did," Pete said.

Coker groaned. "Okay. Misty, I'll put you in the saddle. Hold on to that knob there. Pete, I'll put you ahind Misty. You hold on to her."

He got them on Switchback and led them past the house down a side road. They could see people milling around on Main street and hear drunks yelling. Coker followed the side road until he reached the edge of town where the main street turned. He said, "Hang on, kids. We've gotta move a little faster."

Then he broke into his tireless trot and headed north toward Misty Valley.

10

Viper's Fangs

Vester Speight hurried into the living room. She had heard strange noises, almost as if someone were moving furniture. Sure enough, there was that wretch, Jesse, pushing a sofa across the floor. She stopped and watched him, her eyes narrowed and her jaw clamped.

"Jesse, what are you doing?"

The frightened man spun halfway around almost losing his balance. Surprise and fear showed on his face. Regaining his composure he said, "Jus' cleanin', Miz Speight."

Venom shot from her eyes. "When did you take on cleaning as one of your duties?" she asked. "You know Caroline does the cleaning."

Bowing his head to avoid her inspection, he said, "Yassum, I knows that, but she been ailin' so I'se jus' tryin' to help her out a little bit."

"Caroline hasn't said anything about being sick. Even if she is, don't you ever clean at night again."

Albert Speight came into the room. Standing slightly behind Vester as if to draw power from her, he gave Jesse a hateful look and said, "We were conducting serious business and you interrupted, you dumb bastard."

From years of long practice, Jesse kept a passive face. "Yassuh," he said. "I won't bother you no mo' at night."

The Speights started to speak but stopped. A thumping sound came from above. Vester looked out in the hall at the stairs and said, "What are those brats doing? Jesse, get up there and see what's happening."

The butler shuffled by and climbed the steps with dragging feet. Albert shouted at him, "Don't take all night. Hurry, before those kids tear up the room."

The black man moved only slightly faster. He reached the door, stepped inside and looked around to be sure the children were gone, then untied the guard. While the man tried to get up, Jesse went to the head of the stairs. "The chilluns is gone, Miz Speight."

Albert's mouth worked, but he could not speak. Eventually, he said, "What will we do, Vester?"

Like a cobra Vester stood straight and still, her hard face showing no feeling. "We'll send someone to bring them back, of course. We can't let them get away until the court awards us control of Marshall's money."

"How will we get them back?"

"The man who took the children is Bonnie's father, but he'll return to get her, or he'll try to contact her because she's too weak to make any kind of trip. At least, I don't think . . ." She looked up at the butler.

"What about Mrs. Cook? Is she gone, too?" she asked.

The butler did not move. He said, "I don' rightly know, Miz Speight."

Vester's lips drew tighter. "Go and look."

Jesse went to the room. Expecting to find Bonnie missing, he froze when he saw her figure in the bed. "Miz Cook," he said. "Miz Cook." When she did not answer, he walked over and gently pulled back the covers. Her still figure and open eyes told him she was dead. He whispered, "I'm sorry, Miz Cook. I'se really sorry. You was the only one good to me aroun' here."

He drew the cover over her head, went back to the stairs and stood. The guard came up beside him still rubbing his wrists.

"Well," Vester said. "Is she gone?"

Jesse's eyes filled with tears and his lips trembled. He said, "She still there, but she gone."

Albert shouted at him, "What kind of answer is that? My wife asked you a straight question, and you'd better give her a straight answer."

With ominous calm Vester said to the guard, "Bill, go see if she is there."

The guard walked into the room and then came hurrying out . "She's dead, Mrs. Speight."

Albert looked pleased. Vester gave orders. "Jesse, go home and come back in the morning."

"Yassum, Miz Speight." He hurried down the stairs. When he reached the bottom, Vester stopped him. "Do not say anything about this to anyone. If you do I'll chase you out of Oklahoma. Do you understand me?"

"Yassum, I understans," he said. Immediately he left, shaking his head in sorrow.

"Bill, come down here and tell me what happened," Vester said.

The guard rubbed the knot on his head and tried to think. "I don't know what happened. I heard a noise and woke all tied up."

"He must have done the same thing to Jack at the back of the house," Vester said. "Go see about him and then both of you get back on duty and tell Kendall not to let anyone come in."

"All right," he said.

After he closed the door, Albert smiled. "Our plan is going fine. We've got rid of her."

"Yes," Vester said. "We'll get Dr. Weeks to sign the death certificate, and we'll bury her tomorrow."

"Do you think he will sign the certificate?"

"You know he will," she said. "If he doesn't we'll tell the sheriff how his wife died."

Albert rubbed his hands and laughed. "Then all we have to do is get the kids back."

Vester said sternly. "With her dead we don't need the children back."

"We can't just let them go, can we?"

Vester could not contain her exasperation. "No, we can't let them go, because I'm afraid Marshall's will is going to turn up. The children must go away before it does."

A questioning look crossed his countenance. He said, "You mean?"

"Yes."

"I told you we should have taken care of them already. We had plenty of time."

"Sure, and mess up everything. The sheriff asked us a lot of questions about Marshall so you know he wouldn't have let us off if the kids had suddenly died. Go tell Kendall to come in, but make sure Bill is guarding the front door."

When Kendall hurried into the room, Vester said, "Do you remember that mountain man who took away your rifle?"

With an ashamed look, Kendall said, "You bet I remember him. Why?"

"Would you like to get even with him?"

"You damned right. Bill told me what happened. Do you want me to go after him?"

She looked at him until he dropped his eyes. "No. Obviously, you can't handle him. I want you to tell me who is the most ruthless and cunning man in this territory."

Kendall answered instantly. "That would be either Bert or Vernon Monroe. Those two brothers are downright nasty." He shuddered and shook his shoulders. "Yeah, I stay clear out of their way. They're as mean as a lobo with hydrophobia."

Vester thought for several minutes. "Maybe we can use them both," she said. "Can you find them tonight?"

"Yeah, their little pintos will be tied in front of one of the saloons. Probably looking for trouble. Maybe somebody will kill them some day, but right now everyone's afraid of them, and they ain't afraid of nothin'."

"Go find them and bring them here," she said.

"I'm not sure I want to find them."

Vester's voice dripped poison. "All right. I'll give you ten dollars to do it."

Kendall shrugged his shoulders. "Okay, I'll try, but if they don't like it, I'm going to run."

He left. Albert Speight paced the floor; Vester went into the den and gazed at the wall.

Thirty minutes later they heard loud voices. Kendall brought two men into the room. "These here are the Monroes," he said, and stepped back outside.

Bert and Vernon Monroe stood side by side with their thumbs hooked in their belts. Their sneering lips held self-made cigarettes. Big, black, shapeless felt hats shaded their thin, hard faces.

Albert looked them over and turned to Vester. "They don't look big enough to be as mean as Kendall claims."

He talked too loud and the Monroes heard him. Vernon's hand seemed only to twitch, but he had a forty-five revolver pointed at Albert's head. He cocked the gun. "How mean do you want us to be? We ain't very tall, but these guns make us bigger'n anyone around here."

Vester said, "Put your gun away. If you're as bad as you claim, we've got a job for you."

Showing as little emotion as Vester, Bert said, "What's the job? And how much we gonna get?"

95

"A man from Colorado came and took two children away with him. He's a tough old bird, big and dangerous. Do you think you can handle him?"

Vernon chuckled. "We can handle him. Do you want us to bring him back?"

"No," Vester said. "We don't want you to bring him back."

"What about the kids?" Bert asked.

"We don't want them to come back under any circumstances."

Bert and Vernon looked at each other.

"You want us to kill kids?" Vernon said. "Cost a lot of money to kill kids."

"I'll pay you five hundred dollars apiece," she said.

The men looked at each other and whistled. Vernon said, "You want those kids out of the way bad, don't you? When you gonna pay us?"

"I'll give you a hundred dollars apiece now and the rest when you finish the job." She turned to her husband and said, "Albert, go get two hundred dollars."

He left the room and returned shortly with the money. Vester took it and handed it to the brothers, saying, "I'll pay you the rest when you bring me proof they are dead."

"What kinda proof?" Bert asked.

"Don't be stupid," she said. "Cut off some of their hair or scalp them or cut off their hands. I don't care. Just bring me proof when you come back if you want your money."

Both of them glared at the woman, but she didn't flinch. Vernon said, "Which way do you think they'll head out?"

"I just told you he's from Colorado. Of course, they will go north."

"Yeah, that's probably right," Vernon said. "We'll cut his trail in the morning."

Vester narrowed her eyes and snapped, "Start right now."

"The moon ain't shinin'," Bert said. "We could ride past them in the dark, and if that old mountain man's as sharp as Kendall says, he'd spot us ahead of him. We'll get ready now, but we can't go 'til mornin'."

"All right then," Vester said. "Start as soon as you can. I want them dead as quickly as possible."

The two men turned to leave. Vernon paused at the door and looked back at Vester. He shook his head and said, "And people think we're mean."

Vester listened until the clatter of hooves told her the Monroes had left on their deadly mission.

11

Run, Run, Run

Coker trotted until the dark forced him to slow to a fast walk. The stars gave little light, but he could make out the beaten trail. Misty held on to the saddlehorn and Pete held on to Misty.

They had gone about ten miles when she said, "Hey, Mister, Pete's going to sleep, and I can't keep him from falling."

"Damn," Coker said. "I was hopin' to make twenty miles tonight." He stopped and lifted them gently to the ground. "Guess we'll just have to sleep a while. My mules need to rest some anyway."

He unsaddled the animals a short distance off the road. Those poor kids, losin' their mama and all, must be plumb tuckered out.

"You two just lay down here right nice on this buffalo robe." They were almost asleep when he covered them with an elkskin and patted them softly on their cheeks. "Just go to sleep now. Don't worry 'bout nothin'. We'll get a early start in the mornin'."

He lay by their side and wrapped himself in the remaining elkskin. The children slept soundly, but Coker woke often, listening and watching.

At dawn he had to shake them several times before they opened their eyes. "Wake up," he said. "It's gettin' light. We've got to get goin'."

He ate a piece of jerky and gave the children some sweet rolls he had bought at the grocery store in Freeda. When they finished eating, Misty started to ask Coker a question, then she blushed and looked away.

Finally, she said slowly, "Is there a toilet around anywhere? I'm about to bust."

"Me too," Pete said.

Coker chuckled. "Yeah, there's one for girls ahind those big bushes over there and another'n for boys over the other way."

Misty ran off and then popped out from the brush with her hands on her hips. She saw Coker laughing and went out of sight again. Pete came back with a crooked smile. Misty stomped over and said, "That was not funny."

Coker stopped laughing. "No, guess it wasn't. I won't do that no more."

He lifted them on Thunder Red and trotted up the trail. Misty and Pete slid back and forth, but they hung on. They had gone six miles when Coker pulled them to a stop.

"Why are we stopping?" Pete asked. "To rest, I hope."

"Listen!"

"What do you hear?" Pete asked.

"I said, listen!"

Frightened by his command, they sat quietly. Coker went behind some bushes and tied the mules. He helped the children down and whispered, "Stay out of sight. Somebody's talkin' up ahead. I've gotta find out what's goin' on." With that he disappeared into the bushes.

"All right men," the sheriff said to his posse. "Those two broke out of jail and are supposed to be headin' this way."

"Why do you think they'll be comin' this way?" one deputy asked.

"They used to live between here and Hollis. We've got another posse on the Hollis road south of town. These guys are killers, so if you spot 'em, shoot first and ask questions later."

"How can we tell if they're the men we're after?" another man asked.

"They dropped down into Quanah and stole some horses and some pack mules. They'll probably be leadin' the mules. We'll wait in the trees here a while and then head south if they don't show up."

Coker had crawled close enough to hear the man's last two remarks. "Dammit," he said. "Someone musta rode up here last night. Didn't think nobody'd help those reptiles, much less the sheriff."

He hurried back to the children. "Bunch a men up ahead lookin' for us. I saw a side trail goin' west about a mile back. Come on, we've got to make some tracks."

He had trotted about four miles on the side trail when he saw something move in the trees ahead. Again he stopped and hid the children. He crawled through the bushes until he saw several men hidden on each side of the trail. Then he backtracked to the children.

"What's wrong?" Pete asked.

"Someone's got men ever'where lookin' for us. Got to think 'bout this."

Misty and Pete fidgeted while they waited. Coker sat on his haunches with his back against a tree. After a time he stood up and said, "Seems like lots a men are lookin' for us to go north. Reckon the last place they'd look for us would be south, so we'll head for Texas. We'll try to stay off the trails as much as we can and go around Freeda."

He set the children on Thunder Red again and wound south through the brush.

Bert and Vernon Monroe had gone back to the saloon after leaving the Speights and managed to end up getting drunk. Because they had difficulty shaking off the effects of the whisky, they didn't start until sunup. They lived south of town, so when they got the saddles and rifles on their horses, they rode into Freeda.

At Main street they stopped. "What do you think?" Bert asked. "Did they go toward Olustee or Gould?"

"Well, if it was me and I was goin' to Colorado, I'd go to Gould. Olustee is more northeast."

"I think you're right." They reined their horses left and went toward Gould, soon picking up the mules' tracks.

"From the looks of these, he don't think anyone is followin' him," Bert said.

"Sure enough. He probably don't reckon anyone would help them damn Speights. This job shouldn't take too long."

They could see the tracks well enough to follow them at a fast trot. They found where Coker had spent the night. "He's not too smart," Bert said, "or he'd have kept goin'." After some time they found where he had turned around before he reached Gould.

"He's cagier than I thought," Bert said. "We wasn't payin' enough attention or we'd have noticed he went back the other way."

Wheeling their horses they followed the tracks slowly to make sure they didn't miss anything. They found where the mules followed the side trail. "Hey," Vernon said. "He's goin' to the Hollis road."

They followed the trail and saw where Coker had gone off through the brush. "He's even smarter than I thought," Bert said. "Who would have thought he'd have gone back south? But the tracks are gettin' fresher. It won't take us too long now."

Vernon rode silently for a way. "Who's goin' to shoot the kids? You or me?"

"We'll shoot one apiece, and then we'll both shoot the old man."

"You gonna scalp 'em?"

"We'll do it the same way."

That settled, they rode faster, determined to complete their grim task.

Coker cut through the brush, gradually working west toward where he thought the main road lay. An hour later he came to it and started trotting down the dusty path. Frequently he stepped to one side of Thunder Red to look behind them. The third time he looked back, he stopped and studied their backtrail.

"Yep. Just as I thought. Someone's comin' after us fast."

He hurried on until the road curved. A small knoll lay two hundred yards ahead. On the south side of the knoll he found a place to tie the mules and lifted the children down. Their faces showed they were worried.

"Don't be scared. But remember your mama said for you to do whatever I told you. I want you to hide in these bushes 'til I git back."

He took his shotgun, drifted into the trees out of sight and followed along the road until he found a large tree twenty feet from the trail. He took a look at the knoll and saw two heads sticking out over the crest. "Damn.

Those little skunks didn't mind. I'm gonna haveta take a paddle to their behinds first chancet I get."

He heard horses and got his head out of sight.

Bert and Vernon, always cautious going around curves or over hills, brought their horses around the turn in a slow walk. Bert studied the tracks and said, "They're just barely ahead of us, Vernon."

"Yeah, we're gonna get 'em pretty soon."

Coker's words froze them. "Who you gonna get?"

The brothers looked around far enough to see the shotgun sticking out from the tree.

Vernon said, "We're just lookin' for some stray calves."

"Yeah," Bert nodded. "They got loose last night."

"Sure they did. Ain't seed no calves nowhere. Get down off your horses and keep in mind you cain't hit me ahind this tree, but this splattergun will sure as hell put buckshot through you."

The two dismounted, hoping to get a chance to shoot. "Pull off your gun belts real slow." The Monroes fidgeted with their buckles.

"Hurry up. I ain't a gonna wait all day, and I'd rather kill you than not."

They took off their belts, but stood holding them in their hands. "Okay, move real slow and tie 'em ahind your saddles and don't try to go for 'em."

After they fastened the guns on the horses, Coker said, "Now walk around the turn here and we're gonna have a little talk."

Certain that Coker would kill them, the two looked for an opportunity to bolt into the trees, but he stayed between them and the woods. When he could no longer see the knoll, he ordered them to stop and face him. "I'm fightin' myself to keep from killin' you because I don't want the kids to see it. Now you can tell me why you're foller'n us and do it fast."

The Monroes looked at each other. "We ain't got nothin' to lose now," Bert said. "The Speights paid us to catch you."

"What did they want you to do with us when you caught us? And don't lie or you're dead."

The Monroes squirmed until Vernon said, "They wanted us to kill you."

Coker's gripped the shotgun so hard his knuckles turned white. "So you was gonna kill kids, was you? You worthless sons of a bitches. I'd like t'see your blood on the trail, but those kids'll hear the shots. I may anyway."

His finger twitched, and he almost dispatched the Monroes. He calmed down and said, "Take off your clothes."

Bert sneered. "We can't take off our clothes."

Coker leveled the shotgun at his belly and said, "Take 'em off afore you got a hole instead of a belt buckle."

The Monroes shucked their clothes in record time. "Someday, I'm gonna come back and kill you," Coker said. "Now walk north 'till I cain't see you no more."

Their feet hurting at every step, the Monroes limped up the trail until they got out of sight. Then they jumped for the mesquite bushes and hid to cover their nakedness and get away from the old man. "How did he know we was following him?" Vernon said. "We was careful."

"Yeah, we was careful. That old geezer has just been around too long. Nobody's gonna sneak up on him."

"What are we gonna do?"

"Jake Rierson lives west a couple of miles. If we can pick our way through the rocks and stickers, he'll give us some clothes and maybe loan us some horses to get home. Sure glad we left our money in the shack."

"What then?" Vernon asked. "We gonna go after the old man and the kids?"

"You just went crazy, didn't you? You can go after him if you want to, but I saw that face and those eyes. I think he meant it when he said he was gonna come back and kill us, so I'm takin' my hundred dollars and headin' west."

"Yeah, I saw those eyes too," Vernon said and shivered. "Maybe he won't find us in California if we don't tell anyone where we're goin'."

When they believed Coker had gone, they got up from their hiding place and tiptoed to Jake's place.

Coker picked up the men's clothes and said, "Might be able to use these shirts and pants. Boots ain't no good." He threw the boots into the bushes and tied the clothes over the guns. Leading the horses, Coker ran back to the children.

Pete bubbled over with questions. "What happened to those men? Are we going to ride those horses?"

"What did happen to those men?" Misty asked. "Did you hurt them?"

"Naw," Coker said. "They just decided to go swimmin'."

"In November?" Misty said.

"Just as good a time as any, when you need a bath," Coker said. Then he grabbed them each by the arm and shook them.

"Now listen to me, kids. Your mama told you to mind me and I told you to stay hid and you didn't do that. I don't guess you knowed those guys was tryin' to kill us, so I won't paddle you. But the next time you don't mind you might get kilt."

Misty puckered and nearly cried. "I don't like this running. I thought we were going to a beautiful mountain valley to live."

"That's just what we're gonna do, but it's a long ways off. You gotta be tough if we're goin' to make it."

While he had been talking, he had unlaced the stirrups on the Monroes' saddles. He set Misty on one of the horses and Pete on the other, then adjusted the stirrups to fit them. "Good lookin' little pintos. Leastwise we can all ride when we need to go faster."

He put the reins in their hands and said, "I don't know what these horses is like, so hang on tight and pull these reins back if you want to stop."

He walked toward Thunder Red. Still angry at the Monroes, he mumbled, "Shoulda killed them snakes, but they ain't the big ones."

"What did you say about snakes?" Misty asked.

"Nothin. Come on, let's git goin'."

Not accustomed to riding, Pete dug his heels into the horse's side. The pinto lunged and Pete lost the reins. Coker jumped and grabbed them. Instantly the horse stopped.

"Mighta knowed those guys treated their horses mean. You'll have to be easy on 'em, but they mind, so hang on to the reins."

To be sure they wouldn't lose them completely, he tied the reins together and hooked them over the saddlehorn. As he walked to Misty's horse to do the same, he looked at the saddle. "Hey," he said. "Those guys have got slickers ahind their saddles. We might need those."

He got on Thunder Red and headed south, staying on the trail west of Freeda hoping to go around the town without being seen. He had no trouble figuring distance and time. "I think we're passin' west of Freeda 'bout now," he said.

They had been out of the trees a half mile when he pulled Thunder Red to a sudden stop. Misty and Pete jerked back on their reins, and the pintos stopped so suddenly they nearly fell over their heads. Coker listened. "Big buncha horses comin' our way. We better hide."

He looked around and saw they could not make it back to the trees, but a large barn stood a quarter of a mile ahead. Cows filed down a lane toward a lot where others milled around waiting to be milked.

Coker pulled Thunder Red off the trail into the grass and rode until he got even with the barn. Then he turned back and galloped Thunder Red to a gate at the end of the lane. He jumped off, opened the gate and let the other mules and horses through. He started to leave the gate open but thought better of it. "Iffen I leave it open, they'll know we come in here."

He followed the cows down the lane to the lot. "We'll hide on this end of the barn and hope they go on past," he said. Coker eased the animals against the barn and tried to get them still; but the mules disliked the new horses, and the pintos didn't like the mules.

Suddenly, the barn door swung open and a small boy stood in the opening.

"Come in here," he said. "Hurry."

Coker got the animals inside, and the boy closed the door. "I seen them guys chasin' you. Foller me and I'll put you where they can't find you."

He led them around a maze of alleys to what looked like a blank wall. The boy yanked at the edge of a board, and it came open. "This don't look like no room, but they won't find you in there. Daddy used to hide new calves in here and nobody ever found 'em."

When the boy shut the board behind them, the room was pitch black. "It stinks like cow manure in here," Misty said.

"Right, but it's better'n gettin' caught," Coker said.

In the darkness an eternity passed before the boy came back. He pulled the door open. "You can come out now. They rode by on both sides, but they didn't see nothin'. I opened a gate to make 'em think you'd gone on through, but they didn't stop to look. Who you runnin' from anyway?"

Coker looked at the boy. Black hair lay unkempt on his head, and freckles covered nearly every spot on his face. He was barefooted and wore striped overalls. Deciding he had already saved their lives, Coker said, "I reckon we're runnin' from some snakes named Speight."

The boy's answer set Coker back. "Them goddamned Speights. They ain't worth shit."

Coker grinned. "Purty salty, ain't you boy. What's your name?"

"Bob Bates."

"Well, Bob Bates, they mighta kilt us if you hadn't hid us. Can you tell us how fur we are from Texas?"

"You ain't but about ten miles if you wade Red River and it's low, so shouldn't be any trouble."

Coker fished a five dollar bill out of his pocket. "This ain't worth as much as these kid's lives, but it's somethin' for helpin' us."

The boy stared at the bill. "Yessir," he said. "I'm sure glad I did. I ain't never had this much money in my hand before. I'll have to hide it 'til I can go to town, or paw won't let me keep it." The boy admired the bill some more, then stuck in his pocket.

"Speakin' of paw, he might be back anytime. Y'all better get on out of here."

They rode out of the lot and through the gate the boy had left open. Coker got off and walked as it was easier that way to look out for horse signs.

"I'm glad we're out of that smelly barn," Misty said. "It stunk something awful in there."

Coker remembered they hadn't eaten since the morning. "Bet those kids are hungry. Ain't et nothin' since breakfast. Got to get 'em fed some way."

He went deep into some oak brush to look around. "Huh, there's a crick runnin' through here," he said. "We can water our critters. Let's cross the crick and git on the south side now." Not knowing how the pintos would behave, he gave them water and grain and staked them away from the mules in some tall grass.

He got a ham and a bag of flour out of the pack. Setting the flour on the ground, he stuck his hand into the sack and felt around. "What are you doing?" Misty asked.

Coker pulled an egg out of the flour. "Gettin' some eggs, so we can have ham and eggs for supper."

She asked, "Why are they in the flour?"

"Keeps 'em from breakin'. Or if they do break, you can make bread out of 'em."

"Oh," she said. "I never would have thought of doing that."

He built a small fire and stirred everything together in a tin skillet. Pete swallowed the food quickly, almost without chewing, but Misty forced herself to eat daintily. By the time they finished, dusk had fallen.

Coker looked at the sky and said, "Cloudy. Better cover you kids with elkskins tonight."

"Will my mandolin get wet?" Misty asked. "If it does, it will ruin it. Can you put something around it?"

Coker grunted, got one of the slickers, wrapped it around the mandolin case and tied it. "More trouble'n it's worth," he said under his breath.

He picked out a high spot and told Misty and Pete to lie down on the buffalo robe. Swinging his big knife he cut stakes and drove them into the ground near their heads and then stretched the elkskin over them, weighing it around the edges with rocks.

Another elkskin was fastened around the food packs and the second slicker went over the saddles.

Satisfied that everything was protected, he looked around for a place to sleep and finally picked a huge cottonwood hollowed out at the base on one side. "It looks kinda tight," he said. "I'll sleep outside 'lessen it rains."

Around midnight thunder awakened him and drops spattered on the ground. "Gonna rain all right," he said and crawled into the trunk, barely folding his frame as heavy sheets of water poured down. Fortunately, the wind blew on the back of the tree, so he stayed nearly dry.

Lightning flash after flash lit the sky. Coker stared at the downpour. "Never saw it rain nowhere like this in November. Hope we're fur 'nough away from the crick."

The stream exceeded its banks by ten feet, but they had camped high enough up the hill to escape the water. By dawn the rain had subsided to a drizzle. Coker's muscles were so cramped he had great difficulty prying himself out of the tree and swore as he hobbled around swinging his arms.

Misty gave him a smile. "We were all right inside this," she said when he came over to make sure they were awake. As she and Pete crawled out, he put the slickers on them.

It was too wet for a fire so they ate a cold breakfast of sweet rolls.

Back on the trail the children started laughing at some joke Pete had told. Good kids, he thought, nary a cry during that terrible storm. Guts, they has that, just like their grandma.

They had ridden an hour when the rain started again. Not as heavy as the night before, but nonetheless it caused them to hunker under an elkskin for an hour. When it stopped, they made for the river.

Coker swore softly and growled. "It's a half-mile wide. We'll have to find a bridge."

They followed the bank for two miles until he saw a sign pointing to Quanah. He looked up and down the river for the bridge and finally spotted the end pilings sticking only a foot above the water.

"Well, we cain't cross here," he said. "We'll have to hide out 'til it goes down."

Huge logs rolled down the raging river, their branches churning the water as they turned. A shout came from behind them, and Coker whirled Stranger. He saw the posse, riding in a long semi-circle, charging over the hill three quarters of a mile from them.

They had them pinned against the river.

For a moment he watched, undecided. Then he jumped off Stranger. "Goddammit, they're not goin' to get my kids this time. We'll all die first."

He tied Misty and Pete to the horses with the leather thongs on the sides of the saddles. He attached Misty's lead rope to Stranger, and then connected Pete's horse to Misty's.

"Hang on tight," he yelled. "We're gonna cross the river. Don't try to turn your horses. They'll keep their heads upstream. Iffen you go under, just hold your breath and you'll come back up."

He looped Misty's horse's lead rope around the saddlehorn and rode Stranger to the bank. The mule balked momentarily, but Coker thumped him hard with his heels and whipped him with the reins. Stranger tried to jump as far as he could as if to shorten the time he had to spend in the water he hated.

When the current caught him, it jerked the other animals after him. Immediately, the rampaging river hit the sides of the horses and pulled them all under. Stranger came up first with his head facing upstream. Coker yanked on the pinto's rope and his head broke the surface. One by one the others came to the top blowing water from their noses.

The sheriff and his posse watched them wash downstream and disappear. "I don't guess we'll have to worry about those men anymore," one deputy said. "They'll never make it across."

"No way," the sheriff said. "But you know, we was after two men, and I would have swore I saw three."

Another deputy spoke up and said, "I know I saw three and two of them looked like kids to me."

A rider racing down the hill shouted, "Sheriff!"

The lawman called out, "What's all the hollering?"

The man caught his breath and said, "We just got word they caught those convicts outside of Altus."

"Oh, my God," the sheriff said as he looked back across the river. "I wonder what they was runnin' from. No matter. The poor devils didn't make it. Maybe we'll find their bodies downstream in a couple of weeks."

He led the posse toward Freeda.

A mile downstream Stranger swam into a quiet eddy and struggled up the slimy bank. He found good footing and pulled the others after him into thick woods. Coker jumped off Stranger and hurried to the children who were shivering and blue, their faces white with fear.

Coker untied the thongs and lifted them from the horses. "Jump up and down 'til I git a fire built." But the children did not move.

He dug into the saddlebag for the matches wrapped in oilcloth. Knowing dry wood would lie under the big trees, he found a giant cottonwood and pulled out twigs and leaves from beneath the huge roots. Their luck held. He spied a dry rock under a tree and struck a match on its side, sheltering the blaze with his hands until it burned six inches high. He continued to pile the leaves and dry twigs on the fire until it reached two feet, then, gently so as not to put out the delicate blaze, he laid small, wet limbs across the fire. Gradually they caught, and he kept piling on larger ones until he had a bonfire.

He pulled Misty and Pete close to the flames and shook his head. He had seen men with the same look on their faces many times before, and he knew the children would die unless he could get them warm quickly. The buffalo robe and elkskins had been soaked. He shook Misty until her teeth chattered, then did the same to Pete.

"Can you talk to me?" he shouted. "Can you talk to me?"

Misty said through chattering teeth, "Y-y-yes, I can t-t-t-talk to you. What d-do y-you w-want?"

"Take off your clothes and wring them out." Then he turned to take care of Pete.

He undressed the shivering little boy, pushed him close to the fire and turned back to Misty. She had not made a move. "Misty, take those things off or you're goin' to die! Come on now. You've gotta hurry."

Misty's mouth curled down and she cried. "I can't take my clothes off in front of you. I want to go back to Mother. Even the Speights are better than this."

Coker pulled her close to him and said, "Misty, the Speights tried to have you killed. Don't you believe that?"

She sobbed more and said, "I still can't take my clothes off in front of you."

"Misty, Misty, I changed your mother's diapers a thousand times, and I woulda changed yours if I'da been there."

She was conscious enough to comprehend a little, and she asked, "Why, why did you change my mother's diapers?"

For the first time Coker realized Bonnie had never told Misty and Pete who he was. He hugged her to his chest and said, "Misty, your mama is my girl. I'm your grandaddy."

She leaned her head back and looked at him in disbelief. Tears ran down her cheeks and with quivering lips she said, "You are my grandfather?"

"Yes, Misty. I come all the way from Colorado to keep those Speights from takin' you away from your mama."

"Really? I guess only a grandfather would do that."

She let him take off her clothes, except for the underpants. He told her to sit close to the fire near Pete and then he wrung out the clothing and hung it over a branch to dry. The robe and skins were also set up near the fire.

Soon the heat was so intense, they were forced to move back.

When Misty felt warmer, she looked at her brother. "Pete," she said, "did you know he is our grandfather?"

"Who?" Pete asked. "Who's our grandfather?"

Pointing at Coker she said, "He is."

Pete opened his eyes wide and stared at Coker. He walked around Misty and said, "Are you really our grandfather?"

Coker laid a hand on Pete's shoulder. "I'm 'fraid so Pete. I've been your grandaddy all your life."

Pete grabbed him around the waist and hugged him as hard as he could. Misty moved over close, but didn't touch him.

Unabashed, Pete hopped around with no clothes, shouting, "He's our grandfather. We have a grandfather. I thought maybe Mother made up those stories about Misty Valley."

Their clothes soon dried. They put them on and sat by the fire, one on each side of Coker. After a time Misty said, "We lost our father, but now we have a mother and grandfather, and you have a daughter and grandchildren."

Coker bowed his head and caught his breath. Pete asked, "What's wrong, Grandfather?"

Tears cascaded down Coker's cheeks, and he said, "No, I don't have no daughter, and you don't have no mama. She died afore we left, or I would've brought her too."

Misty's lips trembled, her shoulders slumped and she dropped her head into her hands. "Why didn't you tell us? Why didn't you tell us before we left?"

Coker patted her shoulder. "'Cause your mama wanted me to take you away from them Speights. Now my grandkids is all I've got, and like it or not I'm all you've got."

Pete leaned into Coker's left side and cried. Misty dropped her head against him on the other side. As the dark night wore on they sat by the fire and cried until fatigue lulled them to sleep.

"Oh, Crissy," Coker whispered as he dozed off.

12

Grandfather

Like a restless wolf taking care of its young, Coker got up from time to time to listen and look. The roaring river drowned most of the sounds, but he could hear frogs. "Frogs in November? Ain't never heerd no frogs in November. 'Course I ain't never seen it rain like that in November. Crazy country or crazy year."

He moved the children nearer the fire. He gathered wood, fed the flames and sat watching them.

"Won't be long 'til mornin'. Been a awful hard day and night on my kids. Hope they can stand it when they wake up. Sometimes things seem worse the next day and sometimes better. 'Fraid Misty and Pete ain't had much tough'nin'. Hope they can make this long trip."

Dawn oozed into the trees filtering through a dense mist rising from the ground. As soon as it was light enough, Coker examined the packs. Water still dripped from the canvas, so he took everything out and laid it on the ground. He found the bundle of cartridges and shells and unrolled the oilcloth around them. "Good," he said. "They're dry. Won't haveta buy no more."

Misty woke just as the sun shone on the top of the trees. Startled, she looked around in dismay, saw Coker and jumped up.

"Ready for breakfast?"

When she recognized him, she slumped to the ground. "I don't think I'll ever eat again." She sat, hugged her knees and gazed at the fire.

Coker left her alone. He started going through the gear on the ground. He took the clothes from the bags and hung them on tree branches, dug the wet flour out of the sack and whistled at the sight of six unbroken eggs. "The ham'll be all right iffen I trim the edges," he said.

Before long Pete roused, looked around and cried. Coker went to him and laid a big hand on his shoulder.

"Go ahead and cry, Pete. I know it hurts. I know it hurts bad."

Pete clung to Coker until he finally stifled his sobs.

"I won't cry anymore, Grandaddy. I'll try not to be a baby."

"You ain't no baby. It don't hurt none to cry. Done a lot of it myself."

Coker held him a while longer then said, "Let's see if we can get some breakfast."

He sliced the ham and found the skillet. "Ain't got no bread. Have to eat ham and eggs by theirselves. Cain't make no gravy 'cause the flour's ruined."

The smell of frying ham drew Pete to Coker's side. Coker cooked up six slices and then broke an egg and dropped it into the skillet. Basting it carefully, he pointed to his saddle. "Our tin plates is over there. Get Misty one too."

Misty was still sitting in the same position. Pete brought her food, but she refused to take it.

"Come on, Misty. You've got to eat something, or you'll get sick."

She didn't answer. Pete turned to Coker. "Can you get her to eat?"

"Maybe it'd be better just to leave Misty alone," Coker said. "Maybe she'll come out of it after a while."

Pete's hunger overcame his grief and he had two more eggs and three slices of ham. He wanted another egg, but Coker saved two of them for Misty.

When they finished, Pete helped him spread things out on the ground. "Looks like we're gonna have to stay here all day for stuff to dry out," Coker said. "We only got four cans o' peaches and four cans o' beans. Ain't got nothin' else, so we cain't stay more'n a day."

He untied the Monroes' clothes, hung them and examined their guns. He took the cartridges out, dried the cylinders and the barrels and reloaded them. "Well, they got wet, but some of them shells might shoot. Just wouldn't wanna depend on 'em in a fight."

When he finished with the pistols, he cleaned their rifles and put them back in the scabbards. Next he took care of his own rifle. Pete watched all the time he was working and kept silent. Coker wiped the cartridges, dropped them in a saddlebag and put dry ones in the rifle. He took the shells out of his shotguns and tossed them into the woods.

"Why did you throw those away, Grandaddy?" Pete asked.

"'Cause them shotgun shells is made outa paper, so water got through 'em for sure."

Not a cloud hung in the sky and sun filtering through the trees warmed them until they needed no fire.

"Well, Pete," Coker said. "Let's find us a log to lean against and set in the sun."

Misty saw him walking by. "Did my mandolin get wet?"

"Huh?" Coker said. "What did you say?"

Raising her voice a little, she said, "Is my mandolin all right?"

Coker had laid the mandolin to one side. "I don't know," he said, "but I'll go see."

Gently he unwrapped the package. He could see the lid of the case was wet. He opened it and said, "It's bone dry inside, not hurt atall."

"Would you bring it to me?"

Carrying the mandolin with great care, Coker brought it to her. She took a pick from the strings and strummed a cord. She tuned, played some and sang:

118

"Put me in your pocket
So I'll be close to you.
No more will I be lonesome
No more will I be blue.
Put me in your pocket
So I'll be close to you.
Put me in your pocket, dear,
And I'll go along with you."

She looked wistfully at Pete and then Coker. She spoke in little more than a whisper. "Mother used to sing that song after Daddy died. Oh, how I wish Mother and I both could be in his pocket."

Coker blinked and wiped his eyes. He thought, Maybe it'd do her good to talk about daddy? "How did your daddy die, Misty?"

She laid her chin on her knees and said, "I don't know. He started to Altus in a buggy. Mother fixed him a lunch and brought it to him. Then Aunt Vester came out with a pint jar of coffee. Daddy drove off and we never saw him again. His horse stopped on the other side of Olustee, and he was dead. Dr. Weeks said he had a heart attack, but I don't trust him."

"Maybe his grub was tainted," Coker said. "Had he et his dinner?"

"No. Only the coffee was gone."

"Well, maybe he did have a heart attack."

"He may have, but I don't think so. Mother got sick shortly after he died. and I do think there's some connection, but I don't know what it is."

Coker lifted her chin. "You look a little peaked. Do you want to eat somethin'?"

"I suppose so," she said.

Coker cooked ham and the last two eggs, but she ate only one egg and one slice of meat. Pete grabbed up the rest.

119

They spent the day quietly. Coker watched and listened constantly, but only squirrels and birds came through the thick woods. By late afternoon the sun had dried their goods. Coker packed again.

Just before sundown he cut the remaining ham in chunks and fried it. Then he opened the beans with his Bowie knife and poured them over the ham. Everyone was hungry and wolfed down the food.

"Let's get to bed early tonight," Coker said. "We've got to find a town afore we can eat breakfast."

"Grandfather," Misty said. "It's not 'afore,' it's 'before.'"

Coker looked at her quizzically. "What you talkin' 'bout, Misty?"

"I am talking about the words you use. You shouldn't say 'afore.' You should say 'before.'"

"Don't pay any attention to her, Grandaddy," Pete said. "She went back east to school for two years, so she thinks she's smart. She's always tellin' me what to say."

"There you go again saying tellin' instead of telling," she said. "Won't you ever learn?"

Coker stood abruptly. "Get to bed afore it gits dark."

She sighed and said, "It's 'before.' Oh, well . . ." She went over and lay on the buffalo robe, and Pete followed. Coker took his rifle and stretched out behind a huge log. He could see Misty and Pete through the cracks under the log. He fed the fire through the night, so the light would let him keep an eye on the children.

Before sunrise Coker got them up. He told Misty to put on the smaller pair of the pants. She griped but understood that she couldn't continue to ride in a dress. Coker cinched the belt around her waist, rolled up the pant legs and tied them with a leather thong.

He led the way through the down trees and thick bushes, heading southwest into a brisk wind. Misty looked at the sun behind them and said, "I thought we were going to go north. Aren't we going southwest?"

"Yep," Coker said. "We're goin' southwest. Got to go fur 'nough to find a town."

Misty mocked him. "Fur 'nough.' What is 'fur 'nough?'"

Coker perceived her tone, but he did not understand what she was getting at. He rode on without responding. Before Pete had ridden along behind, content to remain distant from Coker. Now his grandfather fascinated him and he could not keep quiet, firing one question after another.

"What kind of squirrel is that, Grandaddy? Is that an oak tree he's runnin' in? Where are we going? Do you suppose we'll find a store? How far are we from Misty Valley? Huh? Grandaddy, huh? Will we ever go back to Freeda? Do you have any horses? What do you call those saddles with the packs on them? How old are you, Grandaddy? Huh? Grandaddy, huh?"

Misty grew impatient with her brother and said, "For goodness sakes, Pete! You ask questions so fast, nobody could answer them. Slow down or shut up."

"Let 'im be, Misty. He ain't hurtin' nothin'."

"'Ain't hurtin' nothin,'" Misty said. "A double negative after double negative. You should say, 'He isn't hurting anything.'"

Pete resented her criticizing Coker. "I cain't learn nothin' iffen I don't ask no questions, can I?"

Misty glared at him scornfully and said, "What are you trying to do? Imitate his language to irritate me? Go ahead and be a dummy and see if I care."

Their arguments continued until they came to the edge of the trees. There Coker said, "Now, kids, I don't mind your fussin', but don't forget we don't know there ain't somebody lookin' for us over here in Texas. Iffen you keep hollerin' at each other, they can hear you afore

I can hear them. Be quiet for a while 'til we find out iffen they're after us."

While he talked they rounded a point of trees. A horse stood not thirty feet from them. The rider wore a badge and had sixguns on his belt. "Howdy," he said. "Nice lookin' mules and good horses there. Where you headed?"

Coker got off Switchback, went back to Thunder Red and started fiddling with the packs. Standing with Thunder Red between him and the lawman, he said, "Just takin' my grandkids into town to get some grub. Rained on us last night and we had to camp in the timber. Havin' a hard time gettin' back to the trail." He slid his hand under the elkskin on the pack.

"The trail to Quanah is on west about another mile. I'm sheriff of this county and I'm lookin' for some rustlers drivin' some young calves. Haven't seen 'em, have you?"

Coker relaxed some but kept his hand under the skin. "Nope, ain't seen 'em."

The sheriff frowned and looked at them closer. "I got a telegraph message that said some guy run off with some kids over in Freeda night before last." He put his hand on his gun. "You and these kids seem to fit the description I got. You wouldn't be that guy would you?"

Coker slid his hand upward around the grip of the shotgun. He cocked the hammers and pointed it at the sheriff. "Don't reckon we are. Nobody could've crossed the river that night."

"That much is right. The river is still too high to cross, but a man ridin' a mule is not too usual in this part of the country."

He slid his gun slightly up and down in the holster trying to make up his mind. He and Coker locked eyes. No one breathed or moved.

The sheriff said, "Well, I don't have time to fool around with that kind of thing. It sounded like a family mess anyway. I've got to get after those rustlers. I guess you're not the ones."

At that moment the wind blew up the corner of the oilcloth and the sheriff looked into the barrels of Coker's twelve gauge. He gasped and said, "In fact, I'm damn sure you're not the ones they're lookin' for." He spurred his horse into a lope.

They all breathed a sigh of relief as he rode off. "That was close," Misty said. "I thought sure he was going to take us back to Freeda."

"I did too," Pete said. "I could just see Aunt Vester's face when they pushed us through the door. Boy, I'm glad he didn't grab us."

"He wasn't gonna take you back."

"Why not?" Misty said. "He had his hand on his gun. I thought any second he was going to pull it out and make us go with him."

"Misty and Pete, I'm gonna tell you somethin'. I don't know whether your mama ever told you or not, but your grandmama's aunt took your mother away from me when she was eight. Nothin' ever hurt me so bad.

"Your mama wrote me someone was tryin' to take you away from her. I come all the way down here to keep that from happenin'. Now she's gone, and you're mine. Ain't no sheriff or nobody else gonna take you away from me."

"Would you have killed him?" Misty asked.

"He'd a had to kill me afore he'd a got you kids."

The sheriff had told them the truth about the trail. They found it and rode on into Quanah. Coker spied a grocery store and took Misty and Pete in with him. They wanted one of everything, but Coker reminded them the mules couldn't carry the whole store.

They helped Coker carry the goods outside where he packed the parcels into the panniers.

The road from Quanah angled northwest. Coker camped that night alongside it about five miles out. They stayed on the highway the next morning and finally reached Childress.

Coker stopped a farmer driving a wagon and asked the name of the next town. The man told him Memphis lay twenty-five miles ahead. Off they rode again, covering a few more miles until Misty and Pete complained about feeling sore. Coker made camp and the children went to sleep early.

The next morning Coker headed west into the brush. That day they stopped in late afternoon. Misty and Pete, still getting accustomed to riding, went quickly to sleep.

On the following evening when they stopped to camp, Coker led them to the edge of a woodland area. "Y'see those trees out yonder?" he asked them.

They looked where he pointed and Pete said, "Sure, I can see them. What about them?"

"Them mesquite trees is gettin' thicker," Coker said. "They've got thorns. You don't have no chaps, so you'll have to ride careful to keep 'em from pokin' you or pullin' you off."

"Do we have to go through them?" Misty asked.

"Yeah," Pete said. "Couldn't we go back to the main road?"

"No, I reckon not," Coker said. "They ain't no tellin' how fur that sheriff'll ride afore he gets a posse after us. Them Speights'll prob'ly give a reward for gettin' you back or gettin us kilt, so we gotta be hard to find. Them mesquite is hard to ride in, but they're easy to hide in."

Misty and Pete could hardly sit on their sore bottoms, so they went to bed early after eating heartily.

Coker sat and watched the fire, thinking about Rufe and Aspen Hill. But mostly he worried about the hours of riding to come. Were those little tykes up to it? Would be tough, for sure. How long would the weather hold?

"Must be about six hundred miles to those mountains and home. Kids cain't make many miles a day. Gonna take us a month and a half t'git back. It's a long time to stay hid, but I gotta do it."

Suddenly, he smiled and laughed aloud. "I'm a grandfather, how about that! Somethin' I never spected to be, but I guess I'm doing all right at the job. I'd better, fur damn sure. Those two need me."

He felt a lump in his throat as he looked over at them and he was thinking of Bonnie Thankful and Trissy in beautiful Misty Valley when sleep came.

The sun was touching their heads the next morning as Coker led his charges into the dense mesquite on the long journey to Colorado.

13

Hard Riding

Sharp as porcupine quills the mesquite thorns stabbed through the children's clothes and pricked them. After the branches had slapped their faces a few times, they tried to go around the trees without touching them. Often they ducked underneath because the trees grew too close together and sometimes they had to walk.

Fast travel was impossible. Coker fretted about their slow pace, but he had great patience with the cries and whining. "Have to give 'em time to get hard," he would say. Then he would pull back a branch or help them remount their horses.

Brushing off the mesquite branches like flies, Coker rode without complaining. Misty and Pete soon quit griping. They watched how he always seemed to be part of his mule. Before long they leaned forward when they went up a hill and back when they went down. They moved with their horses when they turned, making it easier for the animals.

They were doing less than ten miles a day and Coker had difficulty calculating their whereabouts. Five days after they had cut off the trail, Pete yelled, "Yonder's a town."

Coker looked and saw a small village. Farms lay around the outskirts where the mesquite had been cleared out. "Do you know what town it is?" Misty asked.

"No," he said, "but I think it's fur enough from nowhere that they ain't heerd of us."

He thought about the situation and said, "Tell you what. I'm gonna put on some clothes I bought in Amarilla and go down there. We need some more canned milk and some bacon and eggs."

"What are we goin' to do?" Pete asked.

"I'm gonna put some long ropes on your horses so they can eat grass and I want you to stay here and keep 'em from gettin' tangled up and hurtin' theirselves."

"Grandfather," Misty asked stiffly, "do you ever use correct language?"

Coker frowned. "Don't you understand what I told you about the horses?"

"Yes. I know what you want me to do."

"Then I reckon it's c'rect," he said, and went out of sight to change clothes.

"I'm afraid he's hopeless," Misty said.

"No, he ain't!"

"Yes, he is, and you're getting that way."

Coker came from behind the trees trying to work out the creases in the hat he had bought.

"You didn't change your shoes," Pete said.

"Yeah, I know. I cain't walk in them damn boots." Then he set off for the town.

Misty and Pete waited three hours before he came back carrying a sack over his shoulder. "What did you find out?" Pete asked.

"That little town is called Turkey, but it's too fur south. We gotta work our way more north to get to Amarilla."

"Are we going to Amarillo?" Misty asked.

"No, but we're goin' close to it."

He got the groceries into the packs, and they twisted on through the mesquite. After four more days of painful riding, the mesquite thinned out. By the time they made camp the next day, they had run out of it. "Boy, this is good," Pete said.

Coker shook his head. "Well, it's good because we can make time, but it's bad because we're easy to spot. Them pintos stick out like a sore thumb."

"Yes," said Misty, "they are conspicuous."

"Yep. And besides, they're easy to see."

Misty showed her disgust. "Grandfather, that's what conspicuous means."

Coker had his hands over Switchback's pack thinking about their situation. "One good thing 'bout them pintos. They're hard to see in moonlight. Guess we'd better find somewhere to hole up and wait for the light of the moon. Travelin' at night is a lot safer anyway."

"When's the light of the moon?" Pete asked.

"We been sleepin' at night, so I don't know for sure. Right now we gotta find a spot where we can get the animals some grass and water and stay out of sight."

In the distance Coker could see yellow cliffs extending above a canyon wall. "There might be a good place over there. Let's go have a look see."

They traversed the three miles to the canyon in less than an hour, moving much faster than they had in the mesquite. At the edge Coker could see the canyon ran deeper than he expected. "Let's work our way down and see what we can find," he said.

They wound back and forth along the side of the steep hill. "Goin' like this is what we call a switchback," Coker said.

"Are there switchbacks going to Misty Valley?" Pete asked.

"Bunch of 'em. Only way to get up our mountain."

No water ran in the bottom of the canyon. Coker knelt and pushed his fingers into the sand. "It's damp. Must be a spring up above."

He led them up the canyon a half mile before they found the spring. It came out of a hole a foot wide and four inches deep, ran for twenty feet and went back into the sand. "Good water," Coker said. "'Nough for us and the animals. Bushes along here make a good place to hide our critters. Somebody'd have to be right up there on top to see 'em."

"Are we going to stay down here in the bottom?" Misty asked.

"Not if we can keep from it. We need to be up where we can see."

He showed Pete how to anchor his horse so it could be untied with one pull on the end of the rope. When they got them all tethered to the shrubs, Coker said, "Let's spread out and climb the hill on this side to see if we can spot a place we can sleep without rollin' off."

A few hundred yards up, Coker stopped but saw nothing. Pete had gone farther along. "Grandaddy," he yelled, "I see a cave."

Coker climbed to where the boy stood. Across the canyon he could make out a depression in the side, but he could not tell how deep it was. "I'll go get the mules, Pete, and you go straight across to it so you can holler at me if it's all right."

Misty followed him. By the time Coker reached the animals, Pete had found the cave and motioned for them to come. Coker led the mules to the spot and decided it was much better than he expected. Twenty feet deep in the hill and thirty feet wide, it sloped up gradually some fifty feet above the bottom. The floor itself sloped very little, and a forty foot ledge ran all along the front of the cave, then tapered into the hill.

"Couldn't asked for nothin' better," Coker said.

"This is like bein' in a house," said Pete.

Misty examined the cave. She asked, "Could there be any snakes back in here?"

"Don't think so," Coker said. "It's gettin' down in to November purty good, and the nights're too cold for 'em. Don't think we have to worry 'bout them kinda snakes."

Coker unsaddled the mules and turned them loose. They went back to the horses. "Why do they run back to the horses?" Pete asked.

"Mules is funny that way. They'll always foller horses when they can. Horses always whip 'em. Don't understand it, and it makes me mad to watch a big mule get whipped by a little pony, but that's the way it is."

"Your mules have funny names," Pete said. "How did they get their names?"

"Well, I was leadin' a mare back to the mountains, and she had a colt on one of the switchbacks, so that's where he got his name. Thunder Red's mama had him in a lightnin' storm, and he's red. The big black mule showed up on Aspen Hill one day all skinny and ragged like he was a stranger to the world."

"Their names aren't really so odd then," Pete said.

Coker walked to the front of the cave and looked at the sky. "Damn," he said. "There's the moon here in the middle o' the day. It's gonna be four or five days afore it's light 'nough to ride at night."

"Do you think anyone will be looking for us way out here?" Misty asked.

"With telegraphs them Speights has let ever'one know," he said. "And by now that sheriff in Quanah has told ever' lawman in Texas. We'll just have to settle down here for a few days."

Coker and Pete spent the afternoon gathering wood while Misty arranged the packs and beds in the cave. They built a fire at the edge and the smoke spread along the slope.

After they ate they sat on the ledge in front of the cave and relaxed for the first time since they had left Oklahoma. Suddenly, Pete said, "What's that coming toward us?"

130

"Where?" Misty said.

Pete pointed down the hill. Every now and then something would jump above the weeds. "Do you see that, Grandaddy?"

"I been watchin' 'em."

"Do you see everything, Grandaddy?" Pete asked.

"Ever'thing that moves."

"What are they?" Misty asked.

"Just watch and you'll see."

Before long four heads with big, inquisitive eyes poked over a weed just below their cave. Coker laughed and said, "The first time I seed you, you looked just like them little skunks, 'cept their eyes are brown and yourn are blue."

"Skunks!" Misty glared. "You compared us to skunks."

"Skunks are funny little critters," he said. "Couple of 'em hang around outside our cabin and eat mice. One of 'em lets me rub 'im on the head. Sometimes they're stinkers, but so're you kids."

That night they sat and looked into the darkness. Nearby a coyote howled. "Sounds just like Featherfoot," Coker said. "Wonder what he's doin'? Prob'ly tellin me to come back to Aspen Hill."

"It's a frightening sound," Misty said. "All sounds at night are frightening."

"Don't be scared of night sounds, Misty. Long time ago when buff'los roamed the country, I guided people on trails from Kansas City to Californy and Oregon. Days was hot, but the nights was good. Them sounds which scairt you are sounds which'll keep you from gettin' kilt.

"I always liked to sleep by a stream and go to sleep listenin to 'em. Frogs'n crickets was always a singin' and they told me when anything was comin'."

"How'd they do that?" Pete asked.

131

"When a big animal or person walks by, them frogs quit croakin and the crickets quit singin', so you can tell just how close somethin' is gittin'. They've kept me from gittin' kilt a dozen times."

Another howl came from across the canyon. "That one sounds like a wolf," Coker said. "Ain't many of 'em no more. Better howl while you can, old lobo, cause you're like me. We ain't a gonna be around long. Our time's 'bout gone."

"You're not old," Pete said. "You're going to be around a long time."

"No, I can tell. My skin cuts and scratches easy. My hands ain't as strong and my eyes ain't as good when things is close to me. Cain't have too many more years."

Misty, listening intently, said, "Grandfather, you swear all the time, and you use words only ignorant people use. Didn't you ever go to school? Are you illiterate?"

"Don't know what illit . . . whatever it was you said. Don't know what that means."

"It means someone who can't read and write."

Coker stared at the wall of the cave. "Reckon that's me all right. My daddy kept me home to work on the farm 'cause I was the oldest boy. Never had a chance to learn to read'n write. Trissy tried to learn me, but by then it was too late. Even had to get a schoolteacher to read me your mama's letter."

"Who was your father?" asked Pete. "He sounds mean."

"My daddy's name was Reuben Brown, he..."

"Reuben Brown!" Misty said. "But your last name is Ford!"

"That's what I call myself. But my real name's William Wallace Samuel Brown. I got Coker from a guy readin' a name on a tombstone in Jefferson City, Missouri. Ford Davis was a old man which teached me to pack horses and ride mules. Jimmy Owen rode with me 'til he got kilt. I didn't like my name so just used theirs."

"Why don't you use your own name?" Misty said.

"'Shamed of my daddy."

"Why?" she asked.

"My daddy made a lot o' money raisin' corn in Illinois. He got to bettin' on horse races and drinkin' whisky. He come in drunk one winter day and walked up to the stove and tried to open a new bottle. My little brother, guess he was 'bout six, come up to him wantin' attention and pulled on his pants leg. Daddy dropped the bottle of whisky on the stove and it splashed all over my brother and caught fire. I run to put it out and Daddy knocked me down and told me he'd do it. But he was too drunk and my brother burnt to death.

"First chance I got, I run away and I ain't never been back. Never seen nothin' good come from whisky. Don't never drink none of the stuff."

"How old were you when you ran away?" Misty reached over to take his hand.

"I think I was fourteen, but I ain't sure."

"What did you do after you ran away?" Pete asked.

"Worked from farm to farm gradually gettin' farther west. Started learnin' to guide waggins when I was 'bout eighteen. Loved them mountains we was goin' acrost. Built a house in a place which your grandmother named Misty Valley and stayed.

"Did leave one time durin' the war. Guy named Quondell talked me inta goin' back to Missouri with him. Got hooked up with a captain in the southern army named A. S. Humbard. Northerners chased the southerners out of Missouri. I didn't know nothin' 'bout their fight, so I didn't take sides, but when them people left, a bunch of sorry men just out for theirselves follered 'em to take everything they could.

"Some people named Robinson and a bunch a other families was leavin' for Texas. Humbard was bound and determined he was gonna protect 'em, but he only had sixteen men, so we helped him fight off renegades all the way to Paris, Texas. Come back acrost here goin' back to Colorado. That was over forty year ago, but it's the reason I know a little 'bout this country."

"You could still have learned to read and write if you had wanted to," Misty said.

Coker hung his head and looked at the ground between his legs. "Guess so. Got my words from all over 'cause I been all over. Don't talk like nobody else and nobody else talks like me. I guess I ain't never been good for nothin' or nobody." He got up and walked into the night.

"Misty, you hurt Grandaddy's feelings. You ought to be ashamed."

"Well, I'm not."

Much later, after Misty and Pete had gone to bed, Coker came back, slid under his elkskin and lay staring at the darkness. All those long years ago, but he remembered everything.

The sun shone bright and warm the next day. They ate breakfast and sat quietly under the trees. Coker talked only when he had to answer a question. To break the monotony, the children walked along the ledge of the cave but they said little.

As Coker got things ready for the noon meal, Pete said, "I'm tired of that canned meat. Wish we had some steak or chicken."

Coker stood up and said, "Tell you what. Ain't seen no deer or antelope, but did see some cottontail rabbits when we come up. I'll get my rifle, and see if I can shoot the head off a couple."

"Why don't you take your shotgun?" Pete asked. "Couldn't you hit them easier?"

134

"Them shotguns don't shoot fur 'nough. They're wicked up to 'bout fifty or sixty feet'n that's all."

He walked out on the ledge.

"Come on, Misty," Pete said. "We're gonna shoot rabbits for dinner."

"I don't particularly want to see rabbits get shot," she said and hesitated. "Well, all right. I don't have anything else to do."

Coker studied the slope until he saw some big rocks jutting from the hillside. "There's a spot I think I can set and see over the edge and there's 'nough room for you to watch."

They made their way to the rocks. Coker peeked over the edge and said, "I'll be down here at the end. You stay real quiet."

He walked forward, sat cross-legged on the front of the rock and laid the rifle across his lap. Misty and Pete stood behind him to his right. Then an ominous rattle of a snake broke the stillness.

Coker cut his eyes to the left. A five-foot diamondback, its head even with his arm, poised to strike. Coker felt bumps break out and his flesh crawled in waves where the snake would sink its fangs. He thought, _Damn snake is gonna get me. After all my trouble, Misty'n Pete will die wanderin' 'round in this hellacious country. Damn snake's so big I won't live a hour. Cain't even tell 'em bye. Black pond is gonna get us all._

Pete stared in terror at the diamondback but dared not move. He thought, _We lost our father and mother and I couldn't stand it. Now that snake is going to kill Grandaddy. I don't want to live either._

Misty looked on helplessly. She thought, _My Grandfather is going to die. Pete and I will be left all alone. After he tried to do so much for us, I said mean things to him. But I love him. I love him. Please God don't let the snake kill him._

135

The snake's rattling reached a crescendo. <u>Gotta do</u> <u>somethin'</u>, Coker thought. <u>Maybe</u> <u>I</u> <u>can</u> <u>tell</u> <u>Pete</u> <u>to throw</u> <u>a</u> <u>rock</u> <u>ahind'im</u> <u>and</u> <u>git</u> <u>his</u> <u>attention.</u>

When he steeled himself to talk to Pete, the back of his neck tightened and his throat muscles shut off his speech. Unintentionally, he slid the rifle barrel forward. The snake saw the slight movement, jerked back and put its massive head directly in front of the muzzle. Coker pulled the trigger, and the slug tore through the top of its head. Coker sprang away from the spot. Misty and Pete clung to him so hard, he stumbled backward against the hill.

Coker sighed. "What in hell is a snake doin' out in November? Goes t'show you cain't trust them damned reptiles."

They watched the snake thrash around in its death throes until it lay still. Coker said, "Let me go, kids. I wanna git the rattles off that son-of-a-bitchin' thing."

"No, no," they said, and clung to him.

He waited until their fear subsided, then peeled their arms off. Drawing his knife he went to the snake, cut off the rattles in one vicious swipe and slipped them in his pouch. He swung the body by the bloody tail and smashed it against the ground. Then he whirled it around his head and threw it down the canyon as far as he could.

Trembling he walked slowly toward them. He carried the rifle under his arm, took them by their hands and made the tedious journey back to the cave. He collapsed on the skin, and the children followed suit. For an hour they did not speak.

Then Pete frowned and screwed his face to one side. "Grandaddy, why didn't that snake bite you?"

"I don't know for sure. It mighta been sluggish and was tryin to warm up. Diamondbacks usually bite fast."

"Why did it put its head so close to your rifle?" Misty asked.

"Iffen you can figger snakes out you can do better'n me. I know snakes can tell when somethin' is warm because they bite warm things. He seen my rifle, but maybe he got close tryin' to see if it was warm. But that's all guess. Nobody knows 'bout snakes."

Coker got out the skillet. He mixed Indian bread, fried it and scrambled some eggs. Misty and Pete ate the meal in small bites, still not inclined to talk. After they finished, Coker said, "I've gotta go see 'bout our animals. Will you kids be all right, or do you wanna go with me?"

Pete followed Coker, but Misty stayed in the cave. When he and Pete got back, she had put the buffalo robe in the middle of the cave and laid both elkskins on top. When it came time to go to bed, Coker asked, "Are you gonna put your bed where you had it?"

"No," she said. "Pete is going to sleep on one side of you, and I'm going to sleep on the other. We do think you're worth something, Grandaddy. We're a family."

Coker lay on the robe, pulled up the skins and drew them into his arms.

After breakfast the next morning when Coker went to tend the mules, Pete watched him go, but Misty sat on their bed, hands clasped in her lap. She stared at the ground for a time and then began to cry.

Pete sat down and put his arm around her. "What's wrong?"

"I miss Mother and Daddy. Here we are in a cave in the middle of nowhere. Dirt falls on us and spiders crawl all around. We would have died if the snake had bitten Grandaddy because we don't know where we are. Life seems so miserable and hopeless."

Pete hugged her and cried. When Pete cried Misty tried to stop. She wiped her eyes and nose with her sleeve. "I don't guess it will do us any good to cry. We'll just have to trust Grandaddy to get us somewhere good."

She put her arm around her brother and held him close. Still sniffling she said, "Will you get me my mandolin?"

He brought it over. She strummed and hummed a tune. "I haven't heard that before," Pete said.

"No, you haven't. I'm making up a song for Grandaddy."

"Why do you call him Grandaddy now? You wouldn't before."

"I don't know," she said. "It seems . . . warmer." After a while she sang:

"His hands are not so rough nor his skin so tough.
It's been too long since he's seen the dust.
Stirred by a buffalo,
In the light of the fading sun.
The trails were long, and the days were hot,
So he made friends with the sounds of the night.
Wolves sang their sad, sad songs,
And the rivers rocked him to sleep."

She stopped.Pete asked, "Is that all the song?"

"No. There's got to be more, but I can't get it to come out yet."

"It's really pretty," Pete said, and hummed the tune.

Coker brought back two rabbits, cleaned and ready to cook. "I didn't hear you shoot," Pete said. "How'd you kill those?"

"I got 'em with rocks," he said.

They ate and spent the rest of the day quietly. Coker knew the children needed to settle down.

In the morning he said, "The moon's gonna be out tonight, so you better sleep today."

They all curled up after eating and snoozed until late in the afternoon. A coyote's howl pierced the sky and

Coker sat straight up. "Damn, that sounds like Featherfoot," he said. After the mules were packed he woke Misty and Pete. "Hate to get you little skunks up, but we gotta head on north."

When they stepped outside the cave, it was so cold they could see their breath. He led the mules to the bottom of the canyon, Misty and Pete following with their horses in tow. As he got on Thunder Red, he saw a coyote sitting on the ridge silhouetted in the moonlight. He studied the figure and said, "Naw, he cain't be down here." But he waved anyway.

Misty and Pete shivered and rode two hours before they complained. Finally, Pete called out, "Grandaddy, we're freezing."

"Goodnight, I forgot you and Misty didn't have no coats," he said. "Git off and walk, and that'll warm you."

They went by foot another hour until Misty said, "My arms are cold, and my ears are about to come off."

Coker stopped and put the skins around them. "Hold them horses. I seed a farmhouse still lit up a little way back. I'm gonna do down there and see iffen they've got some coats t'sell."

"Watch out for snakes," Pete said.

"Ain't no snake out in this cold."

In an hour he came back with coats and caps. "They thought I was crazy, and I let 'em think that, but I give 'em twenty dollars, and they was more than happy to sell me the coats and caps. Hope they fit. The caps got flaps to come down over your ears, so they should be warm."

Misty's coat fit well, but the sleeves of Pete's slipped over his fingers. "At least they'll keep my hands warm," he said.

Three nights later they saw the lights of a town. "Is that Amarillo?" Misty asked.

139

"I don't know," said Coker. "We'll camp here and tomorra we'll find out."

At daylight he put on his other outfit and walked to the town, leaving Misty and Pete. He came back with groceries and a somber face. Always perceptive Pete asked, "What's wrong, Grandaddy? You look sad."

"Set down kids. I'm gonna have to tell you somethin' bad."

Misty's face dropped. "What is it? Are people looking for us?"

"No. It might be worse. A feller told me we're down a week into December. I was so wrapped up in gettin' you kids away from them Speights, I done no thinkin' 'bout the time of year. There ain't no way we can get in to Aspen Hill. It's likely waist deep in snow by now."

Misty's eyes opened wide. "What are we going to do then?"

Coker looked at them soberly. "We're gonna have to go to Phoenix and find your daddy's sister."

"We don't want to stay with her," Pete said. "We don't even know her. We want to stay with you."

Misty whimpered and said, "Yes, Grandaddy. We don't want to stay with anyone but you."

Coker thought for a few minutes. "Well, we gotta go there for winter. Next spring, maybe we'll head for Aspen Hill.

"Feller says that town is called Canyon. Funny names down here in Texas. Amarilla is twenty miles north. He says there's a railroad north of here somewhere. We'll angle northwest tomorra and find the railroad. Then we'll foller it 'til we find a whistlestop and ketch it to Phoenix."

His statements pacified Misty and Pete somewhat, but they started for Phoenix with drooping heads and listless eyes.

14

December on Aspen Hill

Snow fell softly on the mountain adding fluffy powder to the two feet on the ground. Rufe watched the big flakes pile up on the rails of the corral until the drifts were six inches deep. He brought out a shovel. "Fourth time I've cleaned the porch off. Winter's comin' for sure. Coker ain't a gonna be back before spring. Glad he got me 'nough meat and grub before he left. Might be able to slide a deer on the snow, but the deer and elk's all gone down anyway. Can't shoot one when they ain't any."

He put on his snowshoes and shuffled to the corral. Blackie whinnied and lifted his head. He forked him some hay and said, "Well, good buddy, they ain't nothin' here but you and me and the camp robbers. Ain't seen Featherfoot in a long time, but he was Coker's coyote I guess. Even hearin' that howl would be some company. It gets godawful lonesome with old Coker gone."

He went part way around the corral to be sure it wasn't down, then headed back to the cabin glad to sit where it was warm. "Must be getting old 'cause I feel the cold more now." he said.

He stopped on the porch to pull off the snowshoes and sank down on a chair he and Coker had fashioned from a log. Selecting a small pole from a pile stacked against the wall, he took out his pocket knife and tested it, making notches in the wood. "Coker never could whittle a chain. Didn't have 'nough patience."

He chuckled as he thought about it. "He'd break 'em ever' time just when he was 'bout through with a link."

A snowshoe rabbit hopped out of a bush near the cabin and stopped. "He's close 'nough I bet I can hit 'im."

He tiptoed inside and got a rifle. It took him some time to focus his eyes on the sights and the white rabbit in the white snow, but he succeeded. "Hot diggity, that'll be a good change from the deer and elk."

He hobbled out, cleaned the rabbit and dropped the intestines in the scarlet circle the rabbit made when it bled. Swarms of camp robbers came swooping down for the feast. By the time Rufe got back to the cabin, all traces of the rabbit had disappeared. He saw them fighting over the last bit and called out, "You coulda left some for Featherfoot, you hungry rascals."

He cooked half the rabbit and put the rest in a box hanging outside on the cabin wall. It would freeze solid and remain frozen until Rufe got it out or until spring came. After eating he bundled up and sat on the porch trying to concentrate on his whittling.

In the mountains darkness usually drops all at once in December. Tonight, however, the moon came up early, its beams reflecting off the snow, making a vivid light except in the deep timber.

"Nothin' purtier than a moon shinin' on the snow," Rufe said. "It makes dark shadows in the trees, but even they look calm and peaceful. I could look at 'em all night. Guess I'll be goin' into those shadows before many more o' these moons pass. Hope Coker ain't gone west."

As he thought he chuckled. "Wish he was here so I could make fun of his damned mules. Don't remember how he got started ridin' them things. Especially, I don't know why when he coulda been ridin' good horses."

He rambled on and on while he admired the moon shining through the ghostly aspen limbs.

"You'd think the light would run down the points of the spruce trees and light up the ground. 'Stead the light seems to stop and leave it dark underneath. Don't understand none of it, but all I know is the snow shinin' beside the black under the spruce and them aspen branches makin' shadows on the snow makes a sight too purty for me to talk 'bout. Them city people don't know what they're missin'."

He was shivering, but managed to stay until the cold bit through his clothes and made his bones ache. Inside he lit a kerosene lamp and sat in a chair with his hands folded in his lap.

"Yeah, it's awful purty, but it's a lonesome moon without old Coker."

15

Fury of the Plains

Westward they went. Coker wanted to travel at night, but Misty and Pete could not bear the cold, so they had to ride during the short days, despite the danger of being spotted.

Many times Coker had told Pete to be quiet to avoid being discovered so he held his tongue for hours. But out on the plains where no one could possibly be near, he rode up alongside Coker, talking and asking questions in rapid fire order.

"There aren't any trees out here at all Why aren't there any trees? Isn't there enough water? How do people live out here without water? Huh, Grandaddy, huh? Why is this land so flat? I can see a hundred miles. Is this sagebrush? Why is so much of it dead?

"Are Indians still out here? I don't see how they could ever have lived out here. Do any animals live out here? I don't see any canyons, so we can't find a cave. I don't see any trees. What are we going to sleep under? Huh, Grandaddy, huh? Doesn't look like there's much grass. Can the horses get enough to eat? It's cold in the day time now. How cold is it going to get? Is it warmer in Phoenix? Where's the railroad? Why can we see light but not the wind? How fast does a train go? Huh, Grandaddy, huh?"

Coker didn't know the answers to many of his questions but no matter. Pete couldn't wait for an answer because he always thought of another question instantly.

Misty dropped back to keep from listening to his patter and only came up when she wanted to ask a question.

The sparse grass made it necessary to stake the horses on long ropes, but Coker let the mules loose as always.

Mesquite and dead sagebrush supplied plenty of firewood. The first night they stopped, after they had cooked supper, Coker carried armloads of wood and built a fire that was six feet across.

"Why are you building it so big?" Pete asked.

"I'll show you after while."

He kept the large fire burning for three hours then let it die to coals. He took green sagebrush and raked the coals to one side, then laid an elkskin where the fire had been. "Okay, little skunks. Let's lay down here, and we'll get to sleep."

"Lay down where the fire has been?" said Pete.

"Yep. That's where we're gonna sleep."

"It's not 'lay' down. It's 'lie' down," said Misty.

Coker sat in the middle of the skin. "Lie down or stand up. Git down here and let's get some sleep."

They settled on each side of Coker in their customary spots. Coker pulled one elkskin over them, but not for long.

"Hey, this ground makes it hot under here," Pete said. "Where did you learn to do this, Grandaddy?"

"I seed a trapper do it the first year I was in the mountains. Iffen your gonna live you gotta take in ever'thing you see."

"You 'saw' a trapper, not 'seed' him," Misty said.

Coker had been trying to learn correct words, but he had begun to tease his granddaughter. "That cain't be right. A saw is somethin' you cut wood with."

"Oh, Grandaddy," she said. "You're exasperating, but I think you may be trying to be funny."

Gradually, the ground cooled and Coker pulled the skin back over them. Later he put the buffalo robe on top so they stayed warm until daybreak.

He started the fire going at dawn and pulled Misty and Pete out. They rushed to stand close to the flames, with their teeth chattering, hugging themselves. "The f-f-fire j-j-just k-keeps me w-warm on one s-s-side," Misty said.

Coker laughed. "Yeah, you gotta keep turnin' 'round and 'round like you're tryin' to cook on both sides."

After they ate Coker said, "Ridin' a horse is mighty nigh the coldest thing you can do. Better walk for a while."

First he had to untangle the horses and untie the ropes stiff with cold. "Damned horses. Don't know why they didn't learn 'em to stay where you stop."

They walked until mid-morning before it turned warm enough to ride. Coker pressed hard and at sundown they hurried to unpack and get a fire going. "How far do you think we came today?" Misty asked.

"I reckon about thirty miles. Thought we'd hit that railroad, but we ain't seen no towns or nothin'."

"Haven't seen any towns," Misty said.

"I just said we ain't seen no towns. Oh, you're talkin' 'bout my words again ain't you . . . isn't you?"

Misty sighed but said no more.

Again they slept on the ground warm from the fire and rose in the cold.

Coker angled north the next day, but though they gained another thirty miles they saw no tracks. They finally found the railroad just before sundown on the third day.

As they walked the next morning, they spotted a tower in the distance.

"What's that?" Pete asked.

"Looks like a tank where the trains take on water," Coker said. "Iffen it is we can ketch a train to Phoenix there."

Before long they could see the long spout slanting upward from the bottom of the tank. "Yep, that's what she is," Coker said.

They mounted and rode the last mile in a trot. A man walked away from the tank as they approached. "Hey, mister," Coker yelled. "Do you have anything to do with this railroad?"

The man came back. "Sure do," he said. "I keep the tank full and fill the engine with water when it stops. This is the Endee station. What can I do for you?"

"We wanna ketch it to Phoenix," Coker said. "Can we get on here?"

"Well, usually you could, but some renegades from Sixgun Siding dynamited the track this mornin', so there aren't any trains runnin'."

"Do you know how long it will take to fix it?" Coker asked.

"As near as they can figure out, about a week or two if it don't get blowed up again."

Coker looked at Misty and Pete and said, "Guess we'll just have t'keep doin' what we been doin'. I reckon we'll have to ride on west."

The man walked beside Stranger and looked up at Coker. "If you are thinkin' about ridin' on west, you better think again, mister. Sixgun Siding is rougher than any place in the west ever has been, and on the other side is nothin' but badlands. I wouldn't try to take young kids through there. And there's another thing. Have you looked north lately?"

The three of them turned in that direction. "You see that blue bank? That storm's comin' fast. Probably be here in two or three hours at the most. If I was you I'd head south as fast as I could and try to find someone to

147

take you in on top of the caprock. You could stay with me, but my little shack's got barely enough room for me and the stove. No way three more could get in."

Coker studied the storm and analyzed their situation. "I guess we'd better get south," he said. "Where's the road?"

"Just after you get to my little shack over there, turn left. If you follow that road, it'll take you clear to Clovis where you might catch a train, but I don't know for sure."

"Much obliged mister," Coker said.

"You're welcome."

Coker was worried. "We better ride hard, kids, 'cause he's right 'bout that storm. I seen a bunch of 'em, and they come fast on the plains."

"Will we make it, Grandaddy?" Misty asked. "And what's a caprock anyway?"

"Sure goin' to try. That caprock is a place where the rocks rise up high sort of like a hill. Maybe find some one there to take us in. Come on, now move those horses."

They trotted the thirteen miles to the foot of the caprock. The jaunt would have been torture for Misty and Pete two weeks earlier, but a month of almost constant riding and camping had made them tough and taught them to sit their horses as well as most cowboys.

A steep, narrow trail led up the incline, so they slowed to a walk. They got to the top and had gone a half mile when the wind whipped over the caprock and hit their backs. Minutes later a few snowflakes, not falling down but blowing horizontally, whistled past them.

"We gotta find a house, kids," Coker hollered and kicked Stranger into a lope.

They galloped another three miles. Then the full fury of the storm enveloped them. Snow blotted out the road, so Coker could no longer follow it.

"Get off your horses," he called out, "and come up here by me so I can see you good."

Knowing his mules would follow, he led the pintos and had Misty and Pete walk in front of him. The raging wind blew from the northeast and, not aware of direction, they drifted southwest ahead of it. The children kept their heads down and clung together. To have turned only slightly into the direction of the blasts would have frozen their faces in minutes.

Visibility decreased until Coker could hardly make out Misty and Pete just in front of him.

"We got to find somethin' to back up against and let the snow blow over us," he yelled. "Only chance we got."

The children moved slower and slower, stumbling along, so cold they no longer cared. Coker kept pulling Misty and Pete up and shoving them forward, cursing himself for the mess they were in.

"Damn," Coker said. "Guess I'm gonna have to kill a couple of these animals and gut 'em out and put the kids inside."

He turned to go back and get the rifle off his saddle and then walked into something about three feet high. He ran his hand along it and could tell it was hard.

"Hey, kids," he said. "This seems to be a wall of some kind. Let's see if we can git on the other side."

He felt his way for about ten feet, then the wall made a right angle. Another ten feet and it made another sharp turn. "There's a wall here all right," he shouted. "Let's get agin' it."

He scooped snow from the wall with his hands and told Misty and Pete to put their backs against it. He tried to get the buffalo robe and elkskins from the packs, but only succeeded in pulling out one skin. He put it around Misty and Pete and sat by them.

"Know I'm gonna freeze. Misty and Pete prob'ly ain't a gonna make it neither, but they might if the snow covers 'em up."

Snow drifted out from them immediately. "Won't be long 'til we have a snow house."

He watched the drifts pile up and felt himself getting drowsy. "Hurry up and cover us up, or we ain't none of us gonna make it."

Another few minutes and he yelled to Misty and Pete, "Are you kids all right?" But there was no answer.

He looked straight ahead waiting for the end. Then he thought he saw a spark. "What in the hell is that? Maybe I'm goin' crazy. Thought I saw a match or somethin'."

He rubbed the icicles off his eyebrows with his sleeve and tried to get a better look. Through the snow he could see a tiny, flickering light only a few feet away.

"Hey," he shouted. "Someone out there?"

The light turned toward them and got brighter.

"What in the world are you doin' out here?" a man called out.

Coker hollered, "Can you help us? I got a couple o' kids here. Do you have a house?"

"Yes. I've got a rope here. Get hold and follow me."

Coker dragged Misty and Pete up and pushed them ahead of him. He grabbed the rope and followed. They went several hundred feet and then the man guided them down some stairs buried in snow. At the bottom, he opened a door and they slipped into a small room with a dirt floor. Gray chips of buffalo manure lay in one corner by a pot bellied stove. The warm air from the stove made their faces ache.

"Maeola," the man called. "Come in here. We've got company."

150

A dark-haired woman with a round face and bright pink cheeks appeared in the doorway. She stood with a puzzled look, wiping her hands on an apron.

"How could we have company in this weather?" she asked. Then she saw the three behind her husband and hurried over.

"My goodness, John," she said. "They're numb with cold."

"I bet they are," he said. "I think you better get these kids covered up quick because they may have some frostbite."

She brought them over to a small bed and tried to get their shoes off, but the laces had frozen. Not wanting to put them between the sheets with their shoes on, she laid them on top of the covers, Misty's head at one end and Pete's at the other.

"I'll go get some quilts. Have to warm them up real quick."

The kids would be all right, Coker just knew it. He turned to the man who had saved them. "I'm Coker Owen Ford. We was in a jam, and I'm sure glad to see you."

"I'm John Carroll. I'm glad I found you. You would have froze before very long. I never saw such a blizzard."

"I got some horses and mules with saddles on out there," Coker said. "Do you have any place I can put 'em?"

"You was only a few feet from a shed," John said. "There's a windbreak runnin' out from it. I don't know whether we can find them in this storm, but we'll try."

He still had the lantern in his hand and led the way up the steps from the dugout house into the storm. "Hold on to this rope," he said. "I ran it to the shed so I could get down and back."

Coker hooked the rope in his elbow because he had no gloves. They had to duck into the vicious wind. The snow seemed to cut Coker's face. When they

151

reached the barn they couldn't see any animals. John yanked on the shed door until he pushed the snow back.

They went into the room and John hung the lantern. Coker could see barrels on the board floor on one side and a bed on the other. John noticed him looking at the bed and said, "I stayed in here while I built the dugout."

He got his lantern and went through a door on the west wall. Coker followed him into another larger room where harness and two riding saddles were stored.

"Let's check out on the west end along the fence," John said. "Horses usually look for other horses."

He opened a large door and held his lantern in front of him. "I see some of them on the outside. Must be yours."

Coker pushed beside him. He could make out several animals coated with snow standing along the fence that started at the southwest corner of the shed. Snow whipped around them. It was impossible to see more than a few feet. Coker whistled. "Hey, there's some long ears sticking up."

"Lead them in here, and we'll take their saddles off," John said.

He opened a wire gate so Coker could bring Thunder Red and the others into the shed.

He took the saddles off the pintos first. He got Stranger's saddle and stood it on its horn against the wall. Then he took the packs off Switchback and Thunder Red and turned them all outside. They found John's horses and lined up in front of a six-foot drift fence.

"You've got some good lookin' mules," John said. "and those pintos ain't bad."

"Good animals all right. 'Course the mules are a hell of a lot better than the horses."

"Do you want to put those packs in the other room where there's a floor?"

"Be better if I could."

John helped him carry the packs. Coker put the buffalo robe and elkskins on the bed. "I can sleep right here."

"Too cold for that. You better come to the house and get somethin' to eat."

"I guess I'd better go see about my kids all right."

Going away from the wind made following the rope to the dugout easier. By the time they got back, Misty and Pete were sitting on the edge of the bed talking to Maeola.

"John," his wife said, "can you believe these kids rode horses and walked all the way across the Texas panhandle?"

John looked quickly at Misty and Pete and then at Coker. "Sure enough?" he said. "That's a long way for kids."

"I've got some hot cornbread and beans fixed," Maeola said. "Come on in the kitchen."

Coker helped Misty and Pete to their feet. They walked tenderly, for their toes had begun to freeze. In the next room Coker could see a bed on one side of the room and a table set with dishes.

Maeola motioned him to a chair at the table. He sat down, then jumped back.

"Thought I heard somethin' under there," he said.

Maeola laughed. "We had to put the chickens somewhere during this storm. Their house blew away, and we couldn't let them die because we've got to have eggs."

Coker peered under the table. A dozen hens and a rooster. John had wrapped net wire around the table legs to keep them penned up.

"I don't like the smell," Maeola said, "but we can't let them die."

"I've never seen chickens in a house before," Misty said.

"I've stayed with a lot worse," Coker said. "This grub smells good. Let's eat it."

Later Coker told the Carrolls how much he appreciated their hospitality. He offered to pay them, but John looked at the state of their clothes and said, "You better keep your money because you're probably goin' to need it. I don't take money anyway for helpin' somebody in a pinch."

Coker saw the pride in John's face and knew better than to insult him by insisting on paying. "We're beholden to you. These kids mean more than the world to me and you saved 'em. Ain't no way I can ever pay you back, but someday afore too long I'll do somethin'."

"My lands, you don't have to do anything for us," Maeola said. "We're proud we can help you, and we're glad to have company."

Pete was nodding in his chair. Coker put a hand on his shoulder and said, "You've had a hard day, ain't you, boy?"

Maeola smiled. "I bet they're plumb give out. Come on. You can use the bed you was on."

She led them back to the front room. "Do you have any nightshirts?" she asked.

"We've just been sleeping in our clothes," Pete said.

"Oh, my!" she said. I'll find you somethin'."

She dug in a small closet and came up with a couple of her gowns. "They're a little big. They'll have to do tonight."

Pete made a face. Coker said, "Put it on, Pete."

He turned red, but obeyed. Maeola tucked them in bed. Then she looked at Coker. "We can make a pallet for you. I hate for you to sleep on the floor, but it's all we can do."

"Thank you, ma'am," Coker said. "However, I'm gonna sleep down in the shed where I won't be no trouble."

"Oh, you can't . . ." she started, but Maeola knew they didn't have enough quilts to make a pallet.

"Do you want to take the lantern?" John asked.

"No. Iffen I can find the rope, I can make it."

"Okay," John said. "Are you sure you will be all right?"

"Reckon so," Coker said. "Got my buff'lo robe and elkskins. I'll be warm 'nough. See you in the mornin'."

John opened the door and helped him find the rope. Coker hooked it under his arm again. Slowly, he headed down to the shed and finally crawled under the skins. Hours went by as he lay with open eyes trying to plan what to do next.

"Seein' tomorra's as hard as seein' through this blindin' blizzard," he said, and finally closed his eyes.

16

After the Storm

Coker woke and heard the wind whistling between the cracks of the boards. He pushed back the buffalo robe and saw snow sifting into the room. It had already covered everything in the shed with a thin coat.

"Bed's too soft. Gotta get up."

His moccasins were stiff as boards so he buried them between the covers next to his body. When they had softened, he put them on and looked around.

He brushed the snow off the packs and rummaged through the meager supplies still left, finding some flour, three cans of beans, two cans of corn and a little bacon.

"We was 'bout out of grub. We would of had to find a store pretty soon."

He put the food in a sack, carried it to the door and pushed with his hand, but the door did not budge. "Am I pushin' on the wall?" He stepped back to look. "No, that's the door all right."

He leaned his shoulder against it and compressed the snow outside about four inches. He got a shovel from the corner, pushed it through the crack and wiggled it back and forth. Little by little he got the door open wide enough so he could slide out and then he found a wall of snow. Not a sign of the rope, even after he shoveled a bit.

Above him he could see drifts driven by the raging wind. He went back into the room and pulled the door shut. "Guess I'll have to eat some froze beans." He got his knife and contemplated the can.

Suddenly, the door opened. John stomped in. He was completely covered with snow and stood there trying to brush some off.

"How the hell did you get down here?" Coker asked.

"I pulled my way with the rope, but the snow is so soft I nearly drowned in it. I had to feed the cows and horses. Can you help me?"

"You bet," Coker said. "Do you have 'nough for my animals?"

"I've got plenty of cane bundles in a stack north of the shed. We made a good row crop."

John took a pair of gloves from his pocket. "Here, I brought you these and some overshoes. I noticed you didn't have any."

Coker put on the boots, slipped his numbed fingers into the gloves and followed John. They went to a door on the north side of the tack room.

John said, "I thought I had done somethin' dumb when I made this door so it opened in, but today it looks pretty smart."

They fought their way out into the wind. Along the north side of the shed, the drifts lay only three feet deep. They ducked to get their faces away from the needles of snow. The cane stack ran parallel to the shed only forty yards away, but John had trouble finding it.

Biting wind tore at their faces. Coker pulled his fur hat as far down as he could, gritted his teeth and stayed close. John finally found the stack, but they had to go to the north side to pull the bundles down.

They hooked the strings of two bundles with each hand and carried them back to the wall, dropping them over the top.

"Hey, there," Coker said. "I sure don't know where I am."

"I've got the stack fenced off," John said. "If you get lost just follow the fence until you get to the wall or the shed."

On their second trip they ran into the west fence and had to follow it to the windbreak. The storm had worsened and Coker could barely make out John three feet away. Struggling, they put the bundles over the wall.

"Got to warm our hands," Coker said.

John nodded and they went back into the barn. They pulled off the gloves and put their hands under their arms.

"I swear it don't never get this cold at Aspen Hill in Colorado." Coker took a swipe at his face where chunks of snow were stuck to his beard,

"You from Colorado? I thought the mountains got colder than it does here."

"They might get colder, but we don't have no wind 'cept on the peaks. Ever' time I get this cold, it's on the damn plains."

They went back to work. After every two trips they had to go into the shed to warm up. Two hours passed before John decided they had given the animals enough bundles. Then they stomped their feet and warmed their hands before starting for the dugout.

Snow had drifted in front of the door again, so they had to force it open.

Coker picked up his sack. "I couldn't figger out where the rope was at."

"I've got it tied to the windmill," John said, "so it's to the left of the door."

"Windmill! I didn't see no windmill."

"That was a tank you was against yesterday. The windmill is just north of it."

"I'll be damned. Ain't seen nothin' since I been here."

158

John found the rope. "At least we'll be goin' away from the wind," he said. They floundered through the drifts. Snow had filled the stairway so they slid to the door. Inside they found Maeola rubbing some salve on the children's feet. She looked up and said, "They have a little frostbite, so their toes may be tender a few days."

She turned to Coker. "Get your shoes off, and I'll tend to yours."

Coker hesitated and said, "Naw, I'll be all right."

She shook her finger at him, and in a tone implying a command rather than a request, she said, "Would you quit being bashful and set down there and get off your shoes?"

He shook his head and sat, pulling off the moccasins. Maeola coated his toes with a soothing salve. Embarrassed, he thanked her several times.

"We'll have breakfast in a little while even if it is the middle of the mornin'." She went into the kitchen.

Coker was impressed. "Never seen a woman so tough and so soft at one time. Here she is livin' in a dugout in the middle of nowhere and puttin' up with this blizzard. Then she rubs a old coot's feet, and I barely felt it. Her fingers is the gentlest I ever felt. Never had anyone do that afore."

"She sure is nice," Pete said.

"She's even more gentle than Mother was," Misty said, and then started to cry.

Maeola called them to breakfast. "Warsh your hands everybody."

"What does 'warsh' mean?" Misty asked.

"You know what it means," Pete said. "Quit tryin' to act like you're smarter than ever'one else."

After they ate John got a shovel and a sack and started outside. "Do you need some help?" Coker asked.

159

"No, I'm a fixin' to shovel off the steps, so I can get to the buffalo chips. We're going to need some for the fire before long."

"What are buffalo chips?" Pete asked.

Maeola laughed and said, "They're dried buffalo manure. They're thick on the grassland. They burn like wood only faster. John hauled in a wagonload of them."

"You bring them in the house and burn them!" Misty said.

"We have coal for the cookstove, but until we can haul some wood up from the breaks, buffalo chips is all we've got."

"What are the breaks?" Pete asked.

"It's what everyone around here calls the land below the caprock. There are lots of cedar growing there, but it's five miles north of here."

"Then we came through the breaks."

John brought in a sack full of chips and put some of them on the fire. "Well, I guess there isn't anything to do now but wait for the storm to quit."

"Grandaddy," Misty said. "Is my mandolin all right?"

"I think so. It's prob'ly a mite cold."

Maeola's eyes lit up and she said, "If you play the mandolin, we can have a lot of fun. I couldn't bring my piano, but I have an old guitar. We can play and sing."

She got the guitar and asked Misty what songs she knew. They went through a few of them. Misty sang soprano and Maeola, alto. Before long Pete and John joined in. Coker listened.

"Why don't you sing with us, Grandaddy?" Pete asked.

Coker wiped at tears running from his eyes. Misty saw him. "What's wrong? Why are you sad?"

He sniffed and said, "The last time I sung was with Trissy and Bonnie, and I ain't never sung since."

160

"We'll stop if it makes you unhappy," Maeola said.

"No, I like to hear you sing. It's really purty," he said. "Just cain't keep from thinkin' 'bout Misty Valley, but don't let me bother you none."

"What is Misty Valley like?" Maeola asked.

Coker spent a few minutes getting control of his emotions. Then in a voice filled with longing, he said, "Right about now the snow lays deep over the valley. Have to use snowshoes to get around. Snow is white and smooth. Trees don't have no leaves, but they're purty stickin' outta the snow.

"When the snow melts, all kinds of flowers bloom right at the edge of the snow. I don't know the names of 'em. Yella ones and blue ones and some other colors I don't know what to call. Trissy knew 'em.

"Me'n Trissy liked it best of all when the aspen leaves turned in late September. We'd walk all 'round the valley and off in the hills, and take Bonnie with us after she's born. Lookin' at them red and yella leaves with Trissy and Bonnie was as close as I'll get to heaven, I reckon.

"Me'n Rufe still ride, and I get choked up thinkin' 'bout Trissy."

He went outside to blow his nose. He came back in and said, "Trissy coulda told you what it was like, 'cause she was real smart. But I don't know 'nough words to tell you what it's really like. You'd have t'see it."

Spellbound by Coker's description, they left off singing. Maeola put away her guitar. "It's been so long since I've played, my fingers are gettin' a little sore. We'll sing some more tomorrow."

By mid-afternoon the storm had passed and the sun broke through the clouds. Coker and John went to see about the animals. "I've got to milk old Blackie," John said. "I couldn't get to her this mornin'."

161

Coker laughed. "You got a cow named Blackie?" Wait'll I tell Rufe Blackie's a good name fer a cow."

"Who is Rufe?"

"He's my partner which is now waitin' for me in Colorado. We argee about horses and mules. Got to get back to 'im afore long."

The animals had backed up to the windbreak during the storm. Snow drifts were piled high around them and made a tunnel by each one. They moved out of their slots when they saw the men coming. Coker checked them over and said, "Looks like all of ours are still kickin'. What about yours?"

"I've got four work horses, two cows and a calf. I see everything but the calf. No, there it is. They're all here."

John got Blackie into the end of the tack room. "I don't usually milk her in here, but the snow's too deep outside," he said.

"I'll give some bundles to 'em while you milk."

"Throw the bundles over the fence," John said, "and make 'em move away from the windbreak. It gets awful messy if they stand around in one spot."

When Coker tossed the first bundles over the fence, the mules heard and charged around, getting several bites before the other animals arrived. The pintos followed and chased them away. Then the workhorses chased the pintos from the bundles, and the pintos chased the mules farther. Last in the pecking order, the cows had to wait until Coker strung the bundles far down the fence.

They all ate for a time, then the workhorses moved to the pintos' feed. The pintos chased the mules, and the mules chased the cows. Every few minutes they rotated to different bundles.

Bitter cold set in the next morning. The two men shoveled a tunnel to the barn so Coker could easily get to his bed.

Coker fretted, but he knew he could not travel with Misty and Pete through drifts in the cold. He reconciled himself to staying until the snow melted.

At supper that night, Maeola said, "John, we've got to have some groceries before long. We have plenty of meat, but we're goin' to be out of everything else in three or four days. If we can afford it, I'd like to have some cocoa to make fudge."

"I don't know if we can get to Clovis or Texico, but we'll have to do somethin'."

"Do you have any sleds?" Coker asked.

"No, I've got a big bundle wagon and a small wagon."

"Can we put runners under the little one?" Coker asked.

John brightened and said, "You know, maybe we can. We've got to give it a try anyway."

The next morning they dug the little wagon out of the snow and looked it over. "It would work all right iffen we had some kinda skids to put under it," Coker said.

"I've got some one-inch oak planks a foot wide."

"You cain't bend oak, and they'd have to be bent up on the front or they'd dig inta the snow. I don't know how we could soak 'em as cold as it is."

John thought for a minute. He looked up quickly and said, "Say, I have some pieces of rims off an old wagon that are worn thin. I think they're wide. Maybe I can bend 'em in the forge."

They spent two days bolting the boards to the wheels and shaping the rims to fit on the front wheels of the wagon. Pete delighted in turning the forge for John. When they finished, Coker said, "It's a godawful lookin' thing, but I think it'll work."

John hooked up two of his horses early one morning. Coker got on the wagon ready to go, but Maeola stopped John. "When do you think you'll be back?" she asked.

"What is today?"

"It's Wednesday, the nineteenth," she said.

"We'll be back, I'd say, by the twenty-second at the latest."

Coker's head jerked up and he said, "I think I was born today."

"We should have baked a cake," Maeola said. "How old are you?"

Coker looked up at the sky as if he were figuring something. "Well, I think I'm seventy-four or seventy-five, around there. I ain't sure. Most often I think I was born in 1831, but I don't 'member for sure."

"My lands," Maeola said. "I thought you was about sixty."

"I wish I was just sixty."

John laughed and got in the wagon. Misty and Pete stood beside Maeola and watched them leave. Coker said, "Take good care of each other."

John whipped the horses with the reins and they wound around the huge drifts. Sometimes they had to shovel to get through and sometimes they went through fields to make headway.

At the junction where they could either go to Clovis or Texico, an old man appeared, driving a team pulling a sled.

"Hello, Mr.Culpepper," John said. "How are you doin'?"

"Oh, fair to middlin'," Culpepper said. "Where you headin'?"

"Gotta get some groceries," John said. "Either to Clovis or Texico."

"Better go to Texico. More people goin' that way. Clovis road is bad."

"Thanks, Mr. Culpepper," John said. "I believe we'll take your advice."

Although they had to wind around drifts, some other wagons had already packed the snow, making their runners slide easily. They saw a number of starving cattle bawling in their helplessness, almost buried in snow. Several of them had pulled the bark off the cedar posts and chewed on the wood itself. One horse, trapped with a single cow, had stripped the hide off her back and bit at her again. Coker took his rifle and shot the animal, putting her out of her misery. "Ain't never seen nothin' like that afore," he said.

"Neither have I. That's a pitiful sight. Oh, by the way, Coker, it would be a good idea to leave your rifle and knife and hatchet in the wagon. They're jumpy down here about people carryin' 'em in town."

Coker grunted and said, "Reckon I can do that."

Well after dark John drove the horses into a wagon yard and paid the attendant. "Be sure and water them good," he said.

Coker and John shared one of the rooms by the yard.

The next morning after breakfast they headed for the grocery store. John picked out canned goods and other supplies.

"Is that goin' to be all?" the grocer asked.

"Yes, that's all."

"No, that ain't all," Coker said. "That grub won't last five people 'til the water gets hot. Go and get two of ever'thing and get a big bag of candy fer the kids and some cocoa so Maeola can make fudge."

John pulled Coker to one side. "Coker, I can't afford all those groceries much less the cocoa."

"Don't worry none. Iffen I wasn't gonna pay for it, I would'na told you to get it. Now get 'nough so we don't have to come back next month."

John shook his head but got the groceries. Coker paid the grocer with twenty dollar bills. They set the supplies in a big box and went to get the wagon. On the way to the yard, they came to a dry goods store. John stopped and looked wistfully at a red dress with lace trim in the window.

"I wish I could buy that for Maeola for Christmas," he said, turning to walk away. "Maybe next year I can make a wheat crop."

Coker grabbed his arm and said, "Come on with me."

He dragged John into the store, went to the clerk and said, "We want that purty red dress hangin' in the winda."

The man looked at his worn leather clothes and said, "That's an expensive dress. Can you afford it?"

Coker looked at the man. "Get the dress, I told you."

The man scurried away. While he was gone, Coker said, "Get Maeola a ever' day dress or two, and find a purty dress fer Misty. I'll get somethin' for Maeola to give you. Pete needs some overshoes and some more pants. Ever' boy needs a pocket knife too, so we'll find a hardware store."

"Coker, that's an awful lot of money. You don't need to get all those things."

Coker's face turned soft and sad. He looked at John and said, "I ain't got to have Christmas since Trissy died and they took Bonnie and this one may be the last one I'll ever have. You just get the things, and more iffen you want, and I'll worry 'bout the money."

The clerk's chin dropped to his chest when Coker paid for the goods from a big roll of twenty dollar bills.

As they left, a smiling Coker asked, "Do you know where a hardware store is?"

John took him around the corner. Coker made him wait outside, went in and picked out a good pocket knife for Pete and a similar larger one for John. As he put them in his pouch, his hand touched the bottle he had taken from Bonnie's room.

"Forgot 'bout that bottle. Oughta throw it away, I guess."

He hesitated, but left the bottle in his pouch. He and John went to the yard where they harnessed the horses and drove back to the stores to pick up their purchases.

"Man alive," John said. "We've about got a wagon load. Good thing this rig we cobbled up slides easy as it does."

That night John was so excited he had trouble sleeping. And for the first time Coker could remember, somebody had to wake him up.

They harnessed the horses in the dark and hit the road for home. John whistled and sang all the time.

About twenty miles from the homestead, the team slowed. John whipped them with the reins, but still the horses lagged. "What's wrong with these horses?" John asked. "Bertha's holdin' back. Strange. She's always full of fire when she's wantin' to go home."

Coker watched her for a while. "That horse is sick."

"I'm afraid she is. Hoyt Clark's place is only a mile ahead. Maybe we can make it there."

He drove into a farmhouse yard and took Bertha out of the harness. Immediately she lay down and rolled and twisted on her back, but didn't get up. "She's got colic," said Coker.

"Sure has. They didn't give her enough water the last two nights."

A man came out of the house. "Got troubles?" he asked.

"Old Bertha's taken with colic, Hoyt," John said. "Do you have any kind of oil?"

"No, I ain't, but I'll heat some water and see if we can get it down her."

"I'd sure appreciate it," John said.

They worked with the horse the rest of the afternoon, but she seemed no better. "We can't make it home tonight," John said. "Can we stay with you, Hoyt?"

"You know you're plenty welcome to stay with me, John. But I sold all my horses so I don't have no feed."

"Well, we can't go any farther tonight with one horse," John said. "Old Jim can make it tonight without feed, and maybe tomorrow someone will come along with a load of bundles."

The next morning Bertha still rolled on the ground. Coker and John took turns getting her up and making her walk, but she lay down writhing in pain as soon as they quit leading her.

Coker was walking Bertha when John saw a wagon carrying bundles. As it approached, he said, "I know that man. Doyle Rutherford. He lives two miles from us."

Coker walked Bertha to the road behind John and looked at the man on the wagon. He was slender, with wrinkles sinking deep in his face. Thin, compressed lips behind a jutting chin and small eyes gave him the appearance of a Hallowe'en witch.

"Hello, Mr. Rutherford," John said.

The man ignored him and looked as if he meant to run over John. At the last minute he reined in the horses.

"Mr. Rutherford," John said. "I've got a sick horse and need some feed for my other one. Would you sell me a couple of bundles?"

Rutherford looked down in contempt. "Hell, no. I need all my bundles."

John held the reins. "I'll pay you twice what they're worth, but I've got to have some feed."

Rutherford gritted his teeth and jerked the reins. "I wouldn't sell you any bundles for love nor money. Now get out of my way."

He whipped the horses and the side of the wagon knocked John into Coker, who fell back a few steps, dropping Bertha's lead rope. "I'll kill you, you son of a bitch!"

Surprised by his fury, John put a hand on his right shoulder to calm him. His action broke the motion of Coker's arm and the throwing knife skittered across the icy road a few feet behind the wagon. Coker jumped over, picked it up and started to throw it, but saw the wagon had gone too far.

Still ranting he walked back to the horse. He saw John shaking and said, "You sick, John?"

"No, I just saw you nearly kill a man over bundles of feed. If the horse starves to death, it ain't worth killing a man over."

"I wasn't gonna kill the sorry bastard over the bundles. I was gonna kill 'im 'cause he wouldn't help a neighbor, and he run over you."

"Coker, you can't do that here. This isn't the wild mountains. Promise me you won't do something like that again."

Coker stared at him as if he were crazy, but finally said, "Okay, I won't do it no more."

Another hour passed and another wagon came down the road with bundles. John went out on the road again. "That's Arvel Rose," he said. The driver was a rotund man with chubby cheeks. He stopped when he saw John.

"Would you sell me a couple of bundles, Mr. Rose?" John asked. "I've got a sick horse and my other one hasn't eaten since yesterday."

"No, I won't sell you any bundles," he said. John heard Coker snort behind him. "But I'll give you some. How many do you need?"

"Throw me down four of five," John said. "I sure do thank you Mister Rose. I've got plenty of bundles at home, and I'll pay you back."

Arvel Rose tossed him twelve bundles. "Well, if I need some, I'll come and get 'em." He waved and clucked to his horses.

"Now there's a good man," Coker said.

"Yes," John said. "He's a good man."

"When was Maeola expectin' us?"

"She was expectin' us today, but I can't leave Bertha."

On the afternoon of the twenty-third, Bertha got worse. A wagon came along leading a big horse. Coker stopped and asked the man if he would sell the horse. They haggled a while, and finally Coker handed over some bills. John, trying to get some warm water down Bertha, didn't see Coker with the new horse which he led into the corral.

Bertha died on the twenty-fourth late in the afternoon. Coker put his arm around John and said, "It's too bad about Bertha. She's gone, but we have to leave early in the mornin'. Maeola and the kids'll be worried sick."

"We can't leave in the morning. We don't have but one horse, and with our load, he can't pull it."

"We've got two horses," Coker said, leading John to the corral and showing him the big bay he had bought.

"Where'd you get that horse? Looks like a good one."

"Bought 'im while you was doctorin' Bertha."

John crawled over the corral fence.

"He's only seven years old and seems to be real gentle. We'll leave tomorrow if he'll work with Jim."

Early the next morning they harnessed the horses and hooked them to the wagon. The bay was well mannered and worked with the other horse as if he had teamed with him all his life.

"He's a dandy," John said. "You can really pick horses."

"Ain't too hard to pick 'em when they ain't but one to pick from."

John laughed and hollered at the horses. "Giddup, let's get home for Christmas."

For two days Maeola milked the cow and fed the animals without worrying. The children pitched in and helped. Pete knew little about farm work, but she found him to be a willing helper.

Maeola watched to make sure they didn't get too cold. She made them remove their shoes at night to check their feet. Darkness came swiftly so they filled the hours with talking.

Once Maeola asked, "Where are you kids from?"

Misty and Pete looked at each other, then Misty said, "Grandaddy told us not to talk about that."

Maeola was still curious, but she changed the subject. "Why do they call you Pete?"

"I don't know," he said. "My daddy called me Pete, but my real name is Richard Lincoln. I may do like Grandaddy and change my name."

"He changed his name?"

"Yeah, it was William something Brown," he said.

Misty sniffed and said, "It was William Wallace Samuel Brown."

"Where did you get your name, Misty?" Maeola asked.

"Mother named me Misty for the valley where Grandmother and Grandaddy lived in Colorado. I guess she liked Cherie too, but I don't know why. What is your name Mrs. Carroll?"

"My full name is Maeola Elizabeth," she said. "It's funny. When I was goin' to school, everyone called me Beth, but John calls me Maeola."

"I like Beth," Misty said. "Mother Beth. Mother Beth. Do you mind if I call you Mother Beth?."

"Why, I'd like that." Maeola began to cry.

Pete usually disagreed with Misty, but he said, "I like it too. You finally did something smart, Misty. Why are you crying, Mama Beth?"

"I had two children, but they died right after they was born, but don't worry about me. I'll be all right in a minute."

Misty decided to think of every way she could to use the new name. "What was your last name before you married, Mother Beth?"

"My last name was Humbard."

Misty gasped. "Grandaddy said something about helping somebody named Humbard go from Missouri to Texas," she said. "I can't think of his first name."

Maeola frowned and said, "That is strange. There aren't many Humbards in the world that I know of. The Yankees forced my parents to move from Missouri to Texas. Wouldn't that be something if Coker rode with them?"

She could hardly contain her excitement. She got her guitar and they sang until bedtime.

Maeola was expecting to see John and Coker by the afternoon of the twenty-first. While she cooked supper, she climbed the stairs several times to look out over the snow. By the twenty-third she was getting worried. Something must have happened. She paced the stairs back and forth. Misty and Pete followed in her steps, also looking worried.

When the men didn't show up by the twenty-fourth, she could no longer keep from talking about it to the children. "Something bad has happened. I'm afraid they may have got stuck in a big drift and froze to death."

Pete shook his head. "Grandaddy wouldn't let 'em freeze. After we got here, he told me he was going to kill two of the animals and put us inside to keep us warm. You can bet he'll figure out some way to keep from freezin'."

"Well, they may have been robbed or killed," she said.

Misty said, "Uh, uh. If someone tried to rob them, they would be the ones in trouble."

"You think your grandaddy is greater than Davy Crockett and Jim Bowie put together, don't you?"

"If you had been with us, you would understand," Misty said.

In spite of their assurances, Maeola expected the worse. On the night of the twenty-fourth, she didn't go to bed, but spent the hours going up and down the stairs looking over the countryside for the light of a lantern.

The next morning she held Misty and Pete and cried. "This will be the first Christmas John and I have been apart. What's worse is we've run out of anything to eat except beef and eggs. Somehow we've got to go for help."

"Where could we go?" Misty asked.

"I don't know. Our closest neighbor is a man named Doyle Rutherford, and he's purdee old and mean."

"Don't give up," Pete said. "Grandaddy will get 'em back."

173

Maeola hugged him and tried to smile. "Pete, it's nice to have that much faith in someone. Don't ever lose it."

After she walked the stairs for several more hours, she said, "We'll wait until dinner time. Then we've got to go somewhere before dark and send someone after them." When Pete said he was hungry, she went to the kitchen to fix the noon meal. Misty took her place on the steps. Suddenly, she bounded into the kitchen and yelled, "Mother Beth, someone is coming down the hill."

Breathlessly, Maeola ran and looked. The child was right! A wagon had topped the hill a half mile south. Maeola studied it and her heart sank. "John took the two gray horses. There is one gray horse, but the other one is a bay. I'm afraid someone is coming to tell us bad news."

They could hardly breathe, so they held hands while they waited. An eon passed before the wagon made the turn past the last drift into the lane. As it did Maeola screamed. "I can see those homemade runners. It is them! It is them!"

Misty and Pete jumped up and down, and they all laughed and cried. Pete said, "I told you. I told you Grandaddy would get 'em home."

As they drove up to the dugout, Coker said, "You got them presents hid?"

"As good as I can. We'll jump out and load 'em all over with groceries, so they won't look in the wagon."

Before they could get down Maeola climbed into the wagon on one side and Misty and Pete on the other. They all talked at the same time until John said, "Hey, simmer down. Help us get the groceries in the house, so we can unharness these tired horses."

Somewhat miffed, Maeola jumped down and John handed her an armload of boxes and bags. Misty and Pete paid no attention to him.

Pete said, "I told Mama Beth you'd be back, but she wouldn't believe me."

"Mother Beth was just worried," John said.

"Who's this Mother Beth?" Coker asked.

"Oh, her name's 'Liz'beth," Pete said, "so we call her Mama Beth."

"Mother Beth," Misty said, "And Mr. Carroll will be Papa John."

Coker and John carried the heavy flour and meal. Then they jumped into the wagon and John drove it to the barn. Standing behind to see if the children were watching, John said, "Put this sack of stuff in your room and bring it up right after dark."

They unharnessed the horses and hurried to the house.

"You could at least have told me why you're so late and where you got that horse," Maeola said.

He went over what had happened, getting some help from Coker. They left out the part about Coker trying to kill Rutherford. When they finished, Maeola said, "Good old Mr. Rose. But how could you buy all those groceries, John? You told me you didn't have near that much money."

"I didn't Maeola, but I'll have to tell you after while."

Coker said, "It's time to feed, isn't it?"

John followed him out. "We'll take it good and slow and drag the feedin' out until dark."

The early December darkness followed John to the dugout. Inside he found Maeola mixing fudge. John sat and watched her and listened to her tell what had

175

happened while they were gone. She stopped stirring and asked, "Where's Coker?"

Pete said, "Yeah, where is Granddaddy?"

"Oh, he said he was awful tired. He said he might just go to bed."

"Oh my, no!" Maeola frowned. "This is Christmas night and we wanted to sing songs together. Couldn't you go get him?"

"I don't know. You know Coker. He's stubborn as a sow in heat."

Maeola stamped her foot and scolded him. "John! You shouldn't say things like that in front of the children."

She stirred her candy and said nothing else. Misty and Pete came to the door, their eyes begging John to go after Coker. He ignored them, so they moved closer and put their hands on his legs.

Stealthy as a mountain lion, Coker carried the sack down the steps and listened. He heard nothing and eased the door open. They were all in the kitchen, so he slid quietly into the room and shouted, "Merry Christmas!"

Maeola jumped up and the children chorused, "Grandaddy!" Then they saw the sack.

"What's in there, Grandaddy?" Pete asked.

"I don't know. I found this on the steps. John, you better help me hand these things out."

Since they had expected nothing, every new gift whether it was overshoes or work pants brought squeals of delight. Coker handed Misty her new dress. She hugged it to her and wouldn't let it go. Pete took his knife and opened it again and again.

"I've got a real pocket knife," he said. "It's mine. It's my pocket knife."

John said, "Maeola, close your eyes."

He held her dress full length in front of her and said, "All right, open them."

She took one look and dropped into a chair. "Oh, John, no," she said. "You can't afford this dress." She began to cry.

John leaned over and whispered, "I picked it out, but Coker bought it all."

"For land's sakes," she cried and ran to Coker and kissed him. "Thank you, Coker. You're our Santa Claus."

Later when the noise had subsided, Maeola took out her guitar. She started to sing and then stopped.

"We're all so happy because we got presents, but Coker didn't get anything."

The old man wiped at his eyes. "Seems like all I do any more is cry," he said. Then he looked at the family around him and said, "I got more than any of you 'cause I waited thirty years to get presents for my family."

Maeola and John lay in bed that night talking about the day's events and their mysterious visitors.

"Misty and Pete told me their granddaddy won't let them talk about where they're from," she said. "Did he tell you anything?"

"Not much. Coker doesn't tell you anything he doesn't want to. I do know he's from Colorado and he's taking the kids somewhere."

"Did he say how long they intended to stay?"

"Didn't say anything about it." He thought for a while. "I suppose they'll be leaving as soon as it warms up."

"Try to find out."

"Why?"

"Because Mother Beth sounds so good," she said. "I hope they stay forever."

17

Discovery

Coker and John came in from breaking the ice on the stock tank and pulled off their coats.

"That stuff is as thick as it gets on the big pond in Misty Valley," Coker said.

"Yeah, it's a foot at least." John blew on his hands. "But I believe the snow is beginning to melt."

"Wouldn't start to melt in the mountains 'til April, and it wouldn't be gone from where me'n Rufe live 'til July."

Maeola came in while they were talking and said, "Sounds awful cold to me. I don't think I could stand snow that long. Come eat." She started into the kitchen, then turned in the doorway.

"Coker, while you was gone, Misty told me you helped a man named Humbard move from Missouri to Texas. What was his first name?"

"Yeah," Coker said. "I 'member him and some Robinsons. He was a captain in the rebel army name of A. S. Humbard."

Maeola twisted her hands in her apron, her eyes opened wide and her chin dropped. "Oh, my goodness," she said. "This can't be true. Captain A. S. Humbard is my father."

It was Coker's turn to be flabbergasted. "You cain't be . . . you're one of Captain Humbard's little girls?"

"Yes, and I should have remembered the mountain man who rode behind us. You took me and Lucy Robinson on your horse a bunch of times."

178

"Leastways I know why you're so tough. Your mama and daddy and them Robinsons was what held that bunch together. They'da all give up if it hadn'a been for them."

"Daddy talked about you a lot, but he called you Sam," she said. "That's the reason I didn't remember you."

She grew strangely sober and went to serve the noon meal. After they ate, Coker took Pete and Misty to exercise the pintos. "Cain't let 'em go too long without ridin' 'em," he said.

When they left, Maeola led John back into the kitchen.

"What's wrong?" he asked. "You look upset.."

She paced the floor and wrung her hands. She sat down and leaned across the table toward John. "I've got to tell you somethin' about Coker. You know I've told you about Papa bringing all those families to Texas with only sixteen men?"

Puzzled by her statement, he said, "Yes, I remember. Why?"

"Before the Robinsons moved farther south, Papa and Emmit Robinson used to talk about how proud they was they got all those people there without losing a person."

"Sure, you've told me all that. What does that have to do with Coker?"

She bit her lip. "Well, Coker, Papa called him Sam, and he and a man named Johnny Quondell rode with our wagon train to Texas. We didn't see them very much, but every day or so they would show up. Renegades stopped us sometimes lookin' for money or anything valuable. One time they took one of the Robinson cows, but the next mornin' that cow was back. Another time they took a little chest Mama had. About a week later she found the chest in the wagon with a spot on it. Papa said the spot was blood. The funny thing was the same renegades never bothered us twice.

"Several years later, Papa told me he thought Coker and Johnny had killed them all. As many battles as he'd been in, Papa said those two scared him the most. They floated around like shadows, he said. They ran like wolves and rode horses like Indians. He said he had an argument or two with them and was afraid they might decide to attack the train. He believed they could have picked off all of his soldiers one at a time if they wanted to.

"John, if what Papa thought is true, Coker Owen Ford is one of the most terrible men I've ever heard of. As much as he's done for us, maybe we ought to ask him to leave."

John thought about Coker and Doyle Rutherford. "Maybe you're ri . . . No, Maeola. Even if what Captain Humbard thought was true, that's been years ago. Besides, sounds like he watched after you all the way from Missouri to Texas even if he had a disagreement with your daddy. He looked after me good. He would have died for you then and I think he would die for us."

"Maybe you're right, but I can't help being a little afraid."

John remembered the knife which could have gone between Rutherford's shoulder blades. He turned to Maeola and put his arm around her.

"I believe he is loyal to anyone he cares for. I don't think there's anything to worry about unless someone tries to hurt us or one of the kids. Then I think he would kill them."

He walked slowly to the door, looked back and said, "I'm goin' out and watch Misty and Pete ride their horses. Think hard before you ask old Coker to leave. Remember, the kids are gonna go with him."

18

The Box Supper

Forty days after the blizzard a patch of brown earth showed through the snow. By the middle of February the largest drifts had become part of the enduring lore of the community. For two weeks mud made the roads impassable for wagons. Travel had to be done early in the morning before the ground thawed or late in the afternoon after it froze.

The still days, accompanied by a sun giving warmth like the glow of a potbellied stove, dried the mud. Everyone was relieved to have survived the big storm. People started visiting each other again.

Maeola hitched Jim to their buggy and drove three miles to see Ona Belle Stafford. In a week three women had come by to see her.

Coker rose at dawn and strolled around the place listening to the birds and animal sounds. A coyote had made himself at home on the hill fifty yards from the dugout. As Coker watched, it trotted to the den and looked at his territory. He howled and sat by the hole with his pointed ears visible in the dim light.

"You sound like Featherfoot, but you don't quite look like 'im. Not 'nough hair on your feet. Close 'nough, I'll call you Featherfoot 'til I see the real one. Hope you quit gettin' chickens or John's gonna put a slug in you. Hadn'a been for me, he'd already a done it."

The coyote howled again and slipped into his den for the day. Coker saw John come out of the dugout. "Out early, ain't you?" he said.

"Coyote always wakes me up. Besides it's gettin' time of the year when I'm goin' to have to milk old Blackie early, so I can get to the field and put the row crop in."

Coker breathed deep and said, "Reckon so. It gets warm early down here."

John shivered and said, "I'm glad you think so." He got his bucket from the dugout and went to milk.

After breakfast Coker helped John mend his harness. They finished that job and started working on the plows to get them ready. Coker examined one of them.

"That's a newfangled piece of 'quipment. Looks like it'll plow two rows."

"Sure will," John said and looked around to see if anyone else was there. "I call it a wiggle tail."

"Why do you call it that?"

"Because you set in the seat and push one way or another with your tail to turn the front wheel to follow the horses. Makes it a lot easier on the horses. It's something I rigged up."

"I'll be damned," Coker said. "Never saw anything like that. Too bad you cain't put a shade over it."

They worked until noon and went to eat. When they sat down, Maeola said, "You've got to quit work now and get ready."

"Ready for what?" Coker asked.

John swallowed a bite. "Everybody around is gettin' together tonight at the Burnetts' barn for a box supper."

"What in the sam hill is a box supper?" Coker asked.

"A box supper is where all the women bring somethin' to eat in a pretty box," Maeola said. "They auction them off to the men and they eat with whoever's box it is."

"Why don't ever'body eat at home?"

"Oh, Coker," she said. "It's a way for everyone to get better acquainted. We're all pretty new to this country."

"Hope you have fun."

"You're going too, Grandaddy," Misty told him.

"Who says?"

"We all say," said Maeola. "We want you to go and wear your leather clothes."

Coker sat straight with his mouth full and said, "No!"

Misty went to him and put her arm around his neck. She looked at him with soft, pleading eyes. "Please go, Grandaddy."

"Misty, that ain't fair. You know I turn to jelly when you turn them sad eyes on me." He shrugged his shoulders and tried to sound disgusted.

"Reckon I'll go."

"Oh, boy," Pete said. "Bet nobody else brings a mountain man."

Late that afternoon Coker, John and Pete waited by the wagon. "How much longer are they gonna be?" Pete asked.

"I don't know," John said. "Seems like we've been standing here two hours." He went to the dugout steps and yelled, "Maeola. You and Misty better hurry up or we're goin' to be the last ones there."

Maeola opened the door a crack and said, "We've got to get our Christmas dresses on and get our hair combed."

"Well, don't take all night."

The three of them talked about plowing and the weather for another half hour. Finally, Maeola and Misty emerged.

"Wow! Look at them," John said. "Ain't they somethin'?"

"Be the purtiest gals there tonight," Coker said.

"Mama Beth looks all right," Pete grinned, "but Misty's ugly as a mud fence."

Coker jerked Pete to face him and said, "Pete, I lost my little brother and it still hurts awful bad. You've just got one sister. Don't never let me hear you talk bad 'bout your Misty no more. Iffen family don't stick together, ain't likely nobody else is gonna help 'em neither."

"Okay, Grandaddy," he said. "I won't do it again, but I was just teasin'."

Coker hugged him. "Right, now let's get goin'."

Maeola and Misty sat in the back on blankets they would use to cover their legs for the return trip. They laughed and sang the whole three miles to the Burnetts.

A number of buggies and wagons were lined up at the hitching rail. John found an open spot to tie the horses and they all walked into the barn.

The loud talk and laughter stopped abruptly as everyone stared at Coker, who looked taller than his six feet three, almost bursting out of his shiny leather clothes. First, there were a few hushed whispers and then everyone began talking at once.

Maeola and Misty in their new dresses soon attracted attention, some of the women looking at them enviously. Not many of them could afford expensive new outfits.

The men clustered on one side of the barn and the women on the other. Boys chattered in a corner and the girls whispered together nearby. Coker followed John and stood listening outside the group as John started talking to the men. They were all sounding off on one thing after another--the weather, their teams and how soon they would plant crops.

John pulled Coker into the circle. "This is Coker Owen Ford," he said. "He's down here visitin' from the mountains of Colorado."

He told Coker the names of the men, but Coker just nodded. John said, "Don't be standoffish. Get in here."

"Yeah," the first man said. "Cat got your tongue?" He laughed at his own platitude. "Why don't you join in?"

Coker said, "Don't know much 'bout farmin' so I'm just listenin'." The conversation turned back to plowing and planting. Coker remained silent.

Bernard Burnett stood on the steps going to the loft of the barn and yelled, "Be quiet everybody. Looks like we've got a big crowd, so let's get on with the auction. Get on up here, Roy, and get after it."

Roy Messenger slipped as he ascended the steps and someone hollered, "Roy, you're as graceful as that little bird you call a cow."

Roy ignored the comment and yelled, "Bring me a box."

Someone handed him a box with a white ribbon and he began his spiel, calling for bids. The first box went quickly. Coker stood to one side and watched the proceedings, but showed no interest. John sidled up beside him, waited for a few minutes, then said, "Coker, I left my money at home. A little girl's box is coming up. I think Pete would like it. Would you buy it for him?"

Frightened by the prospect of getting involved, Coker said, "How do I bid?"

"Just raise your hand when I tell you."

Five more boxes sold before John said, "This is it, Coker. Bid when I tell you."

John waited until the bid slowed at a dollar and a quarter then poked Coker. He raised his hand and bought the box. "What do I do now?" he asked.

"You go pay for the box and come back here and wait."

Trying not to touch anybody, Coker made his way to the table, paid the man collecting the money and got the box. He turned back to find John, but John had disappeared. "Wonder where he went? Guess I'll just wait a bit."

Soon the auction ended. Coker leaned on the wall and kept looking around for Pete or John. A woman who he thought must be about sixty approached him, smiling as she came.

"Mr. Ford, I'm Vera Wharton." Noting Coker's puzzled look, she said, "You bought my box and we're supposed to eat together."

Coker mumbled, "He tricked me. I'll get 'im in the mornin'."

"What did you say?" she asked.

"Nothin' much. Just sayin' as how it was a purty box."

"Thank you," she said. "Let's find a place to sit."

Tables had been set up around the edge of the barn. They found an empty one and she opened the box, taking out two pieces of cake and a covered plate. "Do you like fried chicken?"

She sounded friendly enough. Coker took a deep breath and mumbled, "Yes'm, I do. I order it most times when I go to rest'rants."

"Do you eat in restaurants a lot?"

"Not iffen I can help it."

She laughed and he laughed right along with her. He couldn't figure how it happened, but before long they were talking like old friends. Coker found out she was a widow and she found out Trissy was dead. After he had described some of his trips, she asked him, "How many places in this country have you been?"

186

He shook his head and said, "I've rode trails all over from Car'lina to San Francisco, but I'm too old to 'member 'em all."

"You're not that old. I bet I'm older than you."

"Bet you ain't."

"I'm seventy years old."

Before Coker could catch himself, he said, "You're awful purty to be seventy."

She blushed and smiled. "All right, how old are you?"

"I ain't sure, but I think I'm seventy-five."

Then it was her turn to be surprised. "No," she said.

They talked a while longer and she asked him how long he intended to stay. He said, "Not much longer. I've gotta get back to my partner."

Bernard Burnett stood on the stairs again and said, "Everybody's through eatin', so let's do some visitin'."

Vera Wharton gathered up her dishes and looked into Coker's eyes. "Well, I guess our supper is over, and I enjoyed it. I hope you stay a long time Coker."

As she walked away he said, "She called me Coker. What about that?"

He looked for John, but couldn't find him. Maeola got him by the arm and led him to a man wearing a felt hat.

"Coker, I want you to meet Dr. Hale. We don't see much of him because he lives sixteen miles away, but he always comes when we need him."

Coker shook hands with him and said, "Pleased to meet you, Doc."

Hale seemed friendly enough. He said he had once lived in Denver. They swapped lies for a time and Hale told a joke. Coker laughed, slapped his thigh and then stopped when his hand hit the bottle he had been carrying around in his pouch.

He pulled it out and said, "Doc, I've got some medicine here and I'd like for you to tell me what it is."

The doctor took the bottle, opened it, sniffed and put a little of the liquid on his finger. He tasted the stuff twice and said, "It's not like any medicine I know of." He tasted it again. "In fact I think it's some kind of poison."

"Pizen!" Coker said.

"Well, it might be," he said. "Tell you what. There's an old trapper here who knows more about poison . . . there he is. Come over here, J. W. Got a question for you."

The elderly man smiled as he joined them. "Tell me what is in this bottle," the doctor said.

J.W. sniffed the bottle and took a taste.

"That's arsenic."

"Are you sure?" Hale asked.

"Sure I'm sure. I used a lot of it on wolves, this and strychnine, but strychnine didn't have as much taste. Quit poisonin' wolves when I saw they was thinnin' out faster than the cows."

His answer paralyzed Coker. He found his tongue enough to say "thanks" and then he took the bottle and pushed his way aimlessly through the crowd until he reached the door. Out by the wagon, he started talking to the horse.

"Pizen, Jim, Pizen. Them damned snakes pizened my girl. Pizened her husband too. Pizened 'em both and took 'em to the black pond."

People began to file out of the barn to head home. John and Maeola and Misty and Pete were laughing when they reached the wagon. "Don't wanta break that up," Coker said.

As he lifted Misty into the wagon, he said, "Well, that was quite a party wasn't it?"

"It was really fun," she said.

Maeola climbed into the wagon and said, "I believe you enjoyed eating with Widow Wharton, Coker."

"She's a good looker, Coker," John said. "I know why you liked her chicken."

Coker pretended to be angry. "I got a bone to pick with you when we get home. So I was s'pozed to buy a box fer Pete, huh?"

"You looked mighty interested, Grandaddy," Misty said. "I saw you leaning close to her."

He forced himself to say, "Oh, yeah? Who was that red-headed boy I seed you chasin' after?"

"You didn't see me chase anybody!"

"Yeah, but he chased you a lot," Pete said.

The teasing continued until they got home. Coker told Misty and Pete goodnight and went with John to unhitch the horse.

As he walked beside him, John said, "You didn't really mind eatin' with Widow Wharton, did you Coker?"

"Naw, she's a nice lady."

"I thought you'd like her. See you in the mornin'."

Coker watched until he saw him enter the dugout, then rage filled his entire being. He jerked the door to the shed open and started throwing things in his packs. "I'll kill 'em! I'll kill 'em!"

He checked his shotguns and rifle and got his knives from under the bed. "I'm gonna go tonight and kill 'em."

His rage subsided quickly. Before he saddled his mules, he rolled the problem over. "I could go back and kill 'em, but nobody would know where I was. Misty and Pete would be awful sad, and iffen I got kilt they wouldn't have no grandaddy. Rufe might not make it either. Guess I better let it go. Maybe someone else will kill them bastards."

The next day being Sunday they took a day off. Misty decided she would start a school and teach them all

189

proper speech. She had to be her most persuasive self to overcome Coker's and Pete's protests, but she got them seated and proceeded with her lesson. Coker endured the teacher for an hour, then found an excuse to leave.

Every day after that, she coached Coker in particular because she said he was the biggest offender when it came to the matter of correct language. He tried to say "eat" instead of "et" and "isn't" instead of "ain't," but he struggled in vain. In spite of her criticism he held her hand while she talked and hugged her when she got through.

Pete followed the men constantly, helping all he could and asking endless questions. He kept pestering John to teach him to drive a team. Maeola teased him and called him a rattlebox, but everyone could see she adored the boy.

They all worked through the long, hot days. Coker drove a team and helped John build fence. Together they planted a row of locust trees along the lane.

Coker, dreaming of his cool mountain home, swore at the lack of water and trees on the plains, the hot days and the dusty plowing. He considered farming to be beneath him. He longed for Aspen Hill and knew he should leave, but something was holding him.

"Why don't I get back to Rufe? Got somethin' to do with my kids and John and Maeola. Don't know why, but I cain't seem to leave 'em."

19

Rufe Waits

Rufe hobbled past a snow bank, admired the flowers blooming at the edge and stepped over the glistening water running from under the snow.

"Got a lot o' snow for the middle o' July," he said. "Good winter. Keep everything green all summer."

He ambled along from one bank to the other, smelling the pines and the damp earth. Drinking in the spirits of the high mountains made him forget his loneliness and fears. He walked through the meadows, the aspen, the spruce and the pine until late afternoon.

When he stopped by Featherfoot's den, his malaise returned. "Don't know what happened to Featherfoot. Didn't think he'd leave. Don't believe he could foller Coker."

But the coyote had been gone for months.

The sight of the smooth spots on the porch where he and Coker had sat on the planks and talked, added to his uneasiness. Sitting there, he finished whittling the chain he had been working on and hung it on the wall with a dozen others.

"Not as smooth as I used to make 'em when I had good eyes, but it keeps me busy."

He leaned on the small railing and gazed toward the last switchback.

"Wonder where in the hell Coker went? Next time I go to Ft. Collins, I'll ast the postmaster." His head jerked up and he grinned. "That's what I'll do. He had to get that letter read in Ft. Collins. I'll find out who read it to 'im and, by God, I'll try to foller 'im."

He thought about it to the point of getting his saddle, but then he sat back on the porch. "If I did know where he went to, I couldn't see tracks atall by now."

He went into the cabin and built a fire in the cookstove. While it heated, he cut up a grouse he had killed.

"Got this un t'day. Don't like them damned shotguns, but I can't see 'nough t'shoot their heads off with a rifle no more. Cain't kill a deer lessen it walks right by the cabin where I can see 'im. Cain't haul one in on Blackie 'cause I can't walk back myself."

He placed the pieces of grouse in the skillet and watched them simmer. After he ate he went out and stood on the porch with his hand on the post. "I kin get 'nough to eat this summer. I know Coker'll be back by September to see the aspen if he ain't dead."

He limped to the other end of the porch and then back, where he studied the trail. "Guess they ain't nothin' to do but wait."

He sat watching the trail until darkness forced him to go to bed and he tried to sleep through another lonely night.

Coker....where was his old friend?

20

Coker Lingers

"Weeds gettin' bad?" Coker asked John early one morning.

"Yep. We've gotta take the go-devil to 'em before the row crop gets so tall we can't get over it."

"What's a go-devil?"

John led Coker to a sled-like device with four-foot blades angling back. "This is it, a mighty fine piece of equipment. Knives slant back enough they'll slide through the dirt easy and still cut the weeds. Easier to pull than the lister, so you don't have to rest the horses quite as often. All you have to do is run it down the rows."

"Have two of 'em?"

"No," he said. "Only one."

"You want me to drive it in the mornin' or evenin'?"

"You go ahead this mornin'. I know you hate the heat, so I'll take it after dinner."

While they were hitching the horses to the go-devil, Maeola came out of the dugout tying on a bonnet and carrying a double-barreled shotgun.

"Where are you goin' with the Long Tom?" John asked.

"I saw some ducks light on the lake. I'm goin' to try to get some for dinner."

"Can she hit a duck with that thing?" Coker asked. "It's longer'n my thirty-eight fifty-six."

"Let's watch and see," John said.

They moved to the end of the windbreak. Maeola walked swiftly until she reached a spot on the lake a hundred yards from where the ducks were feeding at the edge. She crouched and eased toward them.

"She's tryin' to get them to fly away," John said.

The ducks took off north, then circled south and flew by Maeola. She waited until they left the lake then raised her shotgun. They saw the puff of black smoke and a duck folded its wings. Just as the sound reached them another puff rose and another duck fell to the ground.

"Damn!" Coker said. "Them ducks was at least fifty yards away. I don't wanna fight no duel with her!"

John chuckled."She kept us in ducks back in Oklahoma."

"Oklahoma? Where in Oklahoma?"

"Marlow and Duncan," John said.

Not wanting to show further interest in Oklahoma, Coker said, "We better get to cuttin' them weeds."

He drove the team until the sun bore down directly overhead, then took them to the barn. John was waiting by the lot to help him unhitch.

As Coker pulled up, he said, "Guess who's here who's never been here before?"

Coker snorted and said, "How in the hell would I know?"

"Widow Wharton pulled in a while ago. Since she never came to see us before, I wonder who she came to see."

"Don't get smart. I owe you a lickin' for that sneaky trick you done pulled on me at the box supper."

John unhitched the horses from the go-devil and drove them around the windbreak to the pasture. As they passed the bundle wagon the rattle of a snake spooked the horses and John fought to keep them from running through the fence.

Coker grabbed a hoe leaning against the windbreak and approached the wagon cautiously. Two prairie rattlers had crawled underneath for shade.

"Sorry, goddamn rattlesnakes! Son-of-a-bitchin things're always waitin' to bite somebody."

He raked them from under the wagon and attacked, chopping off their heads with one vicious stroke after another. He cut them into little pieces.

Maeola had come to call them to dinner. "Coker," she said. "I believe they're dead. Don't break the hoe handle."

Coker looked ashamed, but picked up one of the rattles and put it in his pocket.

"You better calm down before you come in," Maeola said. "The Widow Wharton is here."

"Yeah, John told me."

John had got the harness off the edgy horses and brought it back to hang in the barn. He saw where Coker had chopped the snakes. "Man alive, you made mincemeat out of 'em. There ain't a piece big enough to wiggle 'til sundown."

Coker waited for him to hang the harness and walked with him to the dugout. Coker's mood changed when he saw Vera Wharton. She also showed her pleasure, smiling away when he came in.

While they ate she kept up a running conversation managing to include everyone, but she directed most of her comments to Coker. Subtly she worked around to asking how long he intended to stay. Just as shrewdly he avoided giving a direct answer.

When they had finished eating, Vera Wharton got up to help Maeola with the dishes, and Coker went out with John to harness the other team.

As he left, she said, "I would like to see you again, Coker. I do hope you will stay around."

"Thank you, Vera," he said. He twisted his head, looked at the floor and half mumbled. "I'd like to see you again too." Then he raced out the door and up the stairs without waiting for her response.

195

Outside John said, "Well, well, well! Vera, huh! Looks like our mountain man has a girl friend."

Coker bridled and said, "Watch your mouth or I'll whip you yet."

John laughed and slapped him on the back. "Come on, Coker. You know you like her. Why don't you think about settlin' down here?"

"Don't know. Might be kinda nice to be here with a family and a wife, but I gotta get back to Rufe. He cain't make it through this winter."

"Well, go get Rufe and bring him back with you. Neither one of you can stay much longer in that cold country."

"I lean that way, but I cain't stand this hot country where there ain't no shade, no river and no elk."

"That's right," John said, "but you have a family who loves you."

Coker stared north across the lake for a long time. Finally, he said, "Reckon it's worth thinkin' 'bout."

He did just that, thinking and worrying until the last week of August when John had him breaking out more ground to plant wheat. While he drove the horses, he rolled the problem in his mind, but got no closer to a solution.

Finally, he said, "Dammit, I either gotta go back and stay or bring Rufe back here. I'll go to Aspen Hill and make up my mind after I get there whether I'm gonna come back or not."

He finished breaking the patch by the middle of the morning. When he came in he saw John digging a posthole northwest of the barn. He unharnessed the horses and went to help. "What you doin?" he asked.

"I decided to build a fence down the road by the lake, so we can separate the horses and cows," John said. "Two cows and a calf don't eat much, so this'll be plenty for them."

They took turns on the posthole diggers and finished by three o'clock. As they tamped the post, Coker heard a clatter from the north and saw a wagon approaching.

"Who's that comin'?" he asked.

"It's Emery Sheehan. He lives northwest of here. Don't know why he'd come over to us out of his way."

"Howdy, Emery," John said. "How you doin'?"

"Oh, pretty good," he said. "Looks like you men are doin' some hard work. Sure don't like to dig them postholes."

"Right, not in love with it myself," John said and laughed. "What are you up to?"

Sheehan said, "I rode down here to tell you I was in San Jon and a coupla guys stopped me and was askin' about some runaway kids. They had some pictures which looked a lot like the kids stayin' with you. Where those kids from?"

John thought before he replied. "Their granddaddy here brought them down from Colorado to see us. They're our niece and nephew."

"Don't suppose it matters then," Sheehan said. "Those two guys said the kids they're after are from Oklahoma. Said they was goin' to take 'em back because someone paid 'em to do it. They wore guns and looked mean and hard, so I didn't tell 'em anything about your kinfolk."

"I don't guess it has anything to do with us, Emery, but thanks anyway," John said.

"You bet," Sheehan said. "I gotta get goin'." He clucked to his horses and clattered back up the hill.

As soon as he was out of hearing distance, John said, "What do you think, Coker? Are those men looking for Misty and Pete?"

197

"I don't know. The kid's aunt wasn't all that happy they left, but I don't know why she'd pay someone to find 'em."

"I hope not. I sure would hate to lose Misty and Pete."

"Don't worry none. You ain't gonna lose 'em lessen I take 'em somewhere."

"That's good to know," John said. "Speakin' of Pete, he's over there pickin' tomatoes. I'll go make sure he's gettin' the ripe ones."

As John walked away, Coker said under his breath, "Gonna take 'em back, huh! Wearin' guns to take little kids back with, huh! I bet they got paid all right."

He could feel himself fuming. "Reckon I need to go to San Jon for groceries in the mornin' and find out what kids those gunnies are lookin' for."

21

He Finds Out

Coker ambled to the dugout and acted unconcerned. He looked around in the kitchen where Maeola was taking out pots and pans to start supper.

She gave him a puzzled look and said, "What are you doin', Coker? Do you need somethin'?"

He stooped and looked under the shelf of the cabinet. "Didn't I hear you say we needed some flour? I finished breakin' that patch of ground, so I could go get some in the mornin'."

"We're a little low, but let's all go to Clovis to get groceries and look at the town next week."

Her suggestion stumped him for a moment. Then he said, "I'd like for you to make some o' them cookies like you made Christmas. That'd take a lot of flour for five of us, wouldn't it?"

Sensing Coker was inventing an excuse, she said, "Yes, it would take a lot of flour. Maybe you better go get some in the mornin'. Are you going to Clovis or Texico?"

"Maybe Clovis. I ain't been there yet."

He went back to the shed, cleaned his rifle and shotguns and sharpened the knives and hatchet. "I'll drive the buggy 'cause them guys may be lookin' for mules."

How to hide them though? Must be easily accessible. He looked over the buggy and shook his head. "Well, prob'ly no need to hide m'rifle. Ever'body carries a rifle to shoot coyotes down here, damn their hides, but I gotta do somethin' with my shotguns."

He put some leather straps around the seat and tied his shotguns underneath, using a bow knot so he could release them with one pull. As he set the last one, John, who had been watching him from the barn, came up. "What in the world are you doin', Coker?"

Coker had heard him coming, so he had his reply ready. "Maeola needs some flour for cookies, so I'm gonna go get some in the mornin'."

"Where you goin'?"

"I ain't been to Clovis, so I reckon I'll go there."

"Why do you need shotguns and a rifle?"

"Never know when you're gonna bump inta some problem. Maybe another pore old cow that needs to be shot."

"You remember what I told you about flyin' off the handle, don't you?"

"Yeah, I 'member. I ain't a gonna get in no trouble."

When Misty and Pete went to bed that night, Coker held them longer than usual and kissed them tenderly as he tucked them in. "See you tomorra night," he said.

He sneaked out with the spare lantern figuring he would need it to harness Jim in the dark. By four in the morning he was driving down the lane and soon reached the top of the caprock.

John got up at the call of the coyote and went to milk. When he did not see Coker, he looked in the shed. "Just as I thought. He didn't anymore need to go after flour for cookies than the man in the moon."

He walked to the end of the lane and studied the tracks. He went back and milked Blackie without realizing he had already done that. Engrossed in his thoughts he carried the milk to the dugout without turning the cow loose.

Maeola saw his expression when he came in. To keep from waking the children, she whispered, "What's wrong?"

"Coker's gone."

"Well, he told me he was going for flour this morning."

"Yes, but he didn't say he was goin' to leave in the dark. Where was he goin'?"

"He said probably Clovis. Wait a minute! I heard him tell Misty and Pete he would see them tomorrow night. He couldn't go to Clovis and back in a day."

"No, he couldn't. Besides the buggy tracks go north instead of south. Maeola, I'm afraid there's some unfinished business somewhere he hasn't told us about."

"Oh, my! What do you suppose it is?"

"I don't know, but I've got a feelin' it's mighty serious."

Coker eased Jim down the narrow caprock road. At the bottom he stopped and examined the area. Bushy junipers grew profusely along the gullies running out from the caprock. Behind one of these, he found a small pool of clear water. He maneuvered the buggy to the pool and let Jim drink.

He whipped the horse into a trot for the last ten miles to San Jon. Along the way he studied the terrain. "Ain't much cover after you leave the caprock. Nothin' but cactus and a few mesquite."

At San Jon he stopped behind the line of buildings and slid between two stores so he could see the street. He spotted two men in front of the saloon. They were lounging against the hitching rail and had their thumbs hooked in gunbelts with tied down holsters.

"Them fellows are real tough all right," Coker said. "They look to be fifty-five or sixty years old. They're gonna be hard to fool."

The saloon sat nearly in the center of the block. He saw a grocery store on the west end of town and led Jim there, going behind the buildings. He hurried in, got a fifty-pound sack of flour and carried it back to the buggy. Then he drove Jim to the east end of town, circled the last building and tied him at the first hitching rail on the main street.

He walked nonchalantly along, stopping to peer into stores or look at the sky. Only a few people around. It was still early. The men in front of the saloon saw him coming and stepped onto the boardwalk. Coker acted as if he didn't see them and veered as if to go around them.

"Hey, pardner," one of them said, "we'd like to talk to yuh a minute."

"Sure," Coker said. "What do you want?"

"We're lookin' for some kids that run away from home. Their mama and daddy are awful worried about 'em. Want to know if you seen 'em."

"Seed lots o' kids. Where they from?"

"They're from Oklahoma," the man said.

"Who's their mama and daddy?"

"Some fine people named Speight. Now, how about answerin' some questions for us. You seen any new kids lately?"

"How new is new?"

"We've been lookin' for 'em for nigh on to eight months," he said, "so any time from last December to now."

"What makes you think they're here in San Jon?" Coker asked.

The man said, "No one else in the world could have done it. Sheriff at Quanah, Texas, sent word to the Speights he seen 'em with a guy who's ridin' a mule and leadin' two more. Follered the mules to Turkey and to a farmhouse where the guy bought some kids' clothes. Lost 'em after a big snow covered their tracks.

202

"They was goin' west, so we asked at ever' farmhouse we come to. No one else saw 'em. We spent six months askin' in all the towns from Memphis to Amarillo. Found a man in Canyon who saw 'em go west. Took a chance and come west to Endee.

"Man who watches the water tower there said they went west just before the big snowstorm. We figger if they passed through San Jon someone would have seen 'em. No one has, so we think the man at Endee lied to us. We telegraphed their mama where we are. Tomorrow we're gonna go south up the caprock and look 'til we find 'em."

"What're you gonna do with 'em iffen you find 'em?"

"Oh, we'll take 'em back to their folks," he said.

The second man snickered. "May not make it all the way. Long way to Oklahoma."

The other one whirled. "Shut up, Shorty Bob."

He turned back to Coker. "Can you help us? You seen any kids?"

"Sure, I seed kids," Coker said, "but how'd I know what they look like?"

The man pulled pieces of cardboard from his shirt pocket. He took two pictures from between them. Coker pretended to look at them closely. He said, "Kinda fuzzy," and turned them apparently to get better light. "Wait a minute, I seed these kids all right a couple a weeks ago at a box supper."

Both men pressed forward. The taller one said, "Where are they?"

"They're south of here all right," Coker said. "Your awful smart to figger that out."

"Can you tell us where they're at?" he asked.

"I could take you there, but it's outa my way," Coker said. "Do you reckon you could pay me somethin?"

203

Shorty Bob put his hand on his gun and said, "Sure, we'll pay yuh, won't we, Cled."

Cled pushed him back and said, "We'll give you twenty dollars now and pay you some more when we find 'em."

Coker thought, A bullet in the back'll be my pay. He said, "Sounds fair 'nough. I'll get my buggy and take you there. It's 'bout eighteen miles though, so we'll have to start soon."

"Right. We'll get our horses at the stable," said the one called Cled.

Coker watched them stroll off, then went to the buggy.

He led them south out of San Jon and noticed how the two men split. One rode on each side of the buggy.

"These guys is cold and smart," Coker said under his breath. "Gonna have to be real cagey to fool 'em."

They had gone a mile when Shorty Bob spotted Coker's rifle and yelled, "Hey, Cled, this guy's got a Winchester."

Cled rode close to the buggy and took the gun. "Guess we'd better carry this for you."

"Why you two gonna do that?" Coker asked. "Ever'body has to have a rifle. Now give me mine back."

Cled drew his pistol and said, "I told you we'd carry it, and we will unless you want to argue with this sixgun."

Coker said, "No, no. Go ahead and carry it as long as you give it back to me when we get there. Why are you 'fraid of me?"

Cled grinned at him and said, "We're not really afraid of you. You seem like straight enough guy, but we don't take no chances with anyone. Besides, we'll give your rifle back when you show us the kids."

Coker thought, "Damned right you will."

He rode Jim fast enough to make the other horses trot the ten miles to the bottom of the caprock. There he pulled him off the trail. Cled spurred his horse in front of him and said, "Where do you think you're goin'?"

"Over here to water my horse. He's been trottin' for ten miles, and he needs a breather."

"Watch him, Shorty."

Coker drove Jim to the water and let him drink. Then he got down and drank from the pool. He backed Jim up, turned him around and got back into the buggy. "Good water," he said.

Shorty Bob said, "I am awful thirsty. Let's get a drink too."

Cled thought about it and then said, "Okay, you get a drink while I watch this guy, and then I'll get one."

Shorty Bob took off his hat, lay flat and drank from the pool. "He's right," he said. "That is good water."

Cled stepped to the edge of the pool and said, "Watch this guy close while I get a drink."

"I can drop him before he gets ten feet."

Cled pulled off his hat and lay flat on the ground. When Coker's knife went through his heart, Shorty Bob died without a sound. Coker reached between his legs and put his hand around his shotgun. He untied the strap and pointed the gun across his lap at Cled.

Cled got up and was putting on his hat when he saw Shorty. "What you doin' down there?" he asked.

"He's layin' down there 'cause he's dead."

Cled saw the knife in Shorty's chest and slowly looked up into the barrels of the shotgun.

"So you're gonna kill my grandkids are you?" Coker said. "It takes a real good man to kill kids which cain't fight back."

Cled tried to stall for an opportunity to go for his gun. "It won't do any good to kill me. The Speights said they'd keep sendin' men out 'til they got 'em. They know where we are, so it won't take long."

"How much they payin'you?"

"Five thousand dollars," he said.

"Yeah, that's 'nough to get a rat like you to kill kids. Now it's time to go for your gun, kid killer."

Cled's face sagged and turned chalky white. "You've got the drop on me. Ain't gonna commit..."

The roar of the shotgun cut him off. Coker jumped from the wagon, pulled his knife from Shorty Bob and rolled the two men into a gully behind some juniper trees. He took their gunbelts, pulled their rifles from the scabbards and put them all in the buggy, then retrieved his own rifle where they had leaned it on a tree.

He took the saddles and bridles off the horses and set them on the corpses. Then he took a stick and whacked the horses on the rump. As they trotted away, he fired the other barrel over their heads. They spooked and ran east kicking up dust as they went.

Coker drove up the caprock muttering as he went. "Damned Speights know 'bout where the kids are at, do they? Gonna keep sendin' men out 'til they get 'em. I hate them bastards! Means I gotta take Misty and Pete on to Arizona and don't leave no backtrail."

He drove Jim until he broke into a lather. John heard him coming and immediately saw the white foam on the horse. Coker stopped in front of him.

John asked, "What have you been doin' and why are you drivin' Jim so hard?"

Coker, grim-faced, jumped down from the wagon. "Unharness the horse for me, John. I've gotta talk to Misty and Pete."

With no explanation he handed over the reins and went to look for the children. They were playing hopscotch at the back of the dugout. He took them each by the hand.

"Misty, Pete, get your things. We're leavin'."

"We're leaving?" Misty asked. "Why are we leaving?"

"I cain't tell you now, but somethin' turr'ble has happened and we've gotta go on to Arizona."

Shocked to silence Misty and Pete stared at Coker in disbelief. Pete found his tongue first. He said, "Grandaddy, nothin' could be bad enough for us to leave, could it?"

Misty's lips quivered. "We don't want to leave. We love Mother Beth and Papa John and they love us."

Coker frowned and gave them a stern look. "I know you don't wanna go, but we're goin'. Now get your things. We gotta pack."

They both broke down and wept. Coker put his hands on their shoulders and tried to calm them, but they cried until their noses ran and tears soaked their clothes. Coker wilted. How could he do this to them?

He hugged them both. "All right. Quit cryin' and you can stay."

They stopped, but they sniffled and inhaled sharply after gulping for air.

Coker wiped his own tears and said, "Go on with your game. You're not ever gonna have to leave Mama Beth and Papa John."

Coker walked away and said, "Iffen they're gonna stay, then I gotta do somethin' else."

He moved in great strides to the buggy. John opened his mouth to say something, but Coker spoke first. "John, I gotta job to do. I'm gonna take Thunder Red and Stranger. Gonna leave soon's I get my stuff packed up."

"What job do you have to do?"

"Cain't tell you."

"Are you goin' to Rufe?"

"No, not first anyways."

"How long will you be gone?"

"Don't know for sure. If I get back, it'll be in 'bout two weeks."

"Why can't you tell..." But Coker walked off and stalked into the shed.

John followed and watched him pack the panniers. He put one shotgun in along with the extra cartridges and shells but little else. John asked him, "Ain't you goin' to take your skillet and some grub?"

"Nope. Travelin' light and fast. Ain't gonna take Switchback 'cause his legs is too short." With that he went out and whistled for his mules who ran over to him.

He gave them some feed, tied on a sack of grain and quickly mounted Thunder Red.

"Tell Maeola 'bye' for me," he said, reaching down to shake John's hand. "Don't look for me 'til you see me comin', but don't worry none neither."

"Why not wait 'til mornin' so we can talk this over?"

"Nothin' to talk 'bout no more. I'll ride 'til dark lessen the moon comes out. Gotta get this job done fast. You're a good man, John. Never liked nobody as good as you 'cept for Rufe. So long."

John watched him trot the mules down the lane, turn north, go up the road by the lake and disappear over the crest of the hill.

He headed for the dugout where he found Maeola making jelly.

"Coker's gone," he said, slumping into a chair with his head down.

Maeola stopped stirring the pot on the stove and faced him. "What do you mean, Coker's gone?"

"He said he had a job to do and took off."

"What job?"

"I don't know because he wouldn't tell me."

208

Misty and Pete came into the kitchen. "Misty," John said, "I saw Coker talkin' to you and I heard you cryin'. Do you know where he's goin' and what he's up to?"

Misty shook her head no. "He told us we had to leave and go to Arizona. When we cried so much, he said we could stay."

Stunned by her words, Maeola asked, "Do you know why he was goin' to take you to Arizona?"

"He said something terrible had happened and we had to leave. That's all. He was saying something about a job as he walked away, but I couldn't hear it all."

"Okay," John said. "You and Pete run outside and play. I need to talk to Mother Beth."

Reluctantly, they left. John put his arm around Maeola. "This is the craziest and scariest thing I've ever got into."

"Why?" she asked.

He said, "Believe it or not, he brought flour, but down in that buggy are two rifles and four pistols. When he came with Misty and Pete, he brought two rifles and two pistols, and he took them from those two men who followed them. Something tells me somebody else is walkin' around with no guns or horses or worse."

"I don't know, John. He scares me, but I love him as much as I do the kids. What do you think he's doing?"

"There's no way for me to know, but I'm pretty sure the job he's got to do is gonna hurt somebody somewhere and it may be us. I know it has something to do with Misty and Pete, but I don't know what. We better keep the guns loaded and our eyes peeled for any stranger comin' our way."

"John, you don't like that kind of thing."

"I know, but you and the kids are worth protectin'."

22

Return of the Rattles

Coker stopped below the caprock and rolled up in a single elkskin. By dawn he had passed through Endee and turned east.

Riding hard, he worried little about who saw him. He went directly through towns on the way, stopping to buy something to eat in the restaurants or grocery stores. He was careful about not driving his mules too hard, but pushed on, consumed by the same white hot fury he had experienced when he had first heard about Bonnie, and now she was dead, dammit, victim of those killers!

Ten days after leaving the dugout, he rode into the same grove of trees where he had camped on the earlier trip. "Trees got leaves on 'em now," he said. "Don't look s'much like a damned herd of buzzards."

As he did before, he picketed the mules to be certain they could not be seen. "I'm gonna give you one day's rest," he said. "Then I got to get on with m'bizness."

Coker spent the next day resting and walking through the woodlands. "Trees is purty," he said. "But this godawful sticky heat makes it hard to 'preciate anything."

Late in the afternoon he went to the creek to fill the canteens. More water moved now along the banks, making it easier to reach. As he walked away, he thought of the black pond. "Naw, don't wanna go down there."

Then he got mad. "The hell I don't. I gotta go down and talk to that damnable pond."

His rage drove him down the stream until he climbed the bank encircling the pond.

"Well, I'll be damned," he said. "It's filled up. It ain't black no more, and it don't show no black tree limbs down in it."

Disoriented but calmed by the change in the pond, Coker wandered aimlessly among the trees. He made his way back to camp and sat staring into the woods. "Maybe all this showed me somethin'. I was gonna go in there in the mornin' and bust through the door and shoot ever'body I seen and let 'em kill me. Maybe I don't wanna do that.

"Moon's shinin' tonight so it'll be shinin' tomorra night. Be better to travel at night. That'll give my mules two days rest and make it easier on 'em. Last time they seed me in Quanah, so I'll go west this time."

He rolled up in the skin and lay for hours, planning his moves. The next day he paced back and forth from his camp to the mules, down to the pond, back to the camp, until he had worn a trail. He kept his anger in check, determined to be patient. When the sun dipped behind the highest branches, he saddled the mules and put on his leather clothes. "Want them Speights to know who I am."

Again he guided Stranger down the path to the spot behind the house. "Still got 'nough light to spot them guards."

He dismounted and watched until the moon came up. "Mighty strange," he said. "Don't see no guards, but don't reckon they need any since they ain't no kids to coop up or Bonnie to pizen."

When the moon rose, he followed the shadows cast by the trees right up to the house. He looked around both corners before going down along the west side. He kept his back to the wall, slid slowly to the corner and peeked around. Nobody guarded the front door.

"Purty damned cocky. Since I run afore, I reckon they think they can send men out to kill the kids and nobody's gonna do nothin' 'bout it."

Keeping his back to the front wall, he crept slowly to the door, took another look around and then tried the knob. "I'll be damned," he said, "it ain't even locked."

Easing it open, he peered inside. Jesse stood with his back to Coker, lighting a lamp on a table in the center of the room. He whispered, "Jesse."

The startled man almost dropped the lamp as he turned around. "Mistuh Fo'd," he said. "Whut does... "

Coker held a finger to his lips and motioned for Jesse to come closer. He whispered, "Are the Speights home?"

"Yassuh, they is in the back room."

"Wanna do somethin' for me?"

"Yassuh, I will if I can."

"Go tell 'em someone wants to see 'em, but don't tell 'em who it is."

"Sho' 'nuff, Mistuh Fo'd. Prob'ly lose mah job, but ah'll do it."

Coker went to a corner where he could see the whole room, sat in a big chair and laid his shotgun beside him. Jesse left the door open, so he could hear the conversation in the next room.

"Miz Speight," he said, "someone's here to see you and your husband. They's waitin' in the livin' room."

"Who is it?" Vester asked.

"Why did you let them in?" Albert snapped.

Ignoring Albert's question, Jesse said, "I don't rightly know who it is, but they say they wants to see Mister and Miz Speight right away."

Albert said, "Maybe it's the men we sent to eliminate the kids."

"Perhaps it is," she said.

With expectant looks, the two of them swept into the room. They didn't see Coker sitting in the dark corner.

"Jesse, you had better not be playing jokes on us," Vester said, "or you'll starve."

212

"I ain't playin' no tricks, Miz Speight. They's over there."

When the Speights passed the center table, they saw Coker's dim form in the chair. They mistook him for Cled and hurried closer. "Did you find the brats ?" Vester recognized Coker and stopped. Albert came up beside her and gaped in fear.

"You look like a gopher which got caught out of his hole," Coker said. "Don't blame you none."

Vester drew herself up and snarled, "We haven't done anything to you."

Coker fought to control himself. He rose and advanced toward them leveling his shotgun. "No, you ain't done nothin' to me, I guess. Just pizened my daughter and her husband."

Trying to look indignant, Albert said, "We didn't poison anybody."

Coker reached into his pouch, got the bottle and pitched it to Albert. "Didn't pizen nobody, huh? That's the medicine you goddam reptiles give Bonnie. Go ahead, drink it down."

Jesse tried to get Coker's attention. He pointed up, but Coker didn't see him. The butler went to the fireplace, got a poker and stood by the stairs.

Albert fingered the bottle, then let it drop on the floor and break.

"Don't blame you none for not wantin' to drink yer own pizen," Coker said. "Damned rattlesnakes! You sent men to kill my kids. Wasn't 'nough to kill my daughter, you had to try to kill her kids too."

Shaking with fury, he took the huge rattles from the diamondback and pitched them at Vester. She caught and held them in her hand. "You know your kind, don't you? I cut 'em off a snake which tried to bite me. That snake died and you damned reptiles are gonna die too."

The buckshot caught her in the head, and Vester dropped instantly to the floor while Albert watched in horror. "Don't worry none," Coker said. "Here's yours."

He pitched the second set of rattles to Albert. Reflexively, he reached for them. The buckshot caught him in the chest at the same time.

One of the guards came charging down the stairs. He stood on the bottom step and pointed a pistol at Coker's back. Jesse swung the poker and yelled, "Look out, Mistuh Fo'd."

The butler missed the man's arm, but hit the gun and knocked it from his hand. The guard drew a knife and lunged for Coker who tried too late to draw his Bowie knife.

The blade slashed upward through the leather coat, cutting Coker above the waist. He fell on his back as the man came at him.

Jesse moved forward and hit the guard behind the ear with the poker. He collapsed and hit the floor.

Coker buried his Bowie knife under the man's ribs, pulled it out and wiped it on the fellow's clothes. "Never get too old to be dumb. I knowed better'n to get away from the wall. Got too damned mad."

Jesse had dropped the poker. "You's bleedin', Mistuh Fo'd. I'll get you some clean rags to put on it."

While he went to find them, Coker tried to look at his wound. "Sharp knife," he said. "Cut right through m'jacket. Just a scratch on m'ribs, but deeper down b'low. Been cut a lot worse."

Jesse came back with the rags and staunched the flow of blood. Coker put his hand on his shoulder and said, "Jesse, you saved my life, and I appreciate it. But I guess you done lost your job. What you gonna do now?"

"I don' rightly know, Mistuh Fo'd. The Speights jus' give me 'nough t'get by on so I'se broke."

214

"Don't call me Mister Ford. Call me Coker. I ain't no better'n nobody."

"Yassuh, Mister Cokuh," he said.

"Don't have time to argee," Coker said.

He peeled ten twenty-dollar bills off his roll and handed them to Jesse. "Take these, my friend. Maybe it'll get you somewhere out of this town."

Jesse's eyes opened wide. "I never seen so much money. That'd make me rich, mistuh Cokuh, but I don' want to take your money..."

Coker shoved it in his pocket. "Ain't got time to talk. We hafta get outa here, Jesse. Someone mighta heard the shotgun. Any more men outside?"

"No. The Speights fired 'em all after the chillun got away."

"Jesse, me'n you better get outa here while the gettin's good. Some day maybe I'll see you again."

"Yassuh, I hope so."

Jesse went down the front walk to town and Coker circled to his mules. Holding his side to ease the pain, he rode northwest in the bright moonlight.

23

The Trail Back

Coker kept up a steady pace, not hurrying nor worrying about someone following. He believed the Speights would go undiscovered until morning, so he rode Stranger in a slow trot.

Before the moon set he had passed through Hollis. When morning came, he tried to walk ahead of the mules to rest them, but he had only covered a half mile when the bleeding forced him to ride again.

"Gotta make it to Texas 'cause nobody's seed me in Oklahoma. Iffen I make it outa the state, nobody can prove I ever been there."

He switched saddles and got up on Thunder Red. "Hate t'ride you this hard, but I gotta get out of this here state."

Wincing with pain and gritting his teeth, he kept going until rolling hills and mesquite told him he had entered Texas. Then he pulled off the trail and camped.

The next night he traveled until the trail went through Memphis. He camped close to the town, and when morning came, he found a grocery store and bought supplies to last him two weeks.

"'Nough t'get me to where I'm goin'" he said, and headed for Clarendon.

Uvie Tigert and Larnce Laseman were trailing an escaped bank robber headed north. For two weeks they had gained no ground.

"You know, Larnce," Uvie said, "the way he's headed, this guy's goin' to cross the trail between Memphis and Clarendon. If he turns east and gets to Oklahoma with his kinfolk, we ain't never goin' to get him."

"You're right," Larnce nodded. "We're good, but we ain't goin' to tackle that whole Turnbaugh clan. They're mean as all get out."

"Not on your life. Let's folla him until we get to the Memphis trail and see if he turns If he goes east, ain't no use wastin' our time."

They reached the trail in the afternoon and followed the convict a mile north until his tracks turned east. "Might as well get back to Amarillo," Larnce said. "He's headin' home."

They returned to the main trail to get out of the mesquite and had gone about five miles when Uvie jerked his horse to a stop. "Larnce! I been ridin' along here not payin' no attention to the trail 'cause we ain't after nobody, but you know what I see?"

Larnce looked at the trail. "Yeah, I see mule tracks. What about it?"

"Look good. Them's big tracks for mules, and the left back foot on one of 'em turns in a little. Know whose mule that is?"

"Hell, yes. We trailed that son of a bitch into Clarendon where we lost him at the fairgrounds. It's him, sure as hell. Wonder what he's doin' here nearly a year after we give up on 'im."

"I don't know, but these tracks are fresh, so let's get after 'im."

Coker had decided to travel early in the evening and had mounted Thunder Red when he saw the two men coming in a hard lope. As they neared, they slowed their horses.

"Wonder who those guys are," he muttered. They didn't look familiar.

They stopped three feet from Thunder Red.

"Howdy," Coker said. "Where you headed?"

"Right here," Uvie said.

Larnce put his hand on his gun and said, "We're Texas rangers and we're lookin' for a man who killed a friend of ours last year."

"Yeah," Uvie said. "We swore to trail him to the end of the world to get even for Leonard."

"I don't want no trouble with rangers, but I don't know nothin' 'bout no Leonard," Coker said.

"We believe you do," said Larnce. "We think you killed him about thirty miles this side of Amarillo."

"But that man . . . " Coker started to say then stopped.

"We're goin' to take you in to make sure you're the one," Uvie said. "Give me your rifle."

Coker thought, "<u>They're gonna take me in them mesquites and kill me</u>. <u>Rangers or not I gotta do somethin'</u>."

"Okay," Coker said, "I ain't 'fraid 'cause I ain't done nothin."

He put his hand on the stock of his rifle as though to pull it out of the scabbard, then kicked Thunder Red, ran between both their horses and knocked them sideways. Before they recovered he got into the mesquite and headed west.

He heard them shoot as he rode away and felt the pain under his right arm. "Damn, the son of a bitches hit me. Not too bad don't feel like."

He rode leaning over his mule to make a smaller target. The sun had set and darkness would come soon. "Iffen I can get away 'til dark, I'll lose the bastards."

218

He looked back and could see he led them by nearly half a mile. "Might make it."

As he topped a creek bank, he heard the rifle shots and saw Stranger go down and fall behind a big mesquite. Coker slid off Thunder Red and waited for them in back of the tree. They didn't come so he knew they wouldn't approach directly, but would watch and come for him in daylight.

"Cain't never get away from 'em on one mule," Coker said. "He's already too tired and poor Stranger, he's not moving. Sorry, ole buddy."

He cut the cinch straps on Stranger, got the panniers and threw them over his shoulder. He gave Thunder Red a whack on the rump and said, "Go home, boy, go home."

Many times he had sent his mules home when he wanted to walk in the mountains alone. Thunder Red galloped a mile and then stopped to graze. Home was a long way off.

Coker had one shotgun and his knives. He had unwittingly left his rifle on Thunder Red. "Them rifles'll get me come mornin'."

He looked below him and saw water running in the creek. Several large rocks lay on the edge of the bank. Coker stepped from one rock to the other for forty yards. He stood on one and jumped to the creek fifteen feet below. The jolt opened his wound, and he had to wait on his knees in the creek until the pain subsided. Then he walked down the creek. The moon had gone out of its bright stage, so darkness overtook him and he had to step out of the water. Like a wet, hurt cat he curled in the sand for the night.

Uvie and Larnce waited until morning, then followed the mule tracks slowly across the creek with Uvie in the lead.

219

"I'll be damned," Uvie said. "One of his mules went down here and bled. He got up and went north. The red mule went west."

Larnce rode up beside him. "Did he leave on foot?"

Uvie studied the ground for foot tracks and said, "No, he didn't run off. He's ridin' that mule. With just one mule he won't last too long."

"No, because we can get fresh horses in Clarendon. We'll catch him this time."

They set off after Thunder Red, but since the mule always heard them first, he ran off each time they came close.

They got fresh horses in Clarendon and rode hard on the trail. Thunder Red led them south to the trail Coker had taken with Misty and Pete, then back to the trail between Clarendon and Amarillo. For a week and a half they followed him never seeming to get any closer.

"He is one cagey old man," Larnce said. "I don't know how he keeps that mule goin'."

After riding hard one day, they walked their horses to a ridge overlooking a broad valley. Thunder Red had stopped to graze in the bottom where the grass was sweetest, but he heard them before they topped the ridge. He ran but they saw him before he went out of sight.

"Ain't nobody on that mule," Uvie screamed. "He's empty. No wonder we couldn't catch that damn mule."

"Fooled us again," Larnce said. "We've got to go clear back to where we shot the mule and pick up his trail."

It took them less than a week to reach the place where they had last seen Coker. As they rode along, Uvie said, "You know I bet he got in the creek and walked.

You go up and I'll go down and see if we can find where he come out."

Uvie rode three hundred yards and saw where Coker had spent the night. He hollered for Larnce and they followed the creek a mile. Uvie shook his head. "He got back in the creek, and we don't know whether he kept goin' down or went back up. The creek's too deep and muddy to tell. It'll take us a week to cut his trail ridin' back and forth."

Larnce thought about the situation. He suddenly sat straight. "We're the damndest fools in the world. That mule with the empty saddle is headin' for home. All we gotta do is keep after 'im."

"You're right," Uvie said. "But one thing for sure. That mountain man has made fools out of us for the last time. We're goin' to keep after him 'til we put a dozen bullets through his hide and get that money."

"You're damned right," Larnce said. "Especially that money." They set off to catch up with Thunder Red.

Coker had gone up the creek the next morning because he knew they would find where he got out to spend the night. For two miles he waded, each step sapping his strength. He saw a tunnel going through a large bank. "Wonder what that is? Don't know, but looks like a good place to stop."

On the dry ground he wrung out his moccasins, ate and rolled up in his elkskin. During the night infection set in from his first wound, and he woke in the morning burning with fever. Almost delirious he crawled to the creek and lay in the water until he felt cool, then he pulled himself to the dry sand. Over and over he repeated the process. After four days the fever subsided, but it left

Coker too weak to walk. He sat, unable to eat but a little and sitting there hoping his strength would return.

"S'funny," he said. "While I had fever, kept thinkin' I heard a rumblin' noise. Guess I musta been dreamin'."

Two hours later he heard a rumble in the distance. It grew louder, and a train passed overhead barely moving up the long grade. "A train goin' slow," he said. "Maybe I can catch the next one."

The excitement gave him strength, and he clawed his way up the bank. Five hours he sat in the sun waiting before he heard another train. When he saw it chugging slowly toward him, he stood. The first two cars carried passengers, so he couldn't get on them. The third one was a freight car with an open door. He laid his pack inside and hung on to the side of the car. He had to lean on his stomach where it hurt the most. Inch by inch he pulled himself onto the floor of the car. He rolled and crawled his way to a corner and faded into a dreamlike coma:

Trissy and Bonnie. I see Trissy and Bonnie. Don't see no snake. I can see 'em down in the water. I don't see 'em holdin' hands and laughin'. Wrong pond. They're in the big pond. Water's clear as a bell. Ain't in the black pond no more. They're callin' me. They're callin' me t'come to em, but why're they callin' me mister?

"Mister! Mister!" the boy shouted at him. "Wake up, mister, or you're going to die." He shook Coker by the shoulder until he roused. He saw the boy through a haze and he had trouble remembering where he was. "Need some water," he said.

The boy said, "I'll get some."

He came back with a pitcher of water and a glass. Coker drank four full glasses and it revived him somewhat. "How did you get hurt, mister?"

"Had a run in with some guys which didn't like me."

"You got blood on you. They must have beat you up bad."

"Sure did," Coker said. "Can you get me some beans outa that pack and open 'em fer me?"

"I can do better than that," the boy said.

He came back with two beef sandwiches. Coker could barely chew, but he ate one. "What's your name?"

"Ossie Fryar," he said.

"Well, Ossie," Coker said, "can you tell me where this train is?"

"Sure. We're out west of Amarillo headin' for Albuquerque."

"What?" Coker said and struggled to a sitting position. "Have we come to a water stop called Endee?"

"I don't think so, but I don't know for sure."

Coker felt in his pocket and pulled out a twenty dollar bill. "Iffen you let me know afore we get to Endee, I'll give you this money."

"Yessir!" the boy said and hurried off to find out. He came back shortly. "We passed a place called Vega. They said it will be about two hours before we stop for water at Endee."

"Be sure and let me know," Coker said and dozed off.

When he woke, the boy was shaking him again. "We're stopped," Ossie said. "You better wake up."

Coker got to his feet. "Thank you, Ossie," he said and gave him the bill. He tried to pick up his pack, but gave up.

"When I get off," he said, "throw this off, will you?"

"You bet."

The train stopped. "Which way's south, Ossie?"

The boy led him to the door and pointed. "This is south."

Coker sat down and slid to the ground holding to the side of the boxcar to keep from falling. Ossie handed him the pack, but it fell. He made one feeble attempt to lift it, then left it. He walked to the engine of the train and looked beyond it. Through the haze, he saw the hut of the attendant and knew the trail went right by it.

"Caprock's gotta be south, if I remember right."

He would make it. He had to, for the kids. Staggering he headed for the trail.

24

Falling Leaves

Rufe felt the smooth, white bark and talked while he surveyed the clump of trees. "Aspen has done all turned. Coker didn't make it back to see 'em, and I can't 'magine him missin' his purty leaves."

Going from tree to tree, he touched them in turn, tears coming to his eyes as he admired each one. "Good colors as I ever seen. Always wanted to see 'em before, but now they mean Coker ain't likely comin' back. Leaves are 'bout ready to fall. Still got time though. Iffen he makes it by the end of October, the deer and elk will still be here. Old Coker can get 'em faster'n anybody I ever seen."

As always he completed the circuit around the corral and sat on the porch. He dozed and his head dropped to his chest. Rocks clattering down the hill caused him to jerk his head to look at the switchback. "Horse comin' up the trail."

He backed toward the door in case he needed to get to his rifle. He listened and watched. Each step of the animal seemed measured and slow. Now and then it would stop, but then come a few more steps. After ages, it seemed to Rufe, the animal reached the last switchback where he could see it better.

"Ain't no one on it!" he said. He hobbled down the trail to get a better look. When he got close enough, he said, "It's a skinny black mule." Walking slow enough for Rufe to keep up, the mule went to the cabin and stopped.

Rufe first looked at the mule's head then walked behind him. "Wonder where in the hell he come from.

And why's he so skinny? That's the way Stranger looked when he first come here."

He found himself staring at the mule's back legs. "It is Stranger! I made fun of that crooked hind leg a hundred times to needle Coker."

He ran his hands over the mule feeling his skinny bones. He stopped at the neck when he felt the scab. "Huh, somethin' done poked him in the neck."

When he found the scab on the other side, he said, "A bullet done gone through his neck! Somebody shot 'im."

He paused and stepped back. "Means somebody's been shootin' at Coker."

He threw a rope over Stranger's neck and led him to the corral. Stranger rolled, then got up and fed on the succulent grass. Blackie nickered in recognition and came running over to reestablish his superiority.

Rufe fingered the rope as he made his way back to the cabin. "Ain't got no saddle, but he's got a hole in his neck. Coker wouldn't have turned him loose. Besides he wouldn't have left the other mules. Cain't figger it out."

As he stood there shaking his head, an aspen leaf fluttered to the ground in front of him. He picked it up and turned it over. "It's lost all its color. It's dead."

25

No More Trouble

John carried the washpan to the top of the steps and threw the dirty water down the hill. He looked west where the last light of the sun was barely visible. "'Twas warm today. Bet Maeola and the kids'll want to set outside when it gets a little cooler."

He turned toward the lot by the barn. In the fading light he could see the cows chomping away.

"Huh," he said. "I forgot to let them out. Guess I'd better do that right now." He set the pan on the ground and started down the hill toward the barn.

He was still looking at the cows when he noticed movement out of the corner of his eye.

"What's that?" He peered through the gathering darkness. "Looks like a bear or a mountain lion."

He started to run for the dugout to get his rifle, but stopped when he saw that the thing was barely stirring. The animal moved its front leg a few inches and paused. John dropped down to one knee so he could see it better against the western sky.

"Whatever it is, it's hurt or sick. Doesn't look like it could bother anybody."

He moved closer. When he was ten feet away, the figure collapsed, its head striking the dirt.

"What in . . .? It's a man. Well I'll be damned! It's Coker! It's our mountain man!"

John grabbed the shoulders of the leather shirt and pulled Coker to his feet. He draped him over his shoulders and struggled up the hill to the dugout, turning sideways to go down the stairs so as not to bump Coker's head. He

227

managed to drag his friend into the room and ease him onto the bed.

"Maeola! Maeola!" he yelled. "Bring some cold water!"

Startled, Beth stepped to the kitchen door with Misty and Pete right behind her. "Why, what's wrong?" Then she saw the man on the bed. "Oh! It's Coker! It's Coker! Kids, your grandaddy is home!"

"Grandaddy!" Misty screamed. "Oh, Pete, look it's our Grandaddy."

Pete had already dashed to Coker and was running his fingers over the old man's face. Tears filled his eyes.

"Talk to me, Grandaddy," he said. "Talk to me."

Coker stirred. With John's help, he sat up. "Water," he whispered hoarsely. "Water."

Maeola ran to the kitchen and hurried back with a dipper full of water. Coker was so thirsty he grabbed for it and tried to drink in one gulp, but the wet dipper squirted from his hands and skittered across the dirt floor. Maeola snatched it up and filled it again, rushing back without bothering to wash it. Coker was swallowing hard and reaching out.

This time Maeola kept hold of the dipper handle so that he wouldn't drop it again. "Drink slow," she said. "You'll get cramps if you drink this cold water too fast."

In spite of her efforts, he choked the water down in great swallows and sucked on the dipper to get every drop. Then he wretched and the water came back into his mouth and through his nose. Painful coughs racked his body as the water strangled him. John held his shoulder and slapped him on the back.

When he stopped coughing, Maeola wiped his mouth with her apron and went for more water. This time she brought the dipper back only a third full. He drank as greedily as before, but there wasn't enough water to choke him. After finishing three partial dippers, he was able to slow down and sip.

"That's enough for a while," John said. "He's gonna get sick if he has any more." Gently, he pushed Coker back onto the bed. "You take it easy, old fellow. Everything's all right now."

Coker lay still for a half hour. Then he opened his eyes and looked around. Gradually he recognized the anxious faces watching him. He struggled to get up, but John held him on the bed. "You just lay there and rest. You look pretty used up."

He tried to speak, but it was more of a hoarse, croaking, whisper. "I'm all right." Then he lay back on the bed and seemed to go to sleep.

"Look at those moccasins," Maeola said. "They're worn through, and they're just hanging on his feet. He's been a long ways on foot."

John nodded. "He's crawled a long way too. Those leather pants are worn out."

"Mama Beth!" Pete said. "I can see through his shirt." He spread the leather apart and pointed to the long scab running down Coker's left ribs. "He's hurt! Grandaddy's hurt bad."

John and Maeola leaned over the bed for a better look. She gasped. "There's a hole in the right side of his shirt too."

"Looks like a bullet went through there," John said. "From where it is, it must have gone through him too. We've got to see how badly he's hurt."

Maeola took the bottom of the shirt and tried to lift it enough to see the wound. She jumped as Coker clasped her hand and opened his eyes. "If a little knife cut and a bullet graze was gonna kill me, I'da been dead a long time ago."

229

He swung his tattered feet off the bed and sat on the edge. "I just need me some more water, and I'll be all right."

She brought the dipper. "Now don't drink too fast, or I won't let you have any more."

Coker's head had cleared and he sipped as he had many times before when he had gone for days without a drink. After he had finished two dippers, he asked Maeola, "Have you got anything to eat? I ain't et . . . uh, I haven't ate for three days. At least I think it has been three days."

Misty grabbed his hand and said, "Grandaddy, you may talk any way you want to."

"Goodness!" Maeola said. "I should have known you were hungry. I was just about to put what was left of the stew in the slop bucket, but I think it's still hot. You just set right there, and I'll get you a big bowl."

After she left, Misty stood with her hand on Coker's right knee and Pete pushed against his left leg. Coker put his arm around Pete, but he could only move his right enough to hold Misty's hand. Pete looked at the old man with reverent eyes and said, "I love you, Grandaddy."

Misty's eyes glistened, but she couldn't speak.

Coker waited until the lump in his throat went down. "You don't have no worries now. You ain't a gonna have anybody else after you."

"What do you mean?" John asked. "I didn't know anyone was after them. Who was after them? Why was anyone after them? What happened?"

"It don't matter what happened. They just ain't gonna have no more trouble. That's all I'm gonna say."

John looked into the mountain man's flashing eyes and he knew not to say any more. Maeola came back with a bowl of stew and a chunk of bread. Coker's eyes lit up and his hands trembled as he took the dish from her. He knew all too well the results of eating too fast from several painful experiences, so he forced himself to take a spoonful and chew and swallow it before he took another.

When he finished the stew, he asked, "Is my bed still down in the barn? Think I need to sleep a while."

"You can sleep right where you are," Maeola said. "Misty won't mind the floor."

"No," he said. "This bed's too short, and besides that, my Misty ain't . . . isn't gonna sleep on the floor. That bed in the barn was good 'nough when I left, and it's good 'nough now."

Misty squeezed his hand. "Grandaddy, you can say ain't or anything else you want too. I'm so glad you're alive I don't care how you talk."

Coker pulled her to him and kissed her on the cheek. Then he squeezed Pete tight and kissed him. He kept his arms around them and looked into their eyes. "Can you little skunks take care of Mama Beth and Papa John while I'm gone?"

Misty cried. "Granddaddy, you can't leave. You've got to stay here with us."

Coker fought his tears. "I'll come back," he said, "but I've got to go."

John looked down at him. "You said there was nothing to fear, so why can't you stay?"

Coker looked at him sadly and said, "I said the kids didn't have anything to be afraid of, but if I stay there'll be trouble for ever'body. You know I cain't live in this desert. Besides, Rufe cain't make it through another winter iffen I don't get back."

He frowned and they could see he was considering another problem. "Is Switchback okay?" he asked.

"Yeah, I rode him yesterday," John said.

"Can you let me borrow one of your horses? I'll need to ride fast so I'll need two animals. Stranger is dead, and I let Thunder Red go, so I guess he's lost."

Pete crowded close to Coker. "Thunder Red's not lost, Grandaddy. He came home a long time ago."

Coker stared at him in disbelief. "You ain't a funnin' me are you boy?"

"He's not teasing you," Misty said. "He's out in the pasture."

Coker looked up at John and Maeola and they both nodded. "That big, red son of a gun. I thought he might go back to Aspen Hill, but I never dreamed he'd a come back here. Well, I don't need no horse then. I'm mighty tired. I guess I better get down to my bed."

"John, why don't you help him to the barn?" Maeola asked.

"No," Coker said and struggled to his feet. "I can make it down the hill. I don't need no help." With his back straight as always, he walked slowly but steadily up the stairs.

"I've got to let the cows out of the lot anyway," John said, "so I'll go with you."

Once outside John made another stab at getting information from the mountain man. "Now that we're away from the kids, can you tell me what kind of trouble you're expecting?"

"No, I might never tell you, and I sure ain't a gonna tell you tonight because I'm too tired."

John held the barn door open and watched while Coker crawled under the buffalo skin and pulled it over his head. Then he closed the door softly, opened the gate to let the cows out and went back to the dugout.

When he got there, Maeola was bubbling like a pot of boiling lye soap. "What do you think he's done? What did he mean, the children weren't in danger? I didn't know they were in danger."

"I don't know any of those things," John said. "He wouldn't say any more than he said in here."

Maeola turned her attention to Misty. "Did you know you were in some kind of danger?" she asked.

Misty twisted her face as she tried to decide how to answer. "Grandaddy told us not to talk about anything that happened after we left Oklahoma, but I don't think it would hurt to tell you. I don't really know very much. Two men were following us right after we left Freeda. Grandaddy hid us in some bushes and told us not to watch, but we did. He surprised the men and made them take off their clothes and walk. That's how Pete and I got our horses."

"Goodnight!" Maeola said. "I didn't think he'd steal horses. No wonder someone's after him."

"He's not a horse thief," Misty said. "That's not the reason he took the horses, and I don't think that's why someone is after him. He used to talk to himself a lot when he thought we were asleep. I don't know why, but I know those two men were going to kill Pete and me or take us back to Aunt Vester and Uncle Albert if they could. Grandaddy was looking for horses for us, but he took those horses so the men couldn't follow us any more."

"Do you think your aunt and uncle sent those two?" John asked.

Misty pursed her lips and pulled them to one side and then the other as she thought about his question. "When Grandaddy brought us the pintos, he said he would have killed those snakes except they weren't the big snakes. I'm not sure who the big snakes were, but I think they might be Uncle Albert and Aunt Vester. Just after we crossed the Red River and while I was woozy from being so cold, he said something to me about the Speights and killing, but I don't remember what it was."

"Okay, don't worry about it," John said softly. "I think we've talked enough for tonight, and I've got to plow tomorrow. Let's go to bed."

Maeola tucked Misty and Pete in and kissed them goodnight. Then she and John took the lantern and went to their bed. They lay awake for an hour or more lost in their own thoughts.

Maeola finally said, "What do you think Coker meant about the snakes?"

"I don't know, but from the looks of him and what little he said, I'd guess there's some big reptiles who ain't around this world anymore."

"Surely you don't mean he . . . killed somebody?" she said.

"Just like he killed those rattlesnakes under the wagon."

Maeola shuddered. "What Papa said might be true. If it is, I don't want him lookin' for me."

"I don't think anyone would ever be looking for you."

Maeola was silent for a few minutes. Then she trembled and said, "Do you think he's all right? Do you think he might die tonight?"

"I doubt it. He's tough as a green locust limb, but I'll go see about him anyway."

He slipped out of bed, took the lantern and went quietly out of the dugout. He stopped outside and lit the lantern. Walking to the barn as softly as he could, he stood outside the door and listened for any sound, but he heard nothing. For ten minutes he stood, taut as a new strand of barbed wire, straining to hear. "I'm afraid he didn't make it."

He reached for the door to go inside when he heard a cough. "He's clear down under the buffalo skin. I guess it's best if I leave him alone."

He tiptoed away from the barn and went quickly back to the dugout. As he turned out the lantern, he looked up at the clear sky.

"These New Mexico stars are hard to believe. Right down on top of you. Never saw anything like that in Alabama or Oklahoma. I don't think I can ever leave."

Still shaking his head in wonder, he went back to his bed.

"Is he okay?" Maeola asked.

"I think so. I heard him cough. We'd better get some sleep. Those rows are long enough when I'm not tired."

However, sleep didn't visit them that night. Visions of Coker and his mysterious trip plagued their minds until morning when the coyote howled and light crept through the little dugout window.

26

The Song Is Finished

The next morning as John slipped on his overalls, Maeola whispered, "Go see about Coker, and I'll get some breakfast. Don't wake the kids."

John walked quietly through the kitchen door, but slowed to look down at the children's bed. Four wide-open, blue eyes told him there was no need to worry about waking them.

"Wait a minute, Papa John, and we'll go with you," Misty said. She and Pete bounced out of bed.

John frowned. "When did you get your clothes on? Did you sleep in them?"

Pete avoided his look, but he fidgeted from one foot to the other. "We put 'em on while you and Mother Beth were talking."

"That was right after we went to bed, so you did sleep in your clothes. Maeola won't be too happy about that."

"But we had to see about Grandaddy," Misty said, "and we couldn't go to the barn without our clothes on."

John started to scold them, but their pleading eyes melted him like a snowball on a hot stove. "All right, let's go see about your Grandaddy, but be quiet in case he's still asleep."

They scurried up the stairs and had reached the barn by the time John got out of the dugout. He caught up with them as they were pushing the door slightly open. They peered through the crack like two inquisitive ground squirrels.

"Is he awake?" John asked and stuck his head over theirs in the doorway.

Pete shook his head no. Misty whispered, "I don't think so. At least, I can't tell."

"I'd better take a look." John tiptoed over and carefully pulled the buffalo skin back. He studied the figure for nearly a minute before he laid the skin across Coker's shoulders.

"He's breathing okay. We'd better let him sleep." He slipped out of the room and closed the door. "Let's go get some breakfast. He'll probably wake up soon and be starved to death."

"Maybe he'll just sleep a little longer," Pete said.

"I think we'd better let him rest as long as he can," John said. "He seems to be all right."

They said very little as they waited for Maeola to get breakfast on the table. Then, without a word, they sat down to eat. Misty took two bites of an egg and one bite off a biscuit, looked up and asked, "Mother Beth, may I be excused?"

"Excused? Why you've just started." She patted Misty's shoulder. "All right, go ahead and see about him."

Pete was out of his chair by the time she finished and they sprinted to the barn. Again they looked in, but Coker hadn't moved.

"Let's wake him up," Pete said.

Misty bit her lower lip and shook her head. "No, Papa John said to let him rest. Remember Grandaddy is pretty old so he probably needs to sleep."

They moved slowly to the water tank, hopped up on the flat edge and sat watching the barn. Their little faces were solemn. John studied them and shook his head sorrowfully.

"John, would you kill me a chicken before you go to the field?" Maeola called out.

237

He walked into the kitchen, sat at the table and stared at the window. "I don't think I'll go. At least not for now."

"Why not?" Maeola asked. "Don't you need to get that field plowed? The weeds are getting awful big."

"Yeah, I know," he said. Then he lowered his voice, and he strained to talk. "But you look at those pitiful faces on the tank and tell me you'd go to the field."

Maeola went to the door, stood for a time then came back with a small tear trickling down her cheek. "I'll fix some coffee."

They sat uncomfortably and talked about little things until the coffee was hot. They sipped and tried to perk up, both still weary from the lack of sleep and worrying about Coker.

Maeola asked for the third time, "He is going to be all right, isn't he?"

"He's a tough old son of a gun. I don't know how far he crawled, but it had to be a long way. If he was that determined to see these kids, he's not gonna give up now."

"Then why are we acting as if the world is about to end?"

"Because when he gets all right, he says he's goin' to leave, and that's gonna tear Misty and Pete up somethin' terrible. That is, unless they go with him. Then it's gonna tear us up just as bad. It ain't gonna work out right no matter what."

As he finished talking, Misty ran into the dugout, dived under the bed and pulled out her mandolin.

Maeola asked, "What are you doing, Misty?"

The little girl paused for a moment at the door. "I've got to finish his song." Then she dashed up the steps.

Silently, John and Maeola followed her down the hill. They stopped at the tank where Pete was still sitting.

238

Misty sank down on a gunnysack close to the door of the barn. She played a few notes, then began to work on the song she had begun when they were crossing the prairie. First, the verses she had already finished. Beautiful, Maeola thought. Then she went on, weaving her feelings into new music and words.

All through the morning the four of them kept their vigil. John and Maeola went to the dugout three times for coffee, but Pete and Misty stayed by the barn. Once as Misty sang and played, Pete stared and then shut his eyes, saying, "God, just give him one more ride."

Misty's head jerked up. "That's it. That's it!"

Pete looked at her. "What's it? What are you talkin' about?"

"What you said. It's the last verse of his song."

"Oh," Pete said although he still didn't understand.

At the noon hour John and Maeola settled for some leftover biscuits, but Misty and Pete refused to eat. Maeola took cups and got them each milk from the bucket cooling in the tank.

Since Maeola insisted, they drank the milk, but that was all. They would gaze at the clear water in the tank, but they wouldn't leave. Maeola and John went to the dugout and left them alone. The sun set, and the mountain man slept. John did his chores while Maeola went to the children. She stood by them until she felt the chill of the evening.

Then she said, "Misty and Pete, you've been out here too long. You've got to get some rest."

"No, we've talked it over. We're going to stay here until Grandaddy wakes up," Misty said.

Maeola took each one by the hand and tried to lead them, but they pulled back. When they resisted, she said, "You can't do your grandaddy any more good down here than you can in the dugout. He's asleep and doesn't

239

know where you are. Now come with me, or I'll have to get John to carry you."

Dragging their feet they followed her and, heads nodding, ate some scrambled eggs. She put them to bed and said, "Try to get some sleep, sweethearts, and we'll see about your grandaddy in the morning."

No response.

"I'm awful tired too."

She didn't light the lamp in the other room, but put her gown on in the darkness.

John came in and asked, "Maeola, where are you?"

Her voice sleepy, she said, "I already crawled in."

John got settled down and was drifting off when Featherfoot's howl split the night. He sighed and said, "That ornery critter. I'm gonna shoot him if he don't quit wakin' me up."

"You'd better not ever let Coker hear you say that. You know he might be calling him."

"Yeah, maybe so. I just hope that old rascal can hear his call."

27

Coyote and the Moon

Featherfoot announced the dawn just after John had roused from his sleep. "You're a little early this morning, you old chicken thief. I hope you ate somethin' besides our hens last night."

He remembered Coker and threw off the covers. "Got to get him up this mornin'. If he can't get up, I've got to get a doctor."

He was trying to hook his overall strap as he went up the steps. He stepped outside still working at the stubborn hook.

"You come out to listen to Featherfoot?" said a voice from the shadows.

John jumped back and nearly fell down the steps. "Who . . . Who is it?"

"It's just me. I had to get up and talk to old Featherfoot."

"Coker, you nearly scared me to death. Come on in, man, and let's get some breakfast. You don't know how glad the kids will be to see you."

He put his arm around Coker's shoulder and headed into the dugout. Maeola had her back to them, lighting a lamp when they walked into the kitchen.

She put the globe on the lamp and said, "That was a fast trip. Is Coker all right?"

"Yeh, Coker's okay," the mountain man said and chuckled at her startled look. "My right arm don't seem to work too good, but the rest of me is okay. I'm hungry as hel . . . heck though."

Half in disbelief she hugged him to see if he were real. Then she steered him toward the table. "Set down over here in the big chair and I'll have some breakfast real soon."

"I heard old Featherfoot just as I went to sleep so I musta slept about twelve hours."

He saw the astonished looks on their faces and said, "Well, maybe thirteen or fourteen then."

John told him. "You slept closer to thirty-six hours, Coker. You heard Featherfoot night before last, but you missed him yesterday."

Coker frowned and stared at the table as he digested John's words. Disturbed, he rubbed his chin.

"They may be gettin' close," he said almost inaudibly.

"Who's gettin' close?" John asked.

Coker squirmed in his chair and looked first at John and then at Maeola. "I didn't want to tell you because I didn't want to worry you none. But I know what it's like havin' somethin' hangin' out there you cain't figger out, so I reckon I better tell you enough to keep you from wonderin' the rest of your life.

"I went back to Oklahoma to take care of some business for the kids. Out of Memphis on the way back, a coupla guys wanted to take me in to jail. Claimed they was rangers, but I have my doubts. Sorta think they was bounty hunters."

John was disturbed by his words. "Why would rangers or bounty hunters be after you?"

"They said I kilt a man when I was goin' from Amarilla to Oklahoma."

John looked straight at Coker. "Did you?"

"I kilt him, but he follered me from Amarilla. He was gonna rob me. I would've give him the money in my pocket, but he was gonna take all I had. I had a feelin' he was gonna kill me, so I put a knife in his heart. Some

242

more men was on the trail ahind me, but they never ketched up."

"What happened then?" John asked.

"Nothin 'til I was comin' back this time. I seed a coupla guys follerin' my trail. When they got close, I could see they was wearin' some funny lookin' badges. I didn't think I had done nothin' in Texas to cause any lawmen to foller me, so I rode out just to ask 'em why they was a follerin' me.

"They drawed their guns when I rode up, and then they told me the man I killed was their friend. They claimed to be rangers. I coulda killed 'em, but I didn't want the Texas rangers after me just then."

"Were they goin' to arrest you?" Maeola asked.

"That's what they said, but I had a feelin' they wasn't rangers, and they was gonna' shoot me in the back the first chance they got."

John looked at Maeola then asked,"You didn't kill them, did you?"

"Naw, I didn't kill 'em. Prob'ly shoulda, but I just run old Thunder Red into their horses and knocked 'em down. They got up purty quick and one of 'em put a bullet under my right arm. They started shootin' at me nearly a half mile away. A lucky shot caught old Stranger in the neck and he went down dead. I cut his saddle off, but by the time I did, I knowed they would be close. I chased Thunder Red off and told 'im to go home. Figger'd he'd go to Aspen Hill, and they'd wear their horses out tryin' to ketch him. I jumped in a crick and hid 'til dark. Didn't see 'em no more.

"I went up the crick and hid under a bridge. Then a train come along and I got on it and rode it to Endee. Then I crawled here."

Maeola frowned. "So you think they'll follow Thunder Red here?"

"Sooner or later they will. They shoulda already been here, so I'm guessin' they slowed down and looked at his tracks after a while and knowed I wasn't on 'im, so they backtracked to where I hid. I'm 'fraid they'll be comin' afore long, so I need to get outa here."

Maola frowned and bit her lip. "That tells us why someone might be after you, but who was after the kids? And why aren't they after them any more?"

Coker paused to get his thoughts together. Speaking slowly with much emotion, he said, "My daughter married a man with a lot of money. He died awful funny like. His sister and her husband pizened him to get their hands on his money. Afore he died he told his sister he had made a will and left all his money to Misty and Pete. They wanted to get appointed to be their guardians and get the money, but when they pizened Bonnie and she died, I grabbed the kids and run for it."

"Then they sent some guys after us, and I took their horses away and sent 'em back. Thought ever'thing was okay 'til the day that feller come down and told us about them guys lookin' for the kids. I found two men in San Jon the Speights had paid to kill Misty and Pete."

"Kill the kids! Why those dirty son . . . I can't imagine anyone who'd kill children!" John said.

"Some guys'll kill anyone for a little money," Coker said. "Just afore they died, they told me Aunt Vester and Uncle Albert was gonna keep sendin' men out 'til they got the kids. So I come back here and tried to get the kids to go to Arizona with me, but they didn't want to go, so I seen I had to go back to Oklahoma to visit them reptiles."

John and Maeola were astonished by Coker's story. "You said the men told you just before they died?" John asked.

"Yeah, a minute or two afore."

John felt the icy, ominous sound of his voice and decided not to question him further about the subject.

Maeola was so concerned about the children, she missed the import of Coker's statement about the men. "What happened in Oklahoma when you talked to their aunt and uncle?"

When he spoke, Coker's face was like a stone, cold and hard. "Well, you know what happens to snakes when they bite somethin' too big for 'em to swaller."

John looked at the marble face and said, "I imagine they died."

Maeola's mouth dropped open, and she looked at John for a moment, then turned her attention to Coker. "How did they die?"

Coker shifted his eyes to her without moving his head. "Bad case of lead pizenin'."

John looked at him in disbelief. "You killed a woman?"

For the first time Coker showed rage, and his face contorted with disgust. When he spoke, he seemed to be spitting each word separately. "No, I never have killed no woman, and I ain't goin' to. But I've killed snakes, and they was the worst reptiles I ever knowed."

John and Maeola were looking at him in wonder when his expression changed to one of surprise and pleasure. "I see four big eyes on some little skunks. Come here and see old Grandaddy."

Misty and Pete stumbled over each other getting around the table, but they climbed into his lap, both talking at once. They hugged him, kissed him again and again, and clung to him as if he would suddenly vanish and slip away from them.

Misty held her face close to his and looked into his eyes and said, "Grandaddy, you're not really going to leave us, are you?"

Coker returned her loving gaze then said, "Misty, you turn me into soft moss when you talk like that. But you know old Rufe ain't gonna make it another winter iffen I don't go back. I know he's been watchin' that last switchback ever' day. I'll come back to see you, but me and Rufe been together for thirty years, and he's got a game leg and bad eyes and he cain't hunt no more."

Pete clutched him around the neck and sobbed. "We'll go with you, Grandaddy."

Coker's voice was husky. "I wish you could, Pete, I wish you could, but two old fogies ain't got nothin' for kids. You need schoolin', and you need Mother Beth and Papa John."

With aching hearts, Maeola and John listened knowing there was nothing they could do to ease the unbearable pain. Because of what he had told them, they knew he had to go soon.

Maeola broke the gloom by saying, "Bacon and eggs are ready, and the biscuits should be done. I bet you're starved, Coker, and you children haven't eaten two bites in two days."

"Warsh your hands, kids," John said.

Tenderly, Coker set Pete and Misty down and said, "I reckon I better warsh a little too."

They took turns cleaning up and came back to the table. Misty and Pete hardly ate for looking at Coker, but he devoured biscuits and egg after egg covered with gravy. He stopped chewing once and asked, "Maeola, when is the light of the moon?"

"I'll have to look at the almanac," she said and took it off the nail where it hung by the table. She turned the pages to September and studied for a moment.

"Why, why . . ." Everyone knew she didn't want to continue, but finally she said, "The moon is full tonight."

Coker's head jerked up and he said, "Then I've gotta go tonight. I better get ready."

Abruptly, he left and headed for the barn to pack. He found the saddlebag and took out the extra shirt and pants, the second shotgun and the shells.

He turned to Misty and Pete who had followed him. "Do you know if my rifle was still on Thunder Red when he come in?"

"I don't know," Misty said, "but I'll go ask Papa John."

As she ran out the door, John caught her around the waist. "What are you goin' to ask Papa John?"

"Was Grandaddy's rifle on Thunder Red when he came in?"

John walked into the room and said, "Yep, it was still on the saddle, and some cartridges are in the saddlebags."

Coker grunted his approval. "Well then, all I've got to do is get my bedroll made up and I'm ready to go."

Pete was dismayed. "Are you leaving right now?"

"No," Coker said, "I won't go 'til the moon comes up enough so I can see to ride t'night. We got a while to talk afore I head out."

Misty and Pete squealed.

John brought some chairs to the barn, and the day flashed by as they went over again and again almost everything they had been through together.

Misty would say, "Getting across that river was the most frightening thing in my life." Then she would tell the complete story.

As soon as she finished, Pete would start about the diamondback. Then Misty added another. On and on they went.

Maeola and John couldn't bring themselves to leave the scene. They hadn't heard all the stories and they were fascinated. For a time they forgot Coker's imminent departure. Suddenly, the shadow of the barn moved over them, an unwelcome visitor because it meant late afternoon had come.

Coker walked to the end of the barn and looked closely at the sun sinking behind the cactus on the west ridge.

"I reckon I better get Thunder Red and Switchback saddled." He walked around the barn to look for them.

They were at the edge of the lake bed. When he whistled, their heads jerked up and their ears pointed to him. He whistled again, and they came running.

As they charged up, he talked to them. "Come on, you crazy things. I'm glad to see you lookin' so good." He petted each one and said, "Are you ready to go see old Rufe?"

With Misty and Pete following in his tracks, he let the two mules into the lot and gave them a handful of grain apiece. He could use his right hand to grip things below his waist, but his arm hurt too badly for him to raise it any higher. Because of his injured arm, he struggled to get the saddles on using only his left arm. He finally managed and pulled the cinches tight. By the time he went to get his pack, he was walking slowly.

Watching his every move, Pete realized Coker was having difficulty. "Are you tired, Grandaddy? Because if you're tired, I'll carry the pack. You helped me a lot of times when I was tired, so I'll help you."

Coker looked at him fondly and lied. "No, I was just thinkin' about Rufe and wonderin' if he's still around."

"Sure, he's still around," Pete said. "He'll be waiting for you on the last switchback just like he said he would."

"I 'spect you're right. At least he won't give up `til winter. It ain't quite time yet, so let me hear you and Misty sing again."

Misty got her mandolin, brought it to the barn and she and Pete sang all the songs she could remember, filling the air with music until the sun dipped below the horizon.

Coker stirred from his chair and looked at John. "I didn't think I'd ever need to ask anyone to load for me, but I'm goin' to have to ask you if you'll put my pack on Switchback."

"Sure I'll help you put it on," John said. "but what are you going to do tomorrow night."

Coker bristled. "I could get it on now if I had to. And besides, I'll get plenty strong soon as I see those mountains."

"You probably will, you stubborn old badger," John said and went to help tie on the pack.

Misty and Pete started another song.

Coker pulled the cinches snug and told John how to tie the pack, then leaned his head against Thunder Red's saddle.

"If you're that tired maybe you'd better wait another day."

"I ain't tired," Coker said without looking up. He shook his head. "I've got to go back around that barn and maybe look at my grandkids for the last time. It nearly kilt me when they took Thankful, but I ain't never done nothin' this hard. At least this time I may get to come back."

He stepped away from the mule, raised his head and squared his shoulders. "Well, I've got to play the man even if I ain't."

John followed him around the barn. As they approached Maeola and the children, the light was growing dim on the dark side of the barn. Trying to speak calmly, Coker said, "I reckon I'd better hit the trail as soon as that moon comes up."

"Grandaddy, you've got to wait until I sing your song for you," Misty said.

"A song for me?"

"Yes, I tried to get it in my head all the way across the prairie, but I couldn't finish it until you came back, and I quit worrying about grammar. I just now got the last verse."

"The moon ain't up yet. If you've made a song for me, I can wait."

Misty played a little introduction on her mandolin and looked at Coker.

She sang:
"Well, his hands aren't as rough
Nor his skin so tough,
And it's been too long since he's seen the dust
Stirred by a buffalo
In the light of the noonday sun.

Well, the trails were long
And the days were hot
So he made friends with the sounds of the night.
Wolves sang their sad, sad songs,
While the river it rocked him to sleep.

He can hear the coyote ahowling.
He's calling him back to his home.
Full moon is rising.
He knows time is bringing
His days on the trail to an end.

Just give him one more ride
Over mountains where the air is so clear.
Just one more ride through the valley where his
        heart was broken.
Just one more ride 'cross the prairie that's ready
        to take him

To where he'll be needed again.
This old mountain man's work is done."

Coker stepped away and blew his nose. With his back turned to hide his tears, he pretended to be looking at the trail. After a few minutes, he said, "Misty, that's the purtiest song I ever heard. I know now I'll have to come back to hear you sing it again."

He squatted down and cuddled them tenderly against his chest. "You little skunks take care of Mother Beth and Papa John 'til I get back."

They burst into tears. "Don't cry," he said softly. "I'll be back soon as the snow goes off in the spring. I'll bring old Rufe with me."

He whispered something to Misty then pushed her and Pete away from him. "Misty, keep bein' purty and get as smart as you can. Iffen I'd went to school, I might notta been so illit . . . illit . . . dumb."

"Grandaddy, you're the smartest and best person I'll ever know," Misty said.

Coker took Pete's hand and squeezed it. "Richard Lincoln, keep askin' them questions and keep the sparkle in your eye. And listen to Misty. It won't hurt you none to get some learnin'."

Pete clung to Coker's hand. Awe filled his eyes. "I will, Grandaddy. I promise I will."

"Then it's gotta be so long. I'll be back one a these days. Both of you mind Mama Beth and Papa John."

He walked to Maeola and John. "You're the best people I ever knowed. Take care of my kids 'til I get back."

Coker got Thunder Red and led him around the barn. Switchback followed along as if he were tied to him.

Coker reached for the saddlehorn, but his hand missed it and he almost fell to the ground. He tried two more times before he managed to get into the saddle.

"I'm afraid he's too tired to travel," Maeola said.

"He's awful tired, but I'll bet that old son of a gun could ride a thousand miles if he had too," John said.

"He probably could, and he thinks he's got to."

They turned toward the east where a circle of red was just showing. "It's the first time I didn't want to look at the New Mexico moon," John said.

Coker led Thunder Red away, then stopped and turned to John. "If anyone comes lookin' for me, tell 'em I don't think they're rangers, and I'll kill 'em this time."

"Look, look!" Misty said and pointed at the ridge just south of the dugout.

Featherfoot sat motionless watching the people below him. He turned broadside, glanced their way again and trotted west on the ridge leading around the lake.

"It's time to go," Coker said and guided Thunder Red up the hill, following the coyote.

They watched him until he rode off the ridge into the darkness of the lake bed. He never looked back.

"I haven't seen those aspen leaves he talked about," Maeola whispered, "but if they're more beautiful than that mountain man, they're really somethin'."

"Once he told us he wasn't good for anything or anybody," Misty said.

"He's the best thing that ever happened to us," John said, "because he brought you and Pete."

They kept looking at the spot where he had entered the blackness until a long howl from the northwest hill above the lake echoed around the ridge.

"Featherfoot," Pete said.

Spellbound they stared at the ghostly silhouette of a man and two mules coming out of the blackness and going north over the final ridge toward Colorado and Aspen Hill.

28

The Rangers

The four of them stayed watching the ridge beyond the lake, hoping, yet knowing there was no hope, that a mule bearing the mountain man would slide down the moonbeams and appear by the cactus where it had faded into the night.

It was late before they accepted the reality of his leaving.

John shook from the chill of the fall night. "It gets cold early in New Mexico. No use standin' here lookin' north. He's on his way home."

He shuffled toward the dugout all the time looking back over his shoulder at the spot where Coker had disappeared.

Misty turned wistful eyes away from the ridge. "Mother Beth, will he come back?"

Tears rolled down Maeola's cheeks, and she stifled a sob. "I hope so Misty, I hope so."

Pete stopped and stared at both of them. "Misty, didn't Grandaddy say he was coming back?"

"Yes, I know he said that."

"Did he ever tell us that he was gonna do something that he didn't do?" Pete asked.

"No, he never did."

"Then he'll be back. Ever' day you just watch that ridge and one of these days he'll come over it ridin' Thunder Red and bringing old Rufe along with him. He said he would, and he'll do it. There ain't no use wonderin' 'bout it."

"Don't say . . . No, there ain't. He'll be back."

Maeola, surprised by Misty's choice of words, started to say something but thought better of it.

They caught up with John by the dugout. Misty stopped abruptly. "Mother Beth, Grandaddy told me just before he left there was a leather bag on the bed. He said there was something in it for all of us."

John said, "I'll see if I can find it."

He went into the dark shed and felt around on the mattress until he found the bag. As he brought it out, Maeola said, "What is it John?"

"I don't know. We'll have to take it inside. Too dark out here."

They went into the kitchen, and Maeola lit a lamp. John untied the leather string and dumped the bag's contents on the kitchen table. Maeola gasped and put her hand over her mouth.

"It's money!" Pete said.

"A whole lot of money," Misty said.

"I wonder how much is here," John said.

For a time they busied themselves counting the bills. When they had finished, Maeola and John dropped into chairs, exhausted and amazed.

"John," Maeola said. "There's five thousand dollars there. Where in the world did he get five thousand dollars?"

"He told me he panned a lot of gold," Pete said.

"Maeola," John said, "we can build a house and buy Jacob's land up on the hill."

"We can't use his money. It belongs to the kids."

"Grandaddy wouldn't have left it if he hadn't wanted you to use it. You can bet on that," Misty said. "He said it was for all of us."

John said, "We'll save some of it to send you to college, Misty."

"What a man, what a man," Maeola whispered.

"God, what a man!" John said. "We'll have to hide it until I can get it to a bank."

Emotionally drained they stared at each other until Maeola pushed herself slowly to her feet. "We can't set here all night, so we might as well go to bed."

"Oh, my!" Misty said. "I left my mandolin down by the shed. I've got to get it. Daddy told me not to let it out of my sight."

"I'll go," said John and headed out the door.

"Me, too," Pete said, running after him.

Misty had left the mandolin out of its case. John carried it back and Pete brought the case. "Here it is, Misty," he said, and made as if to throw it to her. When he did, the case slipped out of his hand. He grabbed for it, but his fingers hooked in the wrinkled cover where it had gotten wet. The cover came off and a piece of paper fluttered to the floor.

"What's that?" Misty asked. "It was under the cover. I never saw that before."

She picked it up and read slowly, "'Last will and testament of Marshall R. Cook.'"

"Mother Beth! It's my father's will! It says in here he left everything to Mother, Pete and me. No wonder he didn't want me to let the mandolin out of my sight."

John took the paper and read carefully. "It doesn't talk about the amount. It just says all his property and holdings. How much property and money did he have, Misty?"

"Mother and Father never talked about anything like that where we could hear it, but Aunt Vester and Uncle Albert must have thought it was worth a great deal to try to kill us for it."

"Did Coker know about the will?" John asked.

"No, because I didn't know about it either."

"The only thing I know to do is to write a letter to the courthouse in Altus and ask them what to do about it. You may own a lot of property in Oklahoma."

"I don't ever want to go back to Oklahoma," Pete said.

"I want to stay here too," Misty said, "but we do need to find out about it."

Going to bed was hard, but there wasn't anything left to do. When dawn came, Maeola was putting the last touches on the breakfast. John ate without tasting the food and forced himself to get his hat and head out to work. "I've got to finish shockin' the bundles in the west field. I'll come in at dinner time."

"All right," Maeola said, "I'll milk and have the kids gather the eggs we forgot last night."

John walked toward the barn with his head down, so he failed to see the two horsemen by the edge of the barn until he was only a few feet away. He raised his head sharply and looked them over. One of the men was short, lean and wiry. He was riding a little, tough-looking mustang and leading two pack horses. The other man was taller and was on a rawboned buckskin. Neither of them had shaved for a week or so, he figured. Coker said there'd be somebody comin' pretty soon. These guys look mean so they must be the ones, John thought.

"Hello," he said. "Out early, aren't you?"

The man on the buckskin was looking at the ground around the barn and gave no indication he heard John. With his head tilted back and his deep-set eyes almost hidden by bushy eyebrows, the little man examined John thoroughly before he spoke. "Not for us, we ain't."

John pretended he knew nothing of the reason they were there. "Are you lookin' for a homestead? I think there's still some good land left around Liberty Bell south of here."

The man spit at John's feet. "Naw, we ain't lookin' for no land. We're gonna look around here."

Both men got off their horses. The taller man walked to the shed where Coker had stayed and opened the door.

"Wait just a minute," John said. "Who are you men? You don't have any right to go into my barn."

The little man faced John squarely. "I'm Larnce Laseman." He jerked a thumb over his shoulder at the other man. "This here's Uvie Tigert. We're Texas rangers."

"But this is New Mexico territory. A United States marshal is the only one who has authority here."

Laseman pulled the flaps of his denim jacket back, so John could see two guns. "These Colts give us the right to look anywhere we damn well please."

John tried to hide his anger. "Why are you lookin' around my place?"

"Well, a farmer back over there a couple miles said he seen a man at a box supper wearin' leather clothes. Said he thought he was stayin' with you. Is that right?"

"I don't know what you're talkin' about. We don't have room for anyone to stay here but us and our kids."

Uvie Tigert dropped to the ground on one knee. "Larnce, there're mule tracks goin' up the hill. Made yesterday, looks like."

Laseman fixed John with his cold eyes. "So you don't know no mountain man, huh? Maybe you'd better tell us where he's headin' while you're still in good health."

"I don't know what you're talkin' about. Besides, I don't know whether you are really Texas rangers or not."

Laseman fished a badge from his pocket, flashed it quickly and put it back in his pocket.

"I've been in Texas a lot and saw some rangers. That doesn't look like a ranger badge to me."

As John spoke, he backed toward the dugout, but Tigert had come up and was standing in his way. Laseman moved beside Tigert and slowly pulled one of his guns. "I think this guy needs a gun barrel on the side of his head to make him remember."

Tigert also drew his gun. "Yeah, either that or maybe he'd like to dance to six-gun music."

John looked at the two of them and tried to think of some way out of the predicament, but he knew they were hard men and intended to make him talk any way they could. Sweat ran down his face.

Laseman said, "Hey Uvie, this guy's gonna talk. We ain't gonna have to shoot but one of his feet."

John shuffled his feet and was getting ready to charge the men when he saw something move on the dugout steps. Turning his eyes away he said, "I don't think I'm gonna dance or talk either."

Tigert pointed his gun at John's feet. "Well," he said, "I reckon I'll just shoot both your feet for you bein' so smart."

"Drop those guns!" Maeola shouted from the dugout. "One move and you'll look like a colander."

Laseman slowly turned his head and looked behind him. All he could see was the cannon-like circles in the end of a gun. Maeola had knelt on the dugout step so that only her dark hair was visible over the barrel.

"God damn!" Laseman said. "Throwed down on by a woman. After all these years I didn't check the house."

"Don't talk any more and don't look around again. Take off your gun belts and throw 'em off to one side," she called out.

John backed away from the men. "Better do what she says. She's wicked with that shotgun."

Laseman said, "Guess we better do what she says."

Tigert slid his right hand slowly to his buckle and then paused and his fingers twitched. "Don't do it," Laseman said. "I seen the shotgun, and she's hid so you cain't hit her."

Slowly, they took off their belts and tossed them to one side.

"Take four steps back," Maeola said.

After they did John picked up their guns. Then he shouted, "Pete, bring me my rifle."

In a minute Pete came running with the gun. John levered a cartridge into the barrel. "I never could hit anything with a pistol, but I'm a fair shot with a rifle. Now set down over there by the locust tree and let's talk. I always like to hear stories about Texas rangers."

As the men went to the tree and sat down, Maeola came and stood by John, still holding the shotgun. "What do these men want?" she asked.

"They're after Coker," he whispered.

"Oh, my, that's the reason he was in a hurry. He said someone would be along. Who are they?"

"They claim to be rangers, but I have my doubts."

Laseman said, "Just let us go, and we won't bother you no more."

John didn't answer but took the cartridges out of their guns and gunbelts. When he had finished, he said to Pete. "Go get the forge goin' and put these guns in it until they melt." Pete took them and raced off.

"God o' mighty!" Laseman shouted. "Don't ruin our guns. Those're the onliest guns I've ever had."

"Oh, you'll get 'em back, but they won't shoot. You guys are probably real fast, and you may have more cartridges in your pack. Now tell me. Why are you after the mountain man?"

Laseman's eyes showed hate. "He killed a friend of ours."

"Why did he kill your friend?"

"I don't know," Laseman said. "But he stabbed him to death. Nobody does that to a friend of ours."

John rolled the words around in his mind. "Where did this killin' take place?"

"'Bout twenty miles from Amarillo," Laseman said.

"Out of Amarillo! That friend of yours was tryin' to rob Coker, and he killed him in self defense."

"So his name's Coker, huh?"

John kicked himself for letting the name slip, but he knew it was too late. "Yes, his name is Coker Owen Ford, and let me tell you somethin', I'm doin' you a big favor. You couldn't catch him and his mules if I let you go now, and if you could, you wouldn't want to."

Laseman looked at him sharply. "Why not?"

"Because he knows you're after him, and Coker Owen Ford is the most fearsome man I ever knew. If you catch up with him, you won't know it 'cause you'll be dead."

Laseman spat with contempt. "We caught up with him before, and he didn't kill us."

"That's because you told him you was rangers, and he didn't want to kill lawmen. But before he left he told me he thought you were phonies and he'd have to kill you if you came after him. You can suit yourself. I'm gonna let you go after a while, and if I was you, I'd go back to Texas."

Tigert sneered. "You don't scare us none."

"Okay. That's all I've got to say."

John turned to his wife. "Watch them while I get their rifles and fix them."

Maeola sat with the shotgun across her lap and guarded the men. John got the rifles and put them in the forge. Then he went through their packs and found two

260

more pistols and a knife. By the time he got through heating them until they were useless, it was the middle of the afternoon.

He put the weapons back in the scabbards and packs and told the two men, "I'm gonna let you go now. Don't forget my advice. Besides you don't have any guns."

"We can get more guns along the way," Laseman said.

"By the time you do, for your sake, I hope it's too late for you to catch him. Now get goin'. There's a marshal in Clovis. I'm gonna tell him about you guys. I don't believe you're rangers, so he'll be waitin' for you if you come back."

The men took their horses and began to track Coker's mules up the hill. Cows had walked over the trail marks, but Tigert picked them out. Sometimes he had to get down and crawl, but he found where Coker had turned on the ridge to circle north.

John and Maeola had been watching them. John said, "That guy's good. I thought it would take them until in the mornin' to find where he went. Coker's hurt. If he has to rest too much, they'll catch up with him."

Maeola shook her head sadly. "If they do, I hope they don't have families to miss them."

29

Pursuit

Coker rode hard in the moonlight. The constant trotting jarred him until he winced in pain. By the time he had covered the five miles to the caprock, he was holding his saddlehorn and leaning forward.

Dark shadows filled every turn as he wound his way down the caprock trail. He let Thunder Red walk to the bottom, then kicked him into a trot again.

Another two miles and he doubled over with a cramp where the knife had dug into his side. "Man, that's bad," he said. "Figgered on makin' forty miles tonight, but I'm gonna have to stop. Gotta do better'n that or those damn fake rangers will ketch me in two or three days."

He pitched his camp in the shadow of a large mesquite. Featherfoot howled as he dozed off.

The next morning Coker rode in the daylight to make up time. He passed the railroad tracks at San Jon before the sun came up.

Coker looked at the arid land. "Damn, I don't like desert land, but I'm glad I'm back on a trail I been over. Place called Logan up here about twenty miles. Gotta cross the Canadian River. When was I up this trail? Side hurts and my arm hurts. Cain't 'member when it was."

At noon he held the saddlehorn with both hands. As he rode down a steep canyon he kept himself out of the saddle with his legs. Through gritted teeth he said, "Seems like a crick is in the bottom o' this canyon. Used to be good water."

He crossed the stream, found shade under a cottonwood tree and took the packs off the mules. "Good grass here. Not much water in the crick, but it's clear." He surveyed the trail he had just come down. "Don't think those guys could ketch me this soon, but I cain't be too careful."

After he replenished his canteens, he took off his shirt and examined the wounds. "Bleedin' some. Arm hurts ever' time I move. Been hurt worse, but these hang on longer. Gettin' old I guess."

He washed the blood off, ate some beans Maeola had given him, then took his rifle and sat behind the tree to watch the trail. The coyote posed majestically on the canyon ridge. Coker stared at it for a few minutes before his eyes closed, and he dropped into a deep sleep.

He woke with a start and saw the bright moonlight on the top of the canyon ridge and swore. Loading the mules took longer this time.

The Canadian River ran shallow, so crossing it gave him no problem. Through Logan he rode and found the trail to Mosquero. Ten miles out of Logan he slid to the ground and stopped for the rest of the night.

Coker didn't wake until the middle of the morning. He saddled up, rode a few miles and stopped again. Four days later he rode up the caprock and on into Mosquero. After he passed the little town, he kept going until pain forced him to stop. He rested. When the pain eased, he went on.

No longer could he count on riding at night when he couldn't be seen. He covered as many miles as he could and rested whether day or night. Sometimes ten, sometimes twenty miles he made in a twenty-four hour period. He barely knew when he went through Roy, but because of his uncanny memory of any trail he had been over, he took the right trails.

Four days after leaving Roy he sat on Thunder Red and squinted at the village in front of him. "What town is this? Gotta be Springer. Hope it's Springer anyway."

He shook his head to clear the haze. "Somethin' 'bout Springer I need to 'member. What in the hell was it?" With a start he sat straight in his saddle. "That young feller said he was gonna look for a job down this way. What was his name? Oh yeah, it was Randy somethin' or other."

He tried hard to remember the man's last name, but finally gave up and camped in a clump of junipers. As he lay in his robe, he again tried to think of the name, but fatigue pulled sleep over the pain and halted his thoughts.

Laseman and Tigert followed Coker's trail with little trouble. When they got below the caprock, Tigert said, "He's slowed down a lot, and he's not tryin' to hide his trail. We better go easy or he'll ambush us somewhere."

They could tell Coker had traveled short distances between stops. After they had seen several of Coker's resting places, Laseman said, "Do you suppose he's hurt? He's sure not goin' very far at a time."

"I don't know," Tigert said. "One of us might've hit him back there in Texas, but every time he stops he gets behind a tree or a rock like he's watchin' his back trail. We sure don't want to catch him until we get some guns."

Their caution slowed them. Tigert could tell within an hour or two when a track had been made, so they deliberately stayed behind him. In Logan they could find no place to buy guns, so they followed the trail north.

In Roy the hardware store had a stock of used guns. They bought two pistols and a rifle apiece and rode on after Coker. Outside of town they stopped several hours to practice with the different guns.

After hitting a juniper branch six straight times, Laseman said, "Well, they're all right, but they don't feel quite as good as the ones that farmer ruined. You know, when we finish with this old mountain man, I think we better go back and take care of that son of a bitch."

"I think you're right. I sure hate to be chased off by a woman and I hate worse to have someone take our guns."

"Makes me so damn mad when I think about my guns, I'd almost go back now. But this guy has got to come first."

"That's right. Him and his money is our first job."

They found the camp Coker had made outside Springer. Tigert got off his horse and studied the mule tracks. "We're farther back than I thought," he said. "These tracks was made yesterday. We've got to hurry because if he gets to the mountains, we're through."

They loped through Springer and on north where they picked up Coker's trail and then slowed to a trot. Suddenly Tigert stopped and jumped off his horse to get a closer look at the ground.

"Hey, Larnce," he said. "These tracks was made this mornin', and he ain't movin' fast, and he ain't goin' straight. We're gonna catch up with him before long, so keep your eyes peeled."

They practiced drawing their guns.

Coker had tried to get on Switchback, but the strain was too much. Faltering all the way he walked into Springer with the mules following behind. As he passed a saloon, several men came out and untied their horses. Coker walked up to one and asked, "Is the ranch you work on between here and Raton?"

265

The man laughed and said, "The Eagle Nest ranch is all the way between here and Raton. What do you need, old man?"

"I know a guy which might work on your ranch. His name's Randy."

"Randy Stevens?"

"Yeah, that's his name."

"Sure, I work with him nearly every day. I'll see him tonight when I get back."

"Would you tell him somethin' for me?"

"You bet. What do you want me to tell him?"

"Tell 'em Coker Owen Ford needs his help. Tell 'em I think two gunnies are after me and I'm hurt and I'll be goin' from here to Raton. Will you tell him that?"

"Sure thing," the man said. "I'll tell him."

He looked Coker up and down and noticed the blood on his shirt. "You need some help now, old man."

He motioned to a fellow standing in front of the saloon. "Mr. Coleman, would you help this man? I've got to get back to the ranch, and he can't make it out there."

Coleman came over, took Coker by the arm and led him to his house nearby. "Ain't got much, but I'll give you a place to rest and take care of your mules for you."

The cabin had one room with two beds. He got Coker to lie on one while he put the mules in a corral and fed them hay and grain. Coker dozed off.

Coleman roused him and brought over some steak and eggs. "Good grub," said Coker. "Ain't et this good in a week."

As soon as he finished, he lay back on the bed. Several hours later Coleman woke him for a supper of cornbread and milk. Then Coker slept through the night. The next morning he slipped out while Coleman snored and went to his mules.

"That was good, Switchback. Feel some stronger now, but 'fraid those gunnies ain't far ahind me now. Gonna haveta watch my back."

By the time he saddled up, the strength he had gained left him. He got on Switchback and slumped forward as he rode out of town. Coker couldn't bear to let the mules trot, so he let Switchback follow the trail in a slow meandering walk.

Darkness had fallen before the cowboy delivered Coker's messaage to Randy Stevens.

"When was he coming this way?" Randy asked.

"The shape he was in, I doubt if he could travel before the morning. Mr. Coleman was taking him to his house when I left."

Randy hurried to the foreman's bunkhouse and burst in. "Jeb," he said, "I need a day off tomorrow. Is it all right?"

"What's the problem?"

Randy told him about Coker and the message he had sent. "Take as much time as you need," the foreman said. "You've got to take care of your friends."

Randy spent a restless almost sleepless night. When morning came, he strapped on his old hogleg and rode for the Raton trail, but when he reached it, he saw there were no mule tracks.

"Hasn't got here yet, so I'd better ride down to meet him." He spurred his horse into a fast trot and rode toward Springer.

Coker tried to keep alert and watch his backtrail, but pain dulled his senses. After a time he didn't look back at all and let Switchback take him wherever he would. He paid no attention when Switchback's ears stood erect and the mule looked back over his shoulder. Coker's head rolled back and forth.

The coyote howled a few yards away. Coker awoke and saw Switchback looking over his shoulder. "Uh, oh. Trouble behind. Got to act like I don't know."

He went around some trees where two huge boulders lay by the trail. He turned Switchback towards dense woods behind one rock. Then he got the shotgun and staggered to a position between the boulders. He leaned against the side of the rock nearer the trail and waited.

Growing impatient, Randy rode in a fast lope. "No use looking for tracks because Coker hasn't got this far yet."

As he rounded a big boulder, two men blocked the trail. He yanked hard on the reins and his horse skidded to a stop. Even though they saw him, the riders looked about in every direction. One of them stared at Randy from under big, bushy eyebrows. "Why don't you get out of the trail, partner?"

Randy thought, These are gunnies all right. They must be the ones after Coker. Wonder where he is?

He said, "There's room enough for you to pass. Go ahead. I'm not botherin' you."

"Uvie," the man said, "Don't you think the boy should get out of the trail and let us pass?"

"Yeah, Larnce, I think he oughta get way out of the trail."

A slight movement drew Randy's attention to his right and he saw Coker leaning against the rock. He could see him trying to muster enough strength to step from behind the rock and confront the men.

Quickly, he said, "I'll back up and let you pass."

He made his horse move away a few steps. The men advanced to the edge of the rock. Just a little more, Randy thought.

He backed his horse another two steps and said, "Now you can get by."

The men rode forward and Tigert said, "We don't want to get by, we want you out..." Buckshot tore through his body and terminated his command. The kick of the shotgun pulled it from Coker's weak grasp, so he could not fire a second time. Laseman drew his gun and whirled toward him. Randy shot him in the side just under his right arm and Laseman slid to the ground.

Randy jumped off his horse and ran to the mountain man. "You all right, Coker?"

"Well, they didn't hurt me none, but I ain't all right. I get awful hot. I cain't get 'nough water, and I'm weak as hell."

Randy felt his head. "No wonder you feel weak. You're hot as a pistol. Can you ride?"

"I can ride a ways."

"All right, let's get you to the ranch and get a doctor."

Randy led Switchback across country. He had to stop twice to let Coker rest, but he finally got him into the bunkhouse and in bed. The foreman came in to see what went on.

Randy said, "Jeb, can you send someone for a doctor? I'm afraid my friend is dying."

In a husky, almost inaudible voice, Coker said, "I ain't dyin'. I'm just restin'."

"You probably are. You're too ornery to die."

Jeb said, "I'll send a rider for Doc Wallace right now." He rushed out to find a man.

"Water," Coker croaked. "Randy, get me some water."

Randy brought a bucket. For hours he gave Coker water whenever he wanted it. Darkness came, and a coyote howled.

Coker raised his head a few inches. "Randy, don't let 'em shoot my coyote."

Randy was amazed. "You've got a coyote?"

"Yep, follered me all the way from Aspen Hill and back." Then Coker lost consciousness.

Shortly after dark the doctor strode into the bunkhouse. "What do we have here?" he asked.

"My friend is hurt. I don't know for sure how he's hurt, and I don't think he can tell you."

"Let's get this leather shirt off," the doctor said.

They tried to lift Coker's arms to slide the jacket over his head, but he winced in pain when they tried to lift his right arm. "We'll have to cut it off," the doctor said.

Randy took his knife, started to cut the jacket and saw it had been sewn together, so he cut the threads and pulled the jacket off.

The doctor leaned forward to look at Coker's wounds. "Good God o' mighty! Those are enough to kill anyone."

He soaked the scabs until he got them off and poured whisky into the wounds. Coker jerked. He smelled the alcohol and twisted away. "I don't want no whisky to drink. Don't give me no damned alcyhol." Then he sank on to the bed.

"Well, that's about all I can do for him," the doctor said. "Don't put anything on him so those wounds can get air. Pour whisky on them twice a day, but you'd better send now for a preacher and make funeral arrangements."

After the doctor left, other cowboys came in. "Who's he?" one of them asked.

Randy told him all he knew about Coker. One of the older men said, "I've heard of him. You mean that's Coker Owen Ford?"

"That's the man," Randy said.

The man came closer to look. "Just let me touch him," he said. "He brought my daddy to this country. He's a legend from California to Missouri. I never thought I'd ever see him."

At that moment a coyote howled. "Oh, by the way," Randy said. "He thinks his pet coyote is just outside here. Don't nobody shoot that coyote."

"How will we know which coyote not to shoot?" a man asked.

"Don't shoot any coyote. Because if you shoot one and Coker lives, then you won't."

For three days they watched him. Coker was delirious most of the time. He would shout things like, "Watch out for the log, Misty. Snake gets me, the kids'll die. I'll get the bundles. They ain't goin' into the damn pond. Gotta get back to Rufe. Snakes gotta die. Take care of my kids, John," and on and on.

On the fourth day his fever subsided and he roused and drank a cup of soup. By the fifth day he had regained his faculties and recognized Randy. "Well, I'll be damned. Where'd you come from?"

Randy smiled and said, "I got there just in time for your fracas with those gunmen."

Coker looked puzzled for a minute. "Yeah, I 'member. I shot one guy and lost my shotgun." He grinned. "You're a lot better with that hogleg than I thought you was."

"This is rough country. I've been practicin'. I'm not ready to take on Billy the Kid, but I can shoot pretty straight."

"I noticed that," Coker said. "Best I remember you saved my life, and I wanna thank you."

Randy shook his head. "You don't owe me anything. . . yes, you do. You can tell me where you was going when we parted and what you've been doing since then."

The crew had come in early since it was Saturday. When they heard Coker talking, they gathered around.

Coker went on until midnight and embellished the story very little. When he had finished Randy said, "Just as I thought. You're a hell of a lot meaner and bigger and tougher than the stories."

Coker went to sleep, and the men sat around talking in low voices the rest of the night.

The next morning Coker got up on limber legs. With Randy's help he walked. By the end of the day he was able to make his way with a steady but slow gait.

On the following day he walked an hour. Toward evening, he said, "I've gotta get back to Rufe. Guess I'll go in the mornin'."

Randy protested. "You can't. It's too soon. Those wounds aren't healed, and you're not strong enough. You couldn't fight your way out of a paper sack."

Randy talked for hours and persuaded him to wait one more day.

"You ought to wait at least a week, you stubborn old reprobate. And then you wouldn't be ready."

"It's down into late October and snow's comin'. Rufe cain't make it iffen I don't git back. I gotta go." Knowing no further arguments would help, Randy rose early the next morning and helped him pack.

When he had the mules ready, they shook hands and Randy said, "I hope you're not headed for big trouble like you was last time. Come back and see me, you old rascal."

"Iffen you're still here, I'll come by next spring with Rufe. Have to. Gotta go back to the desert to see my grandkids. By the way, Randy, is anyone after me 'cause of those two dead men?"

"No, I told the sheriff we killed 'em in self defense, but I wasn't too sure he was goin' to believe me until he found wanted posters in their saddlebags. Then he knew they was bounty hunters, and he hates bounty hunters. He said he hoped we killed some more."

Coker went to his mule, and Randy put a hand on his waist to help him up. Coker growled and said, "I don't need no help."

"I knew you wouldn't," Randy laughed.

Coker rode straight up for a quarter of a mile. Then Randy saw him hunch over his saddlehorn, but he kicked Thunder Red into a trot and headed home.

Randy watched him go and said aloud, "He'll never make it. No one in that shape could make another three hundred miles ridin' a mule." Then he thought about what he had said. "Well, Coker might."

30

Aspen Hill

Rufe watched the last aspen leaf flutter to the ground and turned his eyes toward the cabin. He mumbled his thoughts as he hobbled along.

"Naw, Coker ain't a gonna make it back in time to get ready for winter. I'm afraid he ain't a gonna make it back atall."

He sniffed. "Damn, I hate to live in town and eat that slop they fix. Coker got me 'nough for last winter, but I cain't get 'nough for this one, so I reckon I'll have to go on down there as bad as I hate to.

"Old Coker, he ain't comin' back or he'da done been here to watch the quakies turn. Now they's all finished. Featherfoot's done left for good. Naw, Coker's gone. I just kinda wonder if he ever found his girl and her kids."

Tears ran down his wrinkled cheeks as he walked across the porch and looked around the inside of their home. Everything was neat. He had worked hard getting it cleaned up one last time. Chest heaving, he pulled the door shut slowly.

"Well, old cabin, I reckon I'm shuttin' you up for the last time. Thirty years, thirty years. Don't know. Maybe I oughtta die right here 'steada goin' to that damn town. Ain't got much longer anyway."

Already saddled, Blackie stood by the corral. Stranger carried Rufe's meager belongings on his back. Rufe pulled away from the cabin and limped to his horse, but he moved slower than his leg made necessary.

He looked down the trail. "First time I ever wanted to see old Coker's mules. They'd sure be a sight for sore eyes now."

Standing in front of his horse, he looked into its brown eyes and said, "Old Blackie, do you wanna go to town and stand in a corral without no trees to run in? Reckon I oughta turn you loose? No, don't s'pose you and Stranger would make it through the winter without no hay."

Rufe took a deep breath and let out a long sigh. Then he untied Blackie and led him to the porch where it was easier for him to mount. He climbed the three steps and paused to look around one last time.

The corral, the trees, the meat rack, Featherfoot's den and, finally, the corner of the porch where Coker always sat to watch the setting sun and talk to the coyote. Slowly, he hitched his left foot into the stirrup.

He was setting himself to make the final effort to get into the saddle when he saw movement on the trail back in the timber where Coker had faded into the blue so many months ago.

"What's that?" he said, straining to focus his eyes. "Somethin's runnin' up the trail."

He stepped back onto the porch and watched an animal come up the switchback. When it reached the fork and turned toward the cabin, Rufe's face twisted into a smile. He caught his breath as it came closer.

"Featherfoot! God damn, can it be Featherfoot?"

His chest felt as if it were bound with shrinking, green rawhide and he stared at the animal. His heart was beating so hard he could barely breathe.

"How about that! Sure 'nough, it's Featherfoot!"

The coyote stopped a few feet from the porch and fixed his brown eyes on Rufe. The man and the coyote stared at each other for a full minute before Featherfoot turned his head and trotted to the mound at the edge of his den.

There he paused, pointed his nose at the sky and howled long and loud. When he was finished, he stared at the old man again, ducked and crept into his home.

Rufe watched him go and sighed.

"Are you howlin' and tellin' me Coker is comin' or goin' inter yer den tellin' me he ain't?" He jerked his head around quickly to focus on the lower trail again.

Another movement? Yes! Could it be?

"Maybe, maybe...something's comin'!"

Dropping Blackie's reins to the ground, he put his weathered hand on the corner post, sank to the smooth spot on the porch and fixed his eyes on the last switchback.

About the Author

Wesley Arlin Brown, Greeley, Colorado, was born in New Mexico, a few yards from the dugout house described in the book. He has traveled over much of the wilderness areas in the southwest by horse, mule or foot. He received his bachelor's degree from Eastern New Mexico University, did graduate work at Redlands University, received his master's from Western State College and his doctorate from the University of Northern Colorado. He spent thirteen years teaching in public schools of California and Colorado and then taught literature at San Diego University, humanities and composition at the University of Northern Colorado and literature, philosophy, ethics, semantics and humanities at Aims College where he was given the title of professor emeritus. Among other things, he has been a farmer, miner, tank operator in the army and U.S. Forest Service employee.

Dr. Brown has written several short stories and articles and another novel, "Where the Flowers Sing." He is working on two non-fiction books. "Coker" is part of a planned trilogy. Under its original title, "The Last Switchback," the book won honorable mention in The National Writers Club 1991 Novel Manuscript Contest.

The Song

"Just One More Ride," featured in this book, is the work of James Hobbs who wrote the lyrics and music in 1977 while performing in Estes Park, Colorado. He and his wife, Cindy, opened their Flying J Ranch in Ruidoso, New Mexico, in 1982. The song was recorded in 1984 on the second Flying J Wrangler album, "Calling in the Wind." Hobbs is best known in his home state for "Song for New Mexico." His group, the Flying J Wranglers, has appeared all over the country and abroad and has performed guest spots at Grand Ole Opry and the Nashville Network.